ORDINARY PERSON

—

EXTRA ORDINARY LIFE

ORDINARY PERSON

EXTRA ORDINARY LIFE

Funny, strange, amazing, mysterious,
and almost unbelievable stories
from the life and times of

Bob Haddad

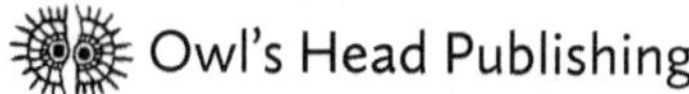 Owl's Head Publishing

Contents

About this book

For you, this may be just another autobiography: one more narrative about the twists and turns, ups and downs, and interesting times of someone's life. But for me, it's more than that: I've been profoundly impacted on a personal level by these life-shaping events.

The fifty stories in this book haven't been embellished or fictionalized. I understand that some may be hard to believe, but they are all true occurrences. Many of them are based on work, travels, and inspiring interactions and adventures with other people. Some are curious, mysterious, funny, strange, and memorable things that have happened to me... and others relate important life lessons and experiences in the extra-physical and spirit realms. In some cases, details are recounted here based on journal entries made over the course of my life, beginning at around twenty years old. Except for the first entry about early childhood, the stories aren't arranged chronologically, so feel free to read them randomly if you wish.

I could never have imagined the amazing patterns of change that my life would take, and I'm thankful for the people, places and things that have formed and shaped me as an individual on planet Earth. I'm especially grateful to the individuals mentioned in this book for providing me with such wonderful and meaningful life experiences, and for opening my mind and deepening my heart. I hope that you enjoy reading these stories as much as I enjoyed writing them.

– Bob Haddad

Help Mighty Mouse, save me!

It was a summer day, and I was sitting in a highchair near the open kitchen window of my parents' two-story walk-up apartment on 57th Street between 12th and 13th Avenues in Brooklyn, New York. Mom had just finished giving me some food, and she'd briefly left the kitchen. My body was firmly in place in the chair, but my three-year-old mind was apparently elsewhere. I felt in danger, or maybe I was just feeling bored, but something was unsettling. I wasn't sure if it was the bogeyman or another unspecified monster that had made plans for my demise, but one thing was clear: someone was coming to get me, and I knew exactly who could come to help me.

I didn't have much time to make my move, and now that Mom had gone to the back of the apartment to make the beds, here was my chance. I wriggled out of the highchair through the half-moon opening of the tray, which was snapped down into place. It was warm outside, and the window was open just enough for me to push the portable screen onto the flat tar roof of the building. I quickly slid through the window and made the easy jump down to the roof. I was afraid, but I was convinced that my only salvation lay in getting help to fight off the monster. The tar roof was warm to the touch, and as I slowly crawled to the edge of the building, my hands and knees were pinched and prodded by small pieces of gravel on the roof's floor. Would there be enough time? How long would it take for me to be rescued? This was my first time asking for help from a superhero, but

I was sure it would happen almost instantaneously, just like in the cartoons. I had to protect myself and Mom, and make sure our house was safe when my brothers and father returned home.

Crawling slowly, moving toward the edge of the roof; yes, this would be a good place because I'd be in clear view. I'll be seen and heard, for sure. "Scream loud," I thought to myself, "there's not much time left." It was scary up there at the edge of the roof, and I couldn't see the concrete steps below where the older kids sometimes played stoop ball. Finally, I decided to make my move. I grabbed hold of the ledge, stood up, craned my neck, and at the top of my lungs, I began screaming: "Help. Help, Mighty Mouse, save me! Help, Mighty Mouse, save me!"

I heard some commotion down on the sidewalk near the neighbor's house. Had the monster already gotten to them? Someone was talking very loudly, and I could hear another voice too, and then a woman began screaming: "Bobby's mother! Bobby is on the roof. Bobby's mother!" A few moments later, I heard more screaming, this time behind me, toward the open kitchen window. It was my mother yelling at the top of her lungs, "Bobby, Bobby." And I was screaming, now even louder, "Help, Mighty Mouse, save me!"

Suddenly, from out of nowhere, I was grabbed and swept upward in one quick movement. A hard hand crashed against my behind, causing immediate pain, as my mother carried me toward the kitchen window. All the while she screamed: "Don't you ever do that again." But why was she hurting me? Didn't she realize that I was saving our entire family from annihilation by an unspecified creature of doom? Her screaming and pinching were a fate worse than the monster! I was crying and confused, and she continued yelling: "Don't you *ever* do that again, do you hear me? Do you *hear* me?"

Bobby at 3½ years old

Mighty Mouse, ©Terrytoons

The shark and
the dolphins

My friend Lue owned a house in Sunset Beach, North Carolina, and I would occasionally go there in the off-season to work remotely and also to relax. One year in springtime, my friend Danny flew from New York to visit me for a week, and as part of our time together, I took him to the beach house. I'd also invited another friend, Sienna, who arrived on the same day in her own car. We had a lovely time together, sharing meals, playing music, reading, and spending time on the beach.

One morning I awoke early, and I couldn't get back to sleep. The others were sleeping soundly in their bedrooms, and I didn't want to disturb them, so around 7:00 a.m., I decided to walk to the beach a few hundred feet away and enjoy the early morning peace and quiet. It was too early for anyone to be there, and I had the long strip of beach entirely to myself. I sat on a towel on the sand for a while, gazing at the ocean. After a few minutes, I became curious to test the temperature of the water. It usually wasn't warm until the early summer, but I was delighted to learn that it was absolutely perfect for an early morning swim. I took off all my clothes, threw them on the beach above the water line, and went in. It was very calm, and once I got beyond the small waves breaking at the shore, the sea was almost motionless. I swam around slowly, and did some twists and turns under the water as I used to do as a child. The water was warm and inviting, and I was so glad I'd come down to the beach alone that morning.

During this period of my life, I'd been experimenting with different types of breathing, or breathwork, as it is also known. I'd been reading books, understanding the dynamics of breath, and had attended a workshop on the topic. Long and protracted breathing through the nose, with relatively long exhalation plateaus, helped to relax the body and mind, and was particularly good for meditation. Holotropic breathing, when you inhale and exhale deeply and rapidly for a long period of time without stopping, was used in group counseling sessions I'd attended. It helped to put people into altered states of consciousness where deep-seated traumas could sometimes be released under guided supervision. Rolling around in the pleasantly warm and tranquil early morning water, with the sun slowly rising on the horizon, I turned over onto my back and took some full and deep breaths into my lungs to become more buoyant. After a quick and short exhale, I rapidly filled my lungs again and held my breath for a long time. When I did this, I noticed that I could stay completely afloat on my back while the front of my body, including my face, remained exposed to air. I continued this pattern of keeping my lungs as full of air as possible and exhaling in short bursts before quickly inhaling again. It felt wonderful, and as I floated aimlessly, I gazed at the morning sky and the drifting clouds above, and I felt at one with the Universe.

I continued to breathe in this way for a minute or so, and as my lungs and body became accustomed to the style and pace of this type of breathing, I closed my eyes for a moment. I felt a certain peace, floating there on my back with my eyes closed in the warm water, and I must have drifted into a slightly altered state. I don't know how long I remained floating with my eyes closed and breathing in this way, but I suppose it could have been three or four minutes. Eventually, I broke through my euphoria, and I realized that it would be a good time to open my eyes and see where I was. I bent my neck forward to take a look, and I was shocked to see that I had drifted far away and was about 400 feet from the shoreline! I panicked, and realized that if I had any chance at all, I'd have to swim as hard and fast as possible, and also to swim parallel to the shore in case I encountered any riptides. I needed to push off somehow, so I flipped onto my side, and as one of my arms came over my head toward the water, my right leg immediately followed by kicking backward... but instead of kicking into water, my foot struck a warm, fleshy substance. I screamed and began to swim as hard and as fast as possible, flailing maniacally in the water and racing to get back to shore. I didn't know what my foot had struck, but I sure as hell wasn't going to linger there any longer in order to find out! I wasn't a trained swimmer, and I wasn't in great physical shape either, but I was swimming with my whole body, thrashing and beating the water as hard as possible. Every once in a while, I glanced at the distant shore to make sure I was swimming in the right direction. Occasionally a wave would glide me forward a bit, and I tried to make best use of the momentum, but after a few minutes I was still very far away. Then, in the distance, I saw the arms of someone at the shoreline gesturing in a wide arc, and I heard a distant voice yelling unintelligible words. I kept swimming with all my might, sometimes choking on small amounts of water that entered my nose and mouth, and occasionally looking toward the shore and feeling encouraged by those waving arms. Now I could hear: "Come on, keep coming. Come on in."

Another little wave rode me forward, and as it broke, my head submerged for a moment, but I came up again. My arms and legs were aching. I'd never swum so hard or for so long in my entire life, and I had to keep going. After another minute, I was almost there. Now I could see the whole body of a man on the beach, still encouraging me with his gestures and words. The waves were breaking against the beach now, and finally, I was able to touch the bottom. "Just a little further," I thought, but as I tried to stand up, my knees buckled and I collapsed back into the water, so I crawled the rest of the way onto the shore like a shipwrecked mariner. Gasping for air, sputtering and spitting, my heart racing, my limbs aching, the concerned man on the beach helped to pull me out of the water, and I collapsed on the sand a few feet from the water's edge.

"Are you OK?" he asked. I don't remember if I answered with words. He continued: "Man, you were so damn lucky. Did you know what was out there? There was a big shark. I could see its dorsal fin poking up through the water right near you." When I heard him say that, I thought to myself that I had kicked a shark, but then he continued: "And then there were three dolphins swimming around you in a circle. Sometimes they would lurch forward in a small arc, but they were definitely swimming around you in a circle. One of them even turned around and rammed the shark. Those dolphins were protecting you from that shark, man! What were you doing out there, anyway? You were so far out!" I tried to blurt out a few words about breathing and floating, but I was still desperately trying to catch my breath, and I couldn't speak very well. "Take it easy, just relax, take some deep breaths," he coached me.

The stranger stayed with me until I gained my composure and was able to sit up and breathe slowly and deeply again. He told me once again what he saw, that the dolphins continued circling around me until I was much closer to shore, and I sat there amazed at the thought that a pod of altruistic dolphins had clearly saved my life. They knew I was alive and not dangerous, and they knew that I was vulnerable to the encroaching shark, so they stepped in to save me. I'll always remember the day I had a deep and meaningful interspecies connection with three life-saving dolphin friends.

"Well, good luck, and thanks for the drink."

During the first years of my early 30s, I was struggling because of an increasingly difficult situation with polyps that had developed on my vocal flaps. The polyps were affecting my ability to earn income, and they were also suppressing my musical expression. I was teaching five classes a day of high school Spanish, working as an Adjunct Professor at several colleges in New York City, and singing two club dates each weekend. For several months, I took expensive voice therapy lessons on the Upper West Side of Manhattan with a famous vocal coach, but the polyps weren't going away. My throat was sore and my voice was hoarse, so I eventually decided to have them surgically removed. After initial consultation with several doctors, I learned that polyps were traditionally excised by microsurgery, but that a new technology involving lasers had also begun to be used. I met with a surgeon at NYU Medical Center who convinced me that laser treatment would be best. I remember in one consultation, he said to me: "Don't worry, you'll be singing like Frank Sinatra in no time."

Hoping that my singing and teaching careers would be restored, I got up the courage and saved enough money to go through with the laser procedure, but a short time after the operation, my hopes were dashed. During the early days of laser excision, it was still unknown that using lasers on mucous membranes can sometimes incur adjacent tissue damage. In my case, a spattering effect had resulted, and my vocal folds became scarred, resulting in a condition that was even worse than I had before the procedure. After a few weeks of voice rest, I was able to speak with a relatively clear voice, but I had lost the strength and clarity of my singing voice, as well as a wide range of notes that I simply couldn't reach any more. I became depressed, began to sell some of my musical instruments, cancelled my singing engagements, and was forced to use a microphone and amplifier to teach in the classroom.

During this period of my life, I was enamored with jazz improvisation, and was listening to great scat singers like Ella Fitzgerald and Mel Tormé, but I was also enchanted by the golden voice of the famous balladeer Johnny Hartman. I played his albums over and over again, especially the classic recording he did with John Coltrane, released in 1963 on MCA Impulse Records. I marveled at Hartman's timbre, strength, and especially his "placement" — the way he could precisely hit notes without sliding upward or downward to reach them. As an avid jazz fan living in New York, I would often go into Manhattan for shows at Bradley's, The Village Gate, The Vanguard, The Blue Note, and others. One day in the summer of 1982, I learned that Johnny Hartman would be performing with his trio for a week in July at the Blue Note on West 3rd Street in Greenwich Village. I jumped at the opportunity to go, but I couldn't afford the full price to sit at a table, so I opted for a cheaper ticket at the bar. I was excited, but I was also sad and depressed because of my wounded singing voice and my lagging music and teaching careers.

Seated at the bar, about thirty feet away from the stage, I settled in with a beer and an open heart to finally hear my idol, 30 years my senior, in a live performance. The curtain opened, and Johnny performed an absolutely amazing first set. Cigarette in hand, his voice floated effortlessly through beautiful arrangements of classic tunes like *My One and Only Love* and *The Nearness of You,* many of which I had learned by listening incessantly to his albums. He had such an amazing voice. The first set ended to a roaring ovation, and as he began to step off the stage, I don't know what got into me. I jumped off my barstool and bounded toward him. Making my way past standing and applauding fans, I came within a few feet of him and blurted out: "Mr. Hartman, could I please buy you a drink?" He stared at me with a startled and perplexed expression, and after an awkward few seconds, he agreed. "Oh my God," I thought. "I'm going to have a personal conversation with Johnny Hartman."

He followed me to the bar, and he sat at an empty stool next to mine. I asked the bartender to give him whatever he wanted, and to put it on my tab. He ordered a shot of whiskey, and then he turned to me, asked my name, and said: "So what do you do?"

I said something like, "I'm a singer, Mr. Hartman, and your music has inspired me very much."

"And what kind of music do you sing?" he asked.

"Pop and jazz, and I love to scat," I replied, "but Mr. Hartman, umm, well..." I began to get emotional, and the words just weren't coming out. He waited patiently as I regained composure. "It's just that... well... I've been having problems with my voice. You see, I had laser surgery to remove some polyps on my vocal cords, and it made my voice even worse, and then I had to go on voice rest, and ever since then I can't sing well anymore, and I get hoarse after about 30 minutes of performing."

I must have rambled on for a few moments, not knowing what to say, or even why I was unloading like this on the great Johnny Hartman during his well-deserved intermission break.

"Well, son," he said, "I'm sorry about that, but we've all had problems along the way." He continued: "Mel was affected for a while, Sinatra went through a rough period, and I also had some problems. So, what are your restrictions?"

I replied that I had lost a fair amount of my volume and that the upper and lower ranges of my voice had been most affected. As we were having this conversation, the bartender placed a drink in front of him. Johnny continued: "How many notes have you lost from your upper range before it doesn't sound good?"

"About five or six whole notes," I answered.

"And from the lower register?" he asked.

"About the same," I said.

"But the notes in between are OK, right?"

I answered that yes, for the most part I was able to control the sound of the notes in the middle of my range.

"So when you improvise," he said, "do you know the notes that you can't reach and sing very well? I mean, do you know which notes to avoid?" I don't think I immediately replied, because I was taken aback by his question. He continued: "If you know which notes you shouldn't go for, because they won't sound good, then just avoid them, and instead, sing only the notes within the central part of your range. Even when you scat, always think ahead, and don't ever improvise on notes that are outside of your range. Stay away from the notes that you can't sing well anymore. Do you know what I mean?"

Stunned and a bit embarrassed by the simplicity and intelligence of his suggestion, something I hadn't fully considered as a way around the problem until then, I think I mumbled "uh-huh." But he wasn't convinced, so he looked me straight in the eyes, and as he held me motionless in his deep, strong and penetrating gaze, he asked again: "Do you know what I mean?"

"Yes, sir," I said.

With that, he lifted the shot glass to his mouth, took the whiskey down in one swallow, slapped the glass on the bar, and stood up. Then he turned to me and said: "Well, good luck, and thanks for the drink."

Johnny Hartman in the 1960s

The classic album

A transcendental
state of mind

I moved with my girlfriend from New York to North Carolina when I was 36 years old. It was a big change for me, but I was ripe for the opportunity to leave the city and start a new life in a friendly place that was more conducive to growth and stability. The last few months living in Brooklyn had been challenging, and there was no doubt in my mind that I was ready to relocate. There weren't many Northerners in North Carolina at that time, and getting used to the southern drawl, excessive courtesies, and the slower pace wasn't always easy for a city boy like me. Soon after the move, I realized that I was perceived by many local people as a "Yankee." Later on, it became apparent that I was a "Damn Yankee," a Northerner who first comes to visit and then permanently relocates there.

I rented a large brick home on ten acres of land for almost the same price as my one-bedroom apartment in Brooklyn, and the plan was to continue growing the new record company I had started. The house had an unfinished basement, and that's where I kept my music gear, microphone cables and stands, and also the growing cassette inventory that I was selling to distributors around the country. One summer evening, I went down to the basement to do some work. It was hot, and I was barefoot and wearing shorts. After descending the stairs, I headed to the area where I kept my inventory. It wasn't yet completely dark outside, and the book I needed was in clear view, so I walked over to my desk without turning on an overhead light. I took the book in my hands, turned around, and then I noticed a dark circle on the floor, just a few feet away from me. I assumed it was one of my microphone cables, but I wondered why it wasn't in its usual place with the rest of the audio equipment. I walked toward it, but before I bent down toward the object on the floor, I reached for the closest overhead light, and I pulled on the cord. What I saw was a very large black snake, coiled in a circle. Its head was erect, and it was looking at me in a defensive posture.

I'd seen Eastern garter snakes in the countryside of Upstate New York a few times in my life, but I certainly never had a snake in my house before! Without knowing exactly what to do, I decided to open the sliding door that led to the backyard, and try to coax the snake outside. I grabbed a broom, and without getting too close, I tried to push it toward the open door, but it quickly slithered away from the door, moved toward the back of the basement, and hid near some cardboard boxes. At that point, I decided to not do anything further, so I climbed the stairs to the ground floor of the building and told my girlfriend what had just happened. It was getting late. Could we find an exterminator that could help us? I looked through the phone book and called a few pest control companies. Several didn't answer the phone, and one said that he didn't work with snakes. Finally, I spoke with a man who said he could come over within an hour, and he advised us to not go into the basement until he arrived.

Later, the doorbell rang, and a short man with a thick Southern accent introduced himself and asked to be shown to the basement. He brought with him all sorts of gear, including a snake pole and a stick with a forked end. I showed him downstairs, and we carefully stepped onto the basement floor, scanning all around to make sure the snake wasn't in view. He asked where it had gone when I tried to sweep it out the door, and I pointed to the back of the room, where the cardboard boxes were stacked. He walked slowly toward the wall, his gear in hand, and we followed behind him, turning on as many overhead lights as possible. He extended a telescoping pole and began tapping on the boxes and moving them slightly from side to side. Suddenly the snake came into view, but it quickly hid behind another box. The exterminator said: "Aw, it's probably just a black snake. Not dangerous. Poor thing's stuck in here. We'll get her out." He moved forward and pushed the box out of the way until the snake was in full view, with its head pointing away from us. "Alright now, that's good; here we go," he said. He moved slowly toward the animal with his snake pole and slowly extended it directly over the body of the snake. Then quickly, he slammed it toward the ground, attempting to grab hold of the snake with the adjustable jaws, but the pole failed to make contact. Suddenly, the snake coiled around, struck the pole, positioned its head upward toward us, and opened its mouth to display its fangs. The snake man jumped back in surprise and said: "Oh man, that ain't no black snake. That's a cottonmouth!"

"A cottonmouth is a water moccasin, right?" I asked. "Aren't they pit vipers?"

"That's right," he said, "more dangerous than a copperhead. You get a bite from one of these things, and you better get to a hospital right quick, or you're in big trouble."

I was a few feet behind him, and at least eight feet away from the large snake, but I felt myself stepping back even further. I heard him murmur a few words, talking to himself in order to decide the best approach to get rid of the snake. He asked if I had a shovel, and I pointed to a few garden tools in the corner of the room. "That one, the drain spade," he said. I grabbed the one with a long narrow blade and brought it over to him.

"OK," he continued – "Here's what we're gonna' do." He then laid out a plan for collaboration among the three of us. I would hold the spade and shine a bright flashlight on the snake at all times. My girlfriend Martha would hold open the heavy door so he and the snake could escape to the outside as quickly as possible. He would trap the snake in the jaws of the snake pole, I would quickly hand him the spade, and he would kill the snake. If there was a problem, he would quickly run outside with the snake in the jaws of the pole, and deal with it outside.

"Do we have to kill it?" I asked.

"You don't wanna' mess with an angry cottonmouth," was his reply.

Once again, we reviewed the plan of attack, and were reminded of our roles. I nervously held the spade in my left hand and the flashlight in my right. He had the forked stick and the snake pole. Martha was far behind us, holding the door open to the woods outside. He would trap and lock onto the snake with the grippers, and then he'd take the spade from my left hand. He reminded me to keep the flashlight focused on the snake at all times, and then he said: "OK, y'all ready?"

I was nervous as hell, a city boy who'd just moved to the southern pine forest and now had a venomous snake in his basement. "Ready?" he asked again, and we replied affirmatively. Then he turned to me and said: "Y'all just give me a minute, OK? I need to get into a tran-scendental state of mind."

"Sure, man, whatever you need," I answered.

He closed his eyes for a second, opened them again, gazed slightly downward, and then took a series of long and deep breaths for about 15 seconds. Then, as if energized by this concentrated moment of focus, he leapt forward, snagged the body of the snake, and quickly pinned it to the floor with the forked stick. Then, with his other hand, he secured the head with the adjustable jaws of the snake pole and locked them into position. Once the animal's head and upper body were secured, he dropped the forked stick, grabbed the spade from my hand, and hacked the poor thing into a few pieces, which continued to wiggle independently for a few moments. He picked up the pole with the severed upper part of the snake still attached, and ran toward the door to bring it outside. Once it finally stopped moving, he showed me the inside of the viper's white mouth, and pointed out the fangs, pits, and the angular head as identifying features. The whole thing was pretty stressful, including the suffering we had caused to the animal.

I thanked the man, paid him for his services, and went back inside to finish cleaning. As I mopped and cleaned the basement floor, I started to laugh at what the snake man had said and done. Here I was, an educated city boy who liked Indian music, yoga and natural foods, and the exterminator was a Southern white guy, perceived by some as an unsophisticated redneck. Yet he had taken a few moments to get into a "transcendental state of mind" before he killed the snake. Those words, and his subsequent moment of meditation, seemed so out of place and inconsistent with my flawed perception of Southerners, and it made me giggle for quite some time.

I never had another cottonmouth in my home, but over the years, I've been in close contact with many snakes, including large and beautiful copperheads, which I have learned to deeply respect.

"¿Estás seguro?"

After two years of college in Ponce, Puerto Rico, I took a year off from school and accepted a full-time job at a non-profit organization in Manhattan. I truly enjoyed my job, and I was able to save some money, but by the end of the year I couldn't wait to get back into college. The year away from school had clarified my goals to get a degree in Latin American Studies, and I enrolled at Queens College to complete my undergraduate work. During the first few months, I learned of a study abroad program at a private university in Mexico City that would grant me full credit for ongoing study, so I applied for the following semester, and I was accepted.

Living in Mexico City was wonderful. I quickly became acquainted with the Metro system and was able to explore the entire city by subway. I lived in a neighborhood called Campestre Churrubusco, where I had a room in the home of a host family, a short walk away from campus. At that time, I was studying Mesoamerican civilization and pre-Hispanic art and archaeology, so I was in the right place at the right time. It was easy to visit the great pyramids of Teotihuacán and the Aztec complexes within Mexico City, and in my spare time I traveled to temples and ruins of the great Olmec, Zapotec, Mixtec and Maya civilizations. I also met Arturo Loreto, a musician my age who played bass guitar. After jamming with him one day, he asked if I would join his band as a singer and piano player. That turned into a wonderful weekly engagement at a restaurant called La Fuente, and my friendship with Arturo and his family lasted for many years.

All was going well until one scary day when I woke up with a throbbing in my genital area. I lowered the covers, pulled down my pajamas, and saw that my testicles had swollen to the size of large lemons. My scrotum had expanded to accommodate the two monstrous things that had somehow enlarged overnight. I wondered what could possibly have happened. I had a girlfriend there at the time, Alicia, and we'd had sex a few times, but how did my balls become so swollen all of a sudden? What else could it have been? The night before, I'd met some friends for dinner, had a few beers and a big bowl of *ceviche mixto* (marinated raw seafood and shellfish), and then I'd returned home and gone straight to bed. Was the shellfish tainted? Was I having an allergic reaction to the *ceviche*? I got out of bed and the whole area down below was red, swollen, throbbing and painful. I hobbled to the bathroom with my legs apart from each other because the gigantic sack I was carrying was interfering with the movement of my legs. *Diós mío*, what was I going to do?

After a while, I realized I needed to go to a doctor, but I was embarrassed to tell my house mother what had happened. I went downstairs for breakfast as usual, and while the *señora* was in the kitchen, I grabbed the telephone book from a table nearby. As I scanned the pages for *médicos*, one of them stood out to me because it said something about *alergias*. I also noticed that the office was located on a street with a name I recognized, which was only a few stops from the Tasqueña metro station closest to the house. I quickly wrote down the doctor's name and address, closed the phone book, returned it to the table, and left the house to take the metro.

I got off the train at the right station and figured out which way to walk. I was in pain down there. I was also very worried. After all, I was only 20 years old, living away from home, and I had a gigantic swollen scrotum that was threatening my manhood. I walked for quite a while down a busy avenue, and finally found the small building on the right side of the street. I rang the bell, and the door opened.

Tasqueña metro stop, Mexico City

It was the doctor himself, a man in his early forties. I explained that I had a problem and that I needed his help. When he asked what kind of a problem I had, I simply pointed to the area between my legs. He let me in, and in a few minutes I was sitting with him in the examination room.

I told him I was a visiting student, and after the usual formalities and health history questions, he asked me what had happened. I replied that I woke up in the morning to an intense throbbing sensation, and that my testicles and scrotum had swollen to about three times their normal size. He asked to see, and I pulled down my pants and underwear. The doctor, now wearing gloves, began to touch and inspect and ask if it hurt here and there. I was very worried, and I hoped that he'd be able to help me right there in his office. He must have sensed that I was nervous and afraid as a young person all alone in Mexico, and he tried to make me feel as comfortable as possible as he examined me. Finally, he said that I was having some sort of allergic reaction. I told him about the *ceviche* of the night before, and he nodded, as if to agree that it could have been the cause of the inflammation. There was a moment of awkward silence, and then he looked at me and said: "*Yo sí te puedo curar, pero…*" (I can cure you, yes, but…)

"*Pero que?*" (But what?) I asked.

He responded by saying: "*Pues, no sé si de verdad quieres que yo te cure. ¿Estás seguro?*" (Well, I don't know if you really want me to cure you. Are you sure?)

I was already terribly afraid, and his remarks and questions made me even more uncomfortable. I couldn't imagine why he would say something like that. Worried and confused, I looked at him and I said: "*Claro que sí doctor, estoy seguro. Ayúdame por favor.*" (Yes, of course, doctor, I'm sure. Please help me.)

Again he asked, "*Pero ¿estás seguro?*" Then he looked me straight in the eye, and with a suppressed smile he said: "*Porque si no, ¡tú podrías tener los cojones más grandes de todo México!*" (Because if not, you could have the biggest balls in all of Mexico!)

Realizing he had set me up, I started laughing, and he also laughed, knowing that he had eased my concern. He told me not to worry, that a simple injection would reduce the swelling, and that I'd be back to normal by the end of the day. As he treated me, he asked about my life, my studies in Mexico, and my life back home In New York, and we continued our conversation even after the injection was administered. I'll never forget that friendly, kind and funny man, and I'll never forget that – if only for a few hours – I once had the biggest *cojones* in all of Mexico.

Sleeping on an Algarve beach

In my life as a young world traveler, I sometimes awoke in the morning in strange places and under strange circumstances. One memorable experience happened when I was about 20 years old. I already spoke Spanish and was beginning to learn Portuguese. My main teacher was fun and inspirational, and I was so excited about my new language learning that when summer vacation came around, I decided to travel to Portugal for three weeks to practice and speak as much as possible. I visited Lisbon and several beautiful inland towns, and then I went to the Algarve, a 100-mile strip of coastline in the southernmost part of the country. I visited with a few friends who had recently moved there, and then I set out to explore a few beach towns before returning to Lisbon and flying home.

Toward the end of the trip, I was running low on money and I was sleeping outside in my sleeping bag, or in protected areas that I considered to be safe. On my last night, after spending a wonderful day at the beach in a small town, I found an area that seemed perfect for sleeping. I positioned my backpack on the sand, unrolled my sleeping bag, and prepared for bed. The moon and the stars were bright, the air was still, and I fell asleep to the sound of the ocean. A short time later, I was awakened by voices and a flashlight in my face. Two policemen politely told me that sleeping on the beach wasn't permitted. During a short conversation, they said that if I needed a place to spend the night, they would take me somewhere, but I wouldn't be allowed to sleep on the beach. When I asked why, they said it was *proibido* (prohibited), and they mentioned something about *os pescadores* (the fishermen). I didn't fully understand everything, and it was already late at night, so I gathered my belongings and followed them along the beach. They brought me to a small stone shelter, a storage shack for maintenance crews on a dune at the edge of the sand. The two young policemen told me I could spend the night there, and then they left. I tossed and turned, but it was smelly and dark in there, and besides, it was filled with mosquitoes that were buzzing in my ears and biting me relentlessly. After about 30 minutes, I decided to return to the beach with my backpack and gear. I found a nice place not too far from the dunes, got into my sleeping bag under the moon and the stars, and fell soundly asleep.

Morning came, and distant sounds of the outside world merged into the borders of my dreams. I realized that the sounds were from the outside world, and I began to wake up. Lying on my side in the sleeping bag, I slowly opened my eyes to greet the morning, and what I saw, just a few inches from my face, were several large squid. I jerked my head back in surprise, and then I noticed more squid to my left and also to my right. Without even lifting my head, I could see squid everywhere within the range of my peripheral vision, just inches away from my head and body. I recoiled, quickly turned onto my back, and came into a sitting position to see that I was completely surrounded by hundreds of large squid, all arranged neatly in concentric circles around me. Struggling through my early morning grogginess, I tried to understand how this could have happened. The tide hadn't reached me... I'd been completely dry while sleeping... so how did these squid wind up on the sand all around me? Then I heard voices, and in the distance, I saw a crew of fishermen and a few small boats near the shore.

I got out of my sleeping bag, carefully tip-toed through the large circles of squid, and walked closer to the shoreline. "*Olá, bom dia,*" one of them said. They were carrying crates of squid and emptying them onto the sand just above the water line. "*Estavas durmindo e não queríamos incomodá-lo.*" I was sleeping, and they didn't want to bother me, so for an hour or so, right at the break of dawn, they left me sleeping there and began to pile their squid in large circles around me. Fascinated by what I was witnessing, and eager to practice my Portuguese, I began to ask questions about their fishing techniques. They brought me to the boat to see their gigantic morning catch, and they showed me how they used nets for trawling and lights to attract the squid closer to the surface of the water. I helped them carry crates to the shore, and a bit later, several motorbikes arrived to pick up and distribute the fresh squid to markets and restaurants in the area. It was a perfectly wonderful way to wake up on the last day of my first visit to Portugal.

Morning catch of squid

Guns in my face

I don't like aggression or violence. I never did. As a kid in grammar school, whenever a bully classmate became confrontational, I'd try to diffuse the situation, or I'd just walk away, even if the other kids called me a sissy. On the few occasions when I was pushed into physical confrontation, I would usually lose the fight and go home with a bloody nose or a swollen face. I never understood why some people believed that violence of any kind could help to resolve a problem. It never does. Almost every time, it simply incites more violence.

Any act of physical violence is terrible, but it's even worse when someone uses a gun to threaten, harm or kill another person. In my mind, people who flaunt guns in this way are either deluded or paranoid, have low self-esteem, suffer from some kind of trauma, and/or are mentally unstable. Ultimately, people who use guns against other people seek to prove to themselves that they're in control, that they're superior to others, or that they will get their way by inciting fear in others.

The USA is at the top of the list for gun ownership, with 120 firearms for every 100 people, or a total of almost 400 million civilian-owned firearms. After that, twelve other countries have between 30 and 50 guns per 100 people, but many of these are war-torn places undergoing social turmoil, or are small nations or territories where a large majority of the guns are used for hunting. The last group comprises about 80% of all countries on the planet, where gun ownership ranges between 0.1 and 0.8 per 100 people, including guns used for hunting. In a number of countries, gun ownership is either heavily restricted, or completely illegal and punishable by imprisonment. Although most developed nations make it difficult to own a gun, in some U.S. States you can walk into a store, buy a gun, and not have to register it. Then you can carry it in your pocket as you have a few drinks at a bar, or buy food at a supermarket, or take your children to a public event. Many people who own guns cite the Second Amendment to the Constitution, which grants citizens the right to bear arms, but having the right to do something doesn't make it ethical, correct or practical.

I've had guns in my face three times in my life. In my late 20s, I stopped at a red light on the corner of Prospect Avenue and 3rd Avenue. Directly ahead was a ramp to get onto the Gowanus Expressway, a stretch of highway that leads to the Brooklyn and Manhattan bridges. Within seconds of stopping at the red light, a car crashed into me from behind. It wasn't a major collision, but it was enough of a jolt to push my body forward against the steering column. I immediately got out of the car to take a look at the damage. As I did so, I turned to the driver of the car that hit me and made a gesture with my open hands in the air. The light turned green and a few cars began to honk their horns, so I signaled to the other driver to pull over to the side so we could discuss things and exchange licenses and information. I pulled over to the shoulder, and the car followed behind me. As I was looking for my license and registration, the other driver approached my car and walked up to my window. He was a dark-haired burly character, older than I.

I lowered the window and exclaimed: "What happened? You crashed into my car at a red light."

He looked at me and said: "No I didn't, you backed up and smashed into my car! You're the one who hit me."

I could hardly believe what he'd said, and as I put my hand on the latch to begin opening the car door, he pulled out a gun and said: "You're the one who backed into my car. If you keep saying it was me, I'll put a hole in your head." As he said this, he pushed the gun into the space of my half-open window and pointed it directly at my head. "Go ahead; say another word and I'll put a bullet between your eyes. Now get outta' here right now!" Trembling and confused, I nodded my head, started the car, and slowly drove around the corner, where I stopped for a while to compose myself.

Many years later, I pulled into a gas station not far from my home in North Carolina, but as I approached the filling area, there was no way that I could access the pumps. A large car had parked at a precarious angle that blocked access to any other vehicle that needed gas. I lowered my window, and politely asked if he would pull alongside the pumps, instead of at a sharp angle, so I could also get some gas. He completely ignored me and didn't even move his head to acknowledge me. Once again, I asked him, still politely: "Sir, could you move your car so you're not blocking the pumps please?" Again, there was a complete lack of response on his part. Irritated at his insensitivity and rudeness, and still seated in my car, I took a photograph of the way he was parked, with a clear view of his license plate. After he finished his transaction at the pump, he walked over to my car, pulled out a gun, pointed it at me, and said: "I'm feeling threatened right now. Don't make me use this on you." I froze in my seat, he smiled wryly, and he quickly returned to his car.

As soon as he sped away, I ran into the filling station store, and the attendant told me that he had seen everything, and that the whole incident was probably recorded by the security cameras. I asked if I could use his telephone to call the police, and he agreed to testify that the man had parked incorrectly and had pulled out a gun. The cops arrived a few minutes later, and I explained the situation to them. They asked me to describe the car, and fortunately I had a photograph on my phone of the vehicle and license plate. They took down all the information, and sent out an alert to track down the driver. Before they left, they said they'd be in touch with me again soon. About 45 minutes later, I received a phone call from one of the officers who told me that they had found the car and driver, and that they felt he was a shady character. They said that he had a license for his handgun, and they had issued him a warning, but without proof of what had happened, they couldn't arrest him. They said that if I decided to make a police report and bring charges against him, he would have access to my name and address, and if he were mentally unstable or sought revenge in any way, he would know my name and where I lived. They told me to think about it carefully, and that if I decided to file a police report, I could do so at the police station. I never did anything further.

The strangest of these incidents happened to me in my early thirties while I was moving things out of a storage facility in Brooklyn. In those days, I kept the physical inventory of cassettes for my music company in a small storage unit of a building a few miles from my apartment. Every few weeks I would go there to retrieve inventory for delivery to various vendors that sold my artists' music. One afternoon I exited the building carrying a large bag filled with cassettes, and I proceeded to walk to my car, which was parked down the street. Halfway down the block, a speeding car screeched its brakes loudly, and stopped directly in front of me. A man jumped out of the back seat, pointed a gun toward me, and yelled: "Freeze."

I did as he said, and he quickly walked up to me while holding the gun, and told me to get into the car. Naturally, I resisted, and I asked him what was going on. "Never mind," he said. The back left door opened mysteriously, and he pushed the gun into my back until I sat down inside the car. The driver of the car told me not to move. The other man got into the back seat beside me, and the car sped away. I felt sure I was being taken hostage, but I couldn't understand why. What did these people want from me? What were they going to do with me and with my bag of music cassettes?

The guy next to me in the back seat started asking me questions while pointing the gun at me. "Where's your gun?" he said. "Give me your gun."

"I don't have a gun," I cried out.

But he insisted: "Give me your gun! What's in the bag?"

"Nothing, just cassettes," I replied.

With that, he pulled the bag out of my hands, and several music cassettes spilled onto the car floor. He rifled through the bag with one hand while he kept the gun trained on me with the other hand. Not finding a gun, he and the other man continued with their line of questioning. "Where are you coming from? Where are you going? Where do you live?" I still had no idea what was going on, what they were looking for, or why they were taking me hostage. I pleaded with them to let me go, that I hadn't done anything. I suggested that if they wanted money, I would go to the bank and get some money for them. Only at that point did they identify themselves as New York City police officers. They told me they were taking me to the scene of a crime, that they had been looking for me for the past hour, and that I would be arrested and taken into custody as soon as I was positively identified. I was slightly relieved that these two men were plainclothes cops, and I tried to console myself with the thought that I was totally innocent... but what if I were falsely accused by someone? What was going on here?

A few minutes later, the car slowed down, and it stopped. I was escorted out of the car by both men, and we walked along the sidewalk. A few yards away, a large black woman was sitting on the stoop of a two-story building. One cop held my arm, and the other pushed his gun against my back as he said to the woman: "We got him. Is this him?" She replied with something I'll never forget, no doubt because of the vindication it provided me, but also because a word she used was quintessentially working-class Brooklynese. She said: "You got the wrong guy. Mineses was black." Not mine, but 'mineses'! The man that had accosted her, or robbed her, or whatever it was that had happened, was black. It was the middle of summer, and I was very dark, but how could the cops forget that little detail?

"Aww, we're sorry man," they said. "We were just trying to do our job. Can we give you a ride home? Could you sign this waiver that says it was a case of mistaken identity, and that you're innocent, and that you agree to not press charges against us?"

Guns! All of us here on planet Earth would be better off without guns in our lives. If nobody had them, why would anyone need them? I'm tired of guns, and I'm tired of living in a society of guns. Guns hurt people. I'm for loving and helping people, not hurting them. I know I may die one day because a crazy person in a society without gun control might shoot me, but that doesn't make me want to own a gun to defend myself! This is one instance where the expression "If you can't beat them, join them" makes no sense at all!

Hitchhiking adventures

In my 20s, I almost always traveled long distances by hitchhiking. Occasionally I would take a bus to a strategic starting point, and then I would continue the rest of the way by thumb. I had a bright yellow backpack with an external aluminum frame, a small red tent, a sleeping bag in a waterproof pouch, and a thin foam pad for extra comfort. I also carried matches, a flashlight, a machete in a sheath, and a *bota*, a leather canteen for water and wine. Whenever evening approached, I'd somehow find a place to sleep, whether at the home or in the garage of someone who'd given me a ride, in a vacant shack off the side of the road, or out under the stars. When it was absolutely necessary, or if I felt uncomfortable or vulnerable, I'd stay at a cheap motel, or I'd pitch my tent at a campground for a few dollars. It was the hippy era when most young people had long hair, shared marijuana freely, and talked about peace, love, and rock n' roll.

After graduating college with a degree in Spanish and Latin American studies, I became part of a team that produced a short documentary film about culture and politics in Puerto Rico, where I had attended college for two years. After the shooting and interviews were done, I traveled to other Caribbean islands, and then flew in a small plane to Caracas, Venezuela. After a few months of traveling through Venezuela and Colombia, I took another small plane from northwestern Colombia over the Darién Gap to Panama. From there, I traveled, met new friends, had affairs with young hippy women, worked at odd jobs to make money along the way, and visited and stayed with people I'd met on the road. I hitched rides all the way through Central America, into Mexico, through the Southwestern United States, across the Great Plains into Canada, and then over Niagara Falls before arriving back in New York City. The whole journey lasted eighteen months, and it made a lasting impression on my life and shaped the way I view other people, languages, cultures, and customs.

I once rode in the back of a truck carrying oranges in Portugal, on top of a load of watermelons in Mexico, and in a crowded cargo vehicle with Quechua-speaking Indians and llamas in the Peruvian Andes. One year, as I was hitching through Central America, a large tractor trailer took me from northwestern Costa Rica to Managua, Nicaragua. We arrived in Managua after dark, and the driver went to a hotel for the night. Before he left, he asked me where I would be sleeping. I said that I didn't know where I'd go, so he offered the back of his trailer as an option. When he opened the back door, he showed me what he was hauling: a giant bed of raw cotton. It was the best night's sleep I'd had in weeks. The next morning, when I emerged from the trailer to explore Managua and to cash a traveler's check, I asked the first person that I saw: "*¿Dónde queda el centro?*" (Where is downtown?) He replied: "*Ya no hay centro.*" (There isn't a downtown any more.) He then pointed to an area in ruins that had been completely leveled by a massive earthquake two years earlier.

Once, while on my way to visit a Canadian sweetie named Annie, whom I'd met in Colombia, I was refused entry into Ontario from Northeastern Michigan. I had only about $30 to my name, which wasn't enough money to qualify for entry into the country, so the customs guards sent me back to the American side of the bridge. At a truck stop nearby, I told my story to a few guys who were going smelt fishing across the border for the day. They piled me into the back of a station wagon, put a fishing hat on my head, and gave me a rod and reel to hold. Once at customs, the driver did all the talking; the customs inspector poked his head into the car; and they let us cross the border.

Once, while hitching through the Midwest, I was dropped off at a highway exit ramp near Kansas City, and rather than wait there for the next ride, I walked a short distance to a gas station. I used the bathroom and bought a snack, and while I was resting outside near the pumps, a hippy guy came up to me and asked where I was headed. We chatted for a while and discovered that we were both musicians. After a few more minutes of conversation, he asked if I needed a place to sleep for the night, and he offered to let me stay at his house. After being on the road all day, and running low on cash, this was great news. A few minutes later we arrived at his house in the country, and I met his wife and two kids. After a shower and some food, we played music and partied until very late. The next morning, at breakfast, they all asked if I could stay for a few more days, and I agreed. That was the beginning of a long friendship with Ted Anderson. Ted wrote some beautiful tunes, including a few that were covered and recorded by well known artists of the day.

On the Caribbean island of Guadeloupe, I once found myself stranded after walking the wrong way on a small mountain road after a ride. It got dark very quickly and there were no cars, people or hotels in sight. With nowhere else to go, I decided to sleep there for the night. I unrolled my sleeping bag onto a patch of grass a few yards from the edge of the road, and I fell asleep. In the morning I was startled awake by a warm, wet, and scratchy sensation on my face. I opened my eyes, and I looked right into the face of a cow. She was licking my face.

One of the most memorable rides I had was on a trip through Texas from Mexico. Dan, someone I'd met on the road, had invited me to stay with him at his parents' home in a suburban neighborhood of Dallas. In an era before cell phones and the internet, we had agreed beforehand that I would arrive at a certain time and place near an exit of Highway I-35 in the Dallas metro area. From there I would call him by pay phone, and he'd come to pick me up. I had been spending a few days outside Austin with Steve and Patty, other hippy friends I'd met on the road, and on the morning of my hitch to Dallas, they dropped me off at an entrance ramp to the highway.

With my Dallas sign in hand, I got a few short northbound rides, but then a long time passed before the next person stopped to pick me up. It was an older man in a flashy red car who told me he'd take me as far as he was going. I gladly got in, and along the way we passed three guys on motorcycles. I waved at them, they flashed me peace signs, and we sped away. A little while later, the man who picked me up started coming on to me, and he said that he'd give me some money, take me out to dinner, and put me up in a fancy hotel if I would agree to have sex with him. I was never a homophobe, and lots of other gay men had come on to me in my travels. Maybe it was because I had an earring in my left ear, which at that time was not at all common among heterosexual men, but regardless, I wasn't interested. As I explained my feelings, and as he continued to try to convince me, the three motorcycles approached in the other lane, and again we gestured to each other. The red car sped forward once again, but a few minutes later, I grew tired of the driver's pestering and the awkwardness I was feeling, and I asked him to pull over and drop me off on the shoulder of the highway. He hesitantly agreed. I grabbed my pack and my sign from the back seat, I thanked him, and he drove away.

A few minutes later, I could hear the motorcycles approaching. As they grew closer, I could see them talking to each other as they rode. Two bikes passed me, and the third one pulled over, asked where I was going, and told me to get on the bike. I'd never gotten a hitch on a motorcycle before, much less with a heavy pack strapped to my back. It was so exhilarating! Our bike caught up with the other two, and once again the three motorbikes rode in tandem, leisurely cruising along in the right lane and enjoying a late afternoon on the road. Later, we stopped to get some food, and after another hour, we arrived at a place where there was food and a few picnic tables. They would be heading home after this stop. We ordered some beer, and the guys pulled out a few joints, which we smoked as the conversation continued. They told me about themselves, and they asked about my travels and my hitching adventures. We went inside the restaurant, shot a game of pool, and when I saw an old upright piano in the corner of the room, I played and sang for them the most recent song I had written. We were having a great time, but they had arrived at their final destination, evening was coming, and I was already pretty wasted. We took some photos, exchanged addresses and phone numbers, and said goodbye. I stumbled back onto the entrance ramp to hitch another ride, but that ride was the last one of the day. When the driver let me off, I realized I couldn't go any further. I walked to a small dingy motel, got the cheapest room available, took a shower, and crashed for the night. The next day, I made it to the rendezvous spot in Dallas, and I had a lovely time with Dan and his family before moving onward to my next stop.

In the days following this adventure, I wrote "Hitching up I-35," a tune with a honky-tonk melody, Texas-inspired lyrics, and a catchy "Take Me Away" refrain. I was 23 years old at the time.

Well it happened a bit past Austin one Monday as I was hitchin' up I-35. I had just gotten over a problem with my lover and I had a lot of things on my mind.

So there I am standing on the side of the road, my mind's been achin' like a horny toad, a pack and a sign are my only load, and I've got to get to Dallas on time....

When along come three big motorcycles rippin' on down so grand. They signaled to me and I thought how free it must be to ride this flat Texas land. Take me away ... take me away.

What a stroke of luck – I was being picked up by this dude in a plush red car. He started getting obscene till I explained that scene and told him he just wouldn't get very far.

So away we sped like a bullet of lead, and it wasn't very long until we passed the same three guys with the wind in their eyes, and they waved a second time at me.

And we left those three big motorcycles chokin' in the red car's dust. About ten miles down he left me off with a frown and I thanked him... just enough. Take me away ...
take me away.

So there I am, a Dallas sign in my hand, hopin' for a straight-through ride. When along came the guys with the wind in their eyes, and one pulled over to the side. He said, "What's your story, man? My name is Cory – Hop on and I'll give you a haul."

I strapped the pack to my back and just like that we were off ... like a fireball. At last I was one of them motorcycles headin' out to the sun. At last one of them three motorcycles headin' to have me some fun. Take me away ... take me away.

From that point on we began to carry on, got some food at a Taco Bell. Later on we made a stop and we smoked a little pot, we were gettin' it on so well, that by the time we got there, we went for a beer, there was pool and a piano there. I played them the song I wrote before this one, We were all without a care.

And by the time I hit the road I was drunker and a-higher than hell. I managed to survive just another ride till I had to ... check into a motel. Take me away ... take me away.

And this all happened past Austin one Monday as I was hitching ... up I-35. Take me away ... take me away.

Hitching up I-35, with my yellow frame pack

The three bikers, with Cory at far right

"You should start a publishing company."

In my early thirties, I was living in Brooklyn, New York, teaching Spanish at a high school, singing and playing piano at local bars and restaurants, and performing with a band at weddings and other social events. I was listening to and learning jazz standards, traditional Indian *ragas*, traditional African melodies, and Latin American and Asian folk music. I had also begun to make recordings of musicians from Africa, India and the Far East on my professional gear, and I was producing small batches of cassettes for artists to sell at their concerts. Eventually, I began to distribute the new cassette line to locally-owned music stores, natural food shops, and just about anyone who would agree to sell them. My passion for world music eventually culminated in the record label I founded, but at this stage I was just having fun, learning about music and business, making a few extra dollars, and helping the great traditional musicians I was meeting.

A big break came when I got a consignment account at the brand-new Tower Records store on 4th Street and Broadway in Manhattan. Once I began supplying that store, I was able to open accounts at other Tower Records stores on the East Coast, and also in California. I hoped to eventually convince a few major independent distributors to take on my line of world music cassettes. On one of my first trips to visit Tower Records buyers on the West Coast, I contacted the owner of Arhoolie Records: a bubbly, knowledgeable and congenial German-born man named Chris Strachwitz. In addition to his record label, Mr. Strachwitz had also begun a distribution company that sold LPs and cassettes to record stores on the West Coast and other parts of the United States. I'd known about Chris's work with American Blues, Cajun and Zydeco artists, as well as Mexican and Tex-Mex musicians. I was hoping to meet him, give him some samples of my world music cassettes, and get his advice about distribution. A few days before I arrived in San Francisco, I found the courage to call him by telephone, and asked if he would join me for lunch one day when I'd be meeting with record stores in the Bay Area. To my surprise, he accepted.

He was already an established record producer and label owner. I was nervous, but I was also excited to meet him and to learn whatever I could in our short time together. We went to a small restaurant with outdoor seating in a trendy part of town. We ordered our food and began to engage in light conversation about the music business. He seemed curious about me, and as he looked at my cassette samples, he asked questions about the artists I'd recorded, especially if he wasn't familiar with a particular type of music tradition or instrument. I remember being very excited by our discussion. Even though he was twenty years older and had much more experience, we both shared similar passions and interests for traditional music. At one point, while asking about one of my recordings, he asked: "Do you have the publishing for these songs?" Not understanding him, I asked what he meant, and he replied: "Are you publishing these compositions?" I replied that no, I wasn't printing sheet music; I was just making and selling cassette recordings. He chuckled at my answer, and then he began to explain to me what it means to "publish" a piece of music. He explained that the intellectual property inherent in a song can be registered with an organization like BMI or ASCAP, which then collects royalties from around the world for the use of that music. He said that many musicians and performers didn't know how to protect their original compositions or understand that publishing companies represent the rights of songwriters. Royalties are paid every time a song is broadcast on radio or television or used in a movie or a TV commercial. That's what he'd meant by "publishing."

It was the first time I had ever heard anything about this part of the music industry. I was still a bit unclear about all of this publishing stuff, and he could probably see it in my eyes, because then he said to me: "Let me tell you a story. One day, in the late sixties, there was a knock on my office door, and a young man appeared with a guitar. He introduced himself as Joe McDonald, and said he knew about my records, and that he wanted to play a song for me."

Recognizing the name, I interjected: "From Country Joe and the Fish?"

"Yep," he responded, and then he continued: "So he came in and sat down, he tuned his guitar, and he started to play this song." Then he sang: "Well it's one, two, three..." and I joined in the singing, "... what are we fighting for? Don't ask me, I don't give a damn. Next stop is Vietnam."

I could hardly believe what he was telling me: that Country Joe McDonald had first played this song to him before it became one of the most important anti-war protest songs of my generation. I was in high school when that song became famous, and I was a serious anti-war activist.

"So what happened?" I asked.

"Well," he said, "I listened to the whole song, and I thought it was great, and he asked me if I could help him to get it recorded. I said I'd try to help him get a record deal, and that if I was successful, I'd want my company to have the publishing rights... and he agreed."

Then Chris looked me straight in the eye, and he said: "Do you know what I did with the money from the publishing royalties of that one song?"

"What?" I replied excitedly.

Then he lifted his left arm and pointed his finger to a large, multi-story building across the street from where we were sitting, and he said: "I bought that building." I remember being shocked by that statement, and I'm sure my eyes grew wide with surprise when he said it. Stunned, I just looked back at him without uttering a word. I didn't know what to say or what to think. And then he said to me: "You should start a publishing company."

When I returned to New York, one of the first things I did was to contact a music attorney. An entertainment lawyer in Manhattan named Larry Fabian helped me register a publishing company with Broadcast Music International, otherwise known as BMI. I named the company after beautiful Owl's Head Park, which was directly across the street from my apartment in Bay Ridge, Brooklyn. Owl's Head Music went on to represent musicians from all over the globe through contract negotiation and licensing.

Although I never made enough money to buy a giant commercial building, Owl's Head was certainly successful, and over the years, I've been happy to have helped many traditional musicians (and also their heirs) around the world. Owl's Head compositions have been featured in television commercials for General Motors and Hewlett Packard; in movies by Warner Brothers, MGM and Netflix; in symphonic pieces; ballet performances; and on television networks like CBS, CNN and PBS. With over 500 compositions, the Owl's Head catalog has generated broadcast and streaming royalties which get paid and distributed to the composers and heirs of musicians I worked with over the years. I owe it all... all of this accumulated good karma, and all of the ways it has positively affected so many people around the world... to Chris Strachwitz.

Chris Strachwitz, Arhoolie Records

Bob Haddad, Music of the World

The angel on the beach

After graduating college, I took time off to do some traveling... serious long-term traveling. I'd worked part time during my high school and college years, and decided to use the money I'd saved. I began my adventure in the Caribbean, explored northern South America for several months, and then slowly moved westward, stopping for weeks or months in Nicaragua, Costa Rica, El Salvador, and Honduras. I spent more than three months in Guatemala, and even took a job there as an English-language editor for an expatriate newspaper. After about ten months on the road in Latin America, my money was dwindling, but I was determined to continue traveling. Sometimes I'd stay with people I met along the way, but more often than not, my home base was a small tent that I carried in my backpack.

At that time in my life I smoked cigarettes. Marlboro, in the red and white hard pack, was my preferred brand. Most people smoked at that time. My father smoked a pipe and cigars; my brothers smoked cigarettes; and many people my age also smoked. Movies, television and advertisements portrayed people smoking on a regular basis. It was considered polite to offer someone a cigarette, and somewhat romantic to light a cigarette for a woman. Clinical studies linking cigarette smoke to cancer weren't available to the public; anti-smoking campaigns simply didn't exist; and printed warnings on cigarette packs hadn't yet been mandated by law. On the contrary, television commercials for tobacco products were rampant, and smoking was generally considered "cool." I'd started smoking in my last year of high school, and continued through my college years, but I also had a love-hate relationship with tobacco. I had developed a "smoker's cough" and a raspy voice, and I noticed that whenever I became sick with a cold or a fever, I had absolutely no desire to smoke. I knew these were indicators that smoking wasn't healthy for me.

At this point in my life, I'd been trying to stop smoking for more than a year. I would stop for a few weeks, only to start again. Then I'd stop for a month or two, but in a vulnerable moment I'd accept a cigarette from someone, and it would trigger my addiction all over again. During the periods when I abstained, I tried everything possible to resist the temptation to smoke, including minimizing interactions with smokers, and always staying upwind of cigarette smoke in public places. When I felt the desire for a cigarette, I'd often put something in my mouth to try to release my nervous energy and satisfy my oral fixation, or I'd place a pen or a small stick between my second and third fingers to simulate the sensation of holding a cigarette in my hands. But inevitably, no matter how much time had passed since my last cigarette, I would start smoking once again... then I'd stop, only to start again a few days, weeks or months later. Stuck in this cycle for over a year, I began to get angry at myself for not being able to permanently stop smoking. I knew in my heart that I wanted to stop, but I couldn't do it, and this contributed to a growing undercurrent of frustration and disappointment.

I was traveling through Central America at the time and had recently spent a few weeks in the company of friends I'd met on the Caribbean coast of Costa Rica. After that, I crossed over to the south of the country, and I pitched my tent on a beautiful Pacific coast beach in a small town. It was mid-morning, and as I lay in the sun in front of my tent, I reached for a cigarette, but the pack was empty. I tried to dismiss the craving, but after a few minutes, I decided to buy a pack of cigarettes. I took some money from my backpack, asked nearby beachgoers to watch my tent for a few minutes, and went to a small store nearby. I returned, sat down on the sand outside my tent, and lit a cigarette. With the first deep inhalation, I succumbed to my nicotine craving, but what also entered my lungs was a dose of self-loathing about my cigarette habit. As I sat there, upset at myself, I noticed a man walking on the shoreline. He looked in my direction, we waved at each other, and I gestured for him to come and say hello. He turned away from the shoreline, walked slowly toward me, and we greeted each other. I invited him to sit down, and we began to chat. I still had the lit cigarette between my fingers, and I took the last drag and then extinguished it in the sand. "Oh, you smoke, huh?" he said.

"Yeah," I answered, "but I've been trying to stop for over a year now, and sometimes I get angry at myself because I know I need to stop, but I just can't do it. I stop and then I start again, you know?"

He then asked me a few questions about how long I'd been smoking, and about how long I'd been trying to stop. I told him about the many times I'd temporarily stopped smoking, and how I'd always started again. I didn't mean to unload my angst on this stranger, but he listened attentively and empathetically. He was a fellow long-haired hippy traveler, and I assumed that he'd understand, and that the conversation would quickly flow into another topic, but when I stopped speaking he looked at me intensely and said: "Well, you'll probably never be able to quit smoking."

Surprised, I looked at him and answered that of course I'd be able to stop smoking. "I already stopped a few times," I said.

"Yeah, but you never really stop," he replied, "because you always start again."

I remember feeling defensive when he said that, and I responded that I knew I could stop and that I would do it soon. Then something life-changing happened. He looked deeply into my eyes, and he said in a soft but resolute voice: "No, you'll never be able to stop smoking until you realize that your mind is not in control of your body." With that, he stood up and said: "OK, man, it was nice to meet you. Take it easy and have a good trip." He made a goodbye gesture with his hand, turned to walk toward the sea, and then slowly continued along the shoreline.

I watched him walk along the beach near the water, and as I thought about what he had said to me right before he left, I began to get angry – angry at myself. I knew in my heart that he was right. I'd been trying to stop smoking for more than a year, and it was my body's craving for the nicotine that was holding me captive. He was absolutely right: my mind wasn't in control of my body. I watched the stranger slowly shrink from view as he walked further into the horizon. My unhappiness and frustration began to ferment in my stomach, and I felt it rising to my chest. I thought about my lack of resolve and willpower to do what I truly wanted for myself. I grabbed the pack of cigarettes that I had just bought, quickly stood up, and walked agitatedly to the water's edge. Once there, I let out a stifled scream, and then, one by one, I ripped apart each of the remaining nineteen cigarettes and threw them into the sea. My actions were accompanied by visceral sounds that emerged from my chest and my throat, and self-affirmations spoken aloud: "I'm never going to smoke again." "That's it, never again. I'm done with smoking." "Do you hear me? I'm never going to smoke again." "Just stop it! – I'm stopping for good." It was a dramatic and cathartic experience that pushed me over the edge, and I assured myself that from now on, my mind would be in control. I reminded myself that I had wanted to stop for a very long time, and that now I was making an active decision and a promise to myself to stop smoking forever. As cotton filters, clumps of tobacco, and torn pieces of cigarette paper rolled in the waves and slowly became consumed by the ocean, I remember looking down the coastline to see the person who had triggered this reaction in me... but he had faded into the horizon.

I never smoked another cigarette for the rest of my life. I often remember that day on the beach in Central America when an unknown angel appeared to me and challenged me to empower myself and to summon the willpower to change my life in a positive way. I don't remember his name or where he was from, but I often thank him and send him blessings, wherever he may be.

Music of the World

In my late twenties, I was living in a fifth floor apartment in Bay Ridge, Brooklyn, and was teaching Spanish at a high school nearby. On weekends and occasionally during the week, I played piano and sang at local restaurants, and led bands at various locations throughout the New York area. These gigs were called "club dates," and playing at weddings and catering hall events was how most professional musicians made enough money to survive. I was a good singer, percussionist, and band leader, but many of my fellow musicians were more talented than I, and this allowed me to grow and learn in wonderful ways.

Over the previous few years, I'd become deeply attracted to traditional music from other cultures. The Beatles had broken up years before, and as I began to move away from pop and rock, I gravitated toward jazz, and also to the traditional music of India and West Africa. My exposure to traditional world music was fueled by my relationship with Robert Browning, a British-born music presenter living in New York. Robert, his wife Helene, and their business partner Geno first opened a place in Manhattan's East Village called ACIA, which later became the World Music Institute. They specialized in presenting concerts of traditional music from India, Africa, Asia, Latin America, and other regions of the world. At first, I simply attended a few concerts there, but within a few months I began to volunteer with pre-concert setup. I learned a lot through Robert, since he put me in contact with some of the most prominent traditional musicians of the day. Over the years I helped with advertising and promotion, and sometimes I picked up artists from incoming flights and let them stay at my apartment for a few days. That would save hotel expenses and allow them to earn more money.

Once, a Senegalese *kora* player named Djimo Kouyate came to perform a concert. While speaking to him after the show, I learned that he didn't have any recordings of his music to sell at concerts, and I asked if he would like to make one together. A few weeks later, he came to my apartment, and we began a series of recording sessions that would result in his first commercial recording, and my first as a producer. These were the days of analog recording, and I used a TEAC four-track open reel machine and several of my best microphones. I passed the signal through a simple mixing board with basic equalization and a spring-type reverb, and when the tracks were finished, I spliced the tape with a razor blade on an editing block, and added several seconds of white leader tape between each track. One side of the large metal reel was side A, and the other was side B. I purchased two more cassette decks, and I connected them "in series" so the output of each machine ran to the input of another. In this way, every time I played the tape deck I could record three cassettes at once. I'd bring the reel to the start of the first song and press the "pause" button. Then I'd load the cassettes to their starting point and hit "record + pause." Finally, when I was ready, I'd quickly press "record" on each of the cassette decks and then press "play" on the open reel machine. I used a kitchen timer to measure the approximate length of each side, and it would beep about one minute beforehand, so I'd have enough time to return to my position. When side A was finished, I'd fast-forward the reel and the cassettes, flip them over to the other side, and repeat the process to record side B.

The cassette insert for the first "Music of the World" recording was made from an image that was photocopied onto cardstock, and then hand-trimmed on a paper cutter. I used the edge of my kitchen counter to fold the thin cardboard so that each insert would fit neatly into a cassette box. Word was beginning to spread about the guy in Brooklyn who was making world music cassettes in his apartment for artists to sell at their concerts. Within a few months I began to receive phone calls from other traditional musicians, asking if I could produce a recording for them. Sometimes, I'd bring the large tape deck to remote locations. Once, while trying to create the right type of reverberation for a Japanese flute, I recorded the sessions in a tiled shower room at the nearby high school where I worked. I continued in this way, recording music from Africa, Asia, and Latin America, making master tapes, reproducing cassettes in my apartment, and selling them to the artists, who would then sell them at their concerts. It was a fun hobby, and I was constantly learning more about traditional music from around the world.

On stage with the first recording artist, Djimo Kouyate

Toward the end of that year, and after surgery to remove vocal polyps, I was forced to go on voice rest, apply for disability compensation from my teaching job, and stop all vocal activity. The small insurance settlement I received was enough to pay my rent for a year or so, and faced with the lack of clarity about my next career, I began to transform my cassette hobby into a more serious business. Instead of simply selling the cassettes to the artists that I was recording, I began to place the products on consignment in natural food stores and small record shops in the New York area. Every few weeks, I'd make the rounds, take inventory, receive payment for the units that had sold since my last visit, and restock the store with more product. Eventually, I landed distribution deals with independently-owned distributors that sold music and other products to natural food stores, New Age shops, and gift stores around the country. In 1983, the California-based Tower Records opened its first megastore in New York on East 4th Street and Broadway. At that time, I had produced about seven cassettes of world music artists, and I was eventually granted a meeting to discuss sales possibilities with the store manager. The buyer seemed interested in the products, but he told me that he couldn't accept anything into the store that wasn't shrink-wrapped. He said that if I sealed the cassettes in plastic wrap, he would allow me to open a consignment account. I didn't know anything about shrink-wrapping, but a few days later I was in a neighborhood delicatessen, and I noticed that their pre-made sandwiches were sealed in plastic wrap. I asked the grocer how he did that, and he showed me a machine with a heating element and sheets of clear plastic. I asked him if he could order a box of those plastic sheets for me; he agreed, and a week later I picked it up. I now had the plastic wrap, but I had no idea how to shrink it neatly around each of the cassette boxes. I tried a hair dryer, but that didn't work because the heat wasn't strong enough, and I couldn't neatly seal all sides of the rectangular cassette box. Then one day I spotted my *comal*, a Mexican tortilla plate that I sometimes used on my gas stove to heat corn tortillas. I removed some plastic sheets from the box, and within a few minutes, I figured out a way to seal a cassette box in plastic wrap by folding the corners in gift-wrap style and holding them against the hot tortilla plate.

Once the corners were sealed, I held the front and back sides of each cassette box against the hot plate until the plastic wrap tightened. After a few hours, I was able to shrink-wrap a good number of cassettes of each of my releases. The following week, I returned to Tower Records in Manhattan with the finished product, and a vendor consignment account was opened for Music of the World. After several months, I stopped making the cassettes at home, and I turned to a professional duplicator in New York City who manufactured the products.

Once a consignment account was opened at the Manhattan store, I traveled with my car to open accounts at other Tower stores in New York, New Jersey, Pennsylvania, Maryland, and Washington, DC. Later that year, I flew to Chicago, Nashville, and California to do the same. After a few years of consignment billing, the rapidly expanding megastore allowed me to open a nationwide commercial account. At that point, I hired several sales reps in New York, California, and Chicago, and paid them a percentage of the total amount of each purchase order they were able to fill. This continued until I opened accounts with distributors in the United States and Canada, who sold my products to record stores in their territories. I joined trade organizations, exhibited my products at conventions, expanded distribution to Canada and Europe, and began advertising campaigns in music magazines and trade journals. During these early years, and before a commercial consciousness of "world music" had developed, Music of the World was the only world music cassette label in the West. In 1989, I moved from New York to North Carolina, and in that same year, with a personal loan from a recording engineer named Ed Haber, the first two compact discs were released on the label. With additional loans from a local bank and also my parents, I converted a barn on my property into a large building with offices and a shipping area, and I hired several employees to work in shipping and publicity. Others were hired on a per-project basis for graphic design, artist promotion, and advertising. Over the next ten years, almost 90 more CD titles were released, and distribution eventually grew to over 20 countries worldwide.

The mid-1990s were peak years for the label, and they were marked by the commercial success of several recordings, including the Grammy-nominated *Raga Aberi* (South Indian classical music); *Vintage Beausoleil* (Cajun music from Louisiana); and one of the label's best-selling recordings, *Talking Spirits*, featuring various Native American artists. In addition to the premier Music of the World label, two other imprints were born during this period of growth. Nomad Records featured modern world music and world jazz, and Latitudes was a mid-price label of single-artist releases and compilations of traditional world music. I attended yearly conventions in the USA and Europe to network with artists, distributors and record labels, and I chaired a world music committee for a major trade organization. Unlike other companies that licensed music from other labels for re-release, Music of the World created almost all its own recordings. I worked closely with the artists, sometimes even contributing to the music arrangements, and I personally produced the great majority of the albums released on the labels.

Everything was going well until two things happened. First, my wife began to have a secret affair with an old boyfriend, and over a period of about several months, I began to discover many painful, unsavory and unimaginable things. As my personal life was changing, so was the music industry. A new technology called Napster had emerged on the scene. It was a web-based platform that allowed users to upload, download and trade digital audio files for free. The technology was unprecedented, and it caught on very quickly. Once a user uploaded a digital song from a compact disc, it could be heard and downloaded by anyone in the world. The website offered a user-friendly interface that allowed music enthusiasts to download copies of songs available on current compact discs, and other songs that were more difficult to obtain, such as unreleased albums and illegal recordings of live concerts. Since this technology had never before been available, it was not yet illegal, and there were no laws in any country to prevent it from continuing. Within a short period of time, the recording industry became severely impacted by a drastic reduction in sales of physical audio products. Millions of units were returned to record labels around the world, and eventually, many record stores, independent record labels, and distributors filed for bankruptcy. By the time the Napster company was sued, and legislation was introduced around the world to ban free downloads of copyright-protected audio, the music business had been changed forever.

My wife and I divorced, I sank deeper into depression, and my creative stimulus was suddenly gone. I still owned my record label, but I had to issue refunds for products that were continuously being returned by my distributors all over the world. With no income, I was forced to terminate all but one of my employees. Suffering financially from marital debt and from the music industry crisis, my only hope was to try to sell whatever was left of my business and move on to a new career. I confided in a few of my record industry colleagues to see if they could help to discreetly spread the news that my label was for sale. One of these, Paul Schulman, told me that he was in touch with a consultant for an emerging dot com that was poised to become the first legal alternative to Napster. It was a company called eMusic.com, which was co-founded by a college student named Gene Hoffman, and venture capitalists began to invest in his new company. Paul phoned me one day, and he asked if I would give him a sales commission if he could connect me to someone who would buy my company. We made a verbal agreement, and he then gave my information to a consultant for eMusic. A few days later, I spoke with a man named Barry Bergman on the phone, and I sent him samples of the compact discs on my label, along with sales figures and press and promotional information. A few weeks later, as a content acquisition consultant for eMusic, Barry flew from New York to visit with me in North Carolina. By then, only my office manager, Michelle, was still working at the company, but I contacted several of my previous employees, and I offered to pay them to pretend that they were busy at work on the day when the representative visited our office.

A few months later, eMusic.com bought the master recordings and copyrights of the entire catalog of recordings that I had produced, and that company continued as a pioneer in subscription-based streaming and download platforms for a number of years. Its structure was based on a user subscription fee for a fixed number of digital downloads per month, and they paid royalties to record labels, artists and publishers. This model became the prototype for all the streaming and download companies that would follow. After the acquisition of my label, eMusic hired me as a salaried consultant for two years. A few years later, eMusic itself was acquired by industry giant Universal Music, and later, the Music of the World catalog was acquired by The Orchard, a leading digital audio distributor. Today, and presumably forever into the future, entire albums and individual tracks from the nearly 100 recordings in the catalog are available through major online streaming platforms.

Music production, distribution, and audio technology changed so rapidly over such a short period of time. I think back on the days of open-reel audio tape, vinyl records, "8-track" players in cars, audio cassettes, telephone answering machines, digital audio tape (DAT), and compact discs. I remember each one of the records I produced, all of the amazing artists I worked with and learned from, and all the places I traveled as I followed my dream of documenting and recording traditional music from around the world. I am grateful to have met and worked with so many amazing artists, and I'm lucky to have had such a rich, creative, multicultural, and rewarding period in my life.

presents this certificate to

Music Of The World Ltd

in recognition of your participation as

Record Company

on the Grammy Nominated Recording

"Raga Aberi"
(Shankar With Zakir Hussain & Vikku Vinayakram)

in

Best World Music Album

for the awards year 1995

Grammy nomination for best world music album

The blind musicians
of Cusco

As a school teacher in my early thirties, I often traveled abroad during summer break. In addition to teaching, I was also recording musicians from around the world. One summer I decided to go to Cusco, Peru. I was collecting information for my master's thesis in Latin American studies, and I'd planned to make field recordings of traditional musicians, and analyze and document the music as part of the project. I was already familiar with the more commercial types of Andean music, but I was hoping to find, meet, and record traditional musicians in their native settings. In preparation for the trip, I bought new recording equipment, including a portable cassette recorder, microphones, cables, and other audio gear.

After landing in Lima, where I'd planned to spend a few days before flying on to Cusco, I took a bus from the airport to downtown. My clothing was in a large backpack strapped to my back, but all my expensive recording equipment, money, passport and other valuable items were in a small day pack. I wore it backward – with the bag resting on my chest – so I could keep track of it at all times. While walking down a busy pedestrian street called Jirón de la Unión, I noticed something wet on the front of my jacket, but I thought nothing of it and I continued onward. A few moments later, a mestizo woman came up to me and said: "*Oye señor, te ensuciaste.*" She pointed to a gooey substance on the left sleeve of my jacket, and offered to help me clean it. I wondered where the soapy liquid had come from, but I took the napkin she offered to me, thanked her, and began to clean my sleeve. As I was doing this, she said there was more on my large backpack, and I felt the pressure of her hand against my back as she rubbed from behind me. After a moment, she suggested that I remove my backpacks so we could clean them properly. For some reason, I complied. I first placed the small backpack on the ground in front of me near my feet, and then I turned around to remove the larger pack from my back. She encouraged me to turn my body toward her as she continued to wipe my jacket for a few seconds. By the time I turned around once again, my small backpack was gone. I panicked, and frantically scanned the busy crowd ahead of me to see if I could spot someone running away with my backpack. A moment later, when I turned around again, the woman was also gone. Within one hour of my arrival in Peru, I had lost all of my valuables, including my passport, camera, flight tickets, traveler's checks, and recording equipment. I had worked and saved for many months to prepare for this trip, and now all my valuables and identification were gone.

The next few days were spent at the police department, at the American Express office to report the stolen traveler's checks, and at the U.S. Consulate, since I had to apply for a new passport. Needless to say, I was devastated, and I stayed at a hostel for a few days to compose myself and ponder my options. I still had my wallet, credit cards, and all my clothing, but I felt defeated and depressed. I had wanted more than anything to make field recordings of traditional musicians in the Andes, yet all of my newly-purchased equipment had been stolen on the first day of my trip. Within a few days I was granted a new passport, and I decided to contact the airlines and request a return ticket back to JFK Airport. One week after leaving for a two-month Peruvian adventure, I was back home in my apartment, confused and without a cause. After a few days of considering my options, I decided to confront my defeat and follow through with my original plan. I went to J&R Audio in Manhattan and I purchased all new gear, including a professional field recorder, new microphones and cables, and a new camera. I purchased another round-trip ticket, this time with an open return flight. I didn't need to repack my main bag: I simply washed a few items of clothing and reinserted them. Three days later, I landed once again in Lima, but this time I made a direct connection to Cusco, and I stayed at a hostel that was recommended to me by someone I'd met ten days before. My journal entry from that day reads: "It's a bit expensive, about $3.50 per day, but it seems safe, and it's only a 15-minute walk to the Plaza de Armas."

For the next day or two, I wandered around the amazing city of Cusco, the ancient capital of the Incan empire, and I visited a few historic sites. One afternoon, I walked to a street named *Jatun Rumiyoc* to look at the foundations of an ancient Incan palace made of giant hand-hewn blocks of stone. The mortarless joints of the interlocked stones are so tight that even a knife blade can't pass through them. As I entered the long, winding street paved with cobblestones, I heard a stringed instrument ahead of me, and then someone singing. As I got closer, I saw a small round man, wearing a golden-brown poncho and a *chullo*, a traditional woven llama wool hat with ear flaps. His eyes were closed, and he was playing a harp and singing in Quechua. Delighted, I leaned against the opposite wall to listen for a while as people passed by and occasionally threw coins into his cup. At one point, he lifted his head to say *gracias* to someone, and that's when I noticed he was blind. While he was taking a sip of water in between songs, I approached him, put some money in his cup, introduced myself, and we began to speak. I explained that I was hoping to record some traditional music while in Cusco, and I offered to pay him if he would record for me one day. He happily agreed, and we made arrangements to meet again at that very spot. We met as planned the next day, and we slowly walked to a nearby shop where, for a small fee, the owner let us use a private room to record. After doing tests for microphone placement, equalization and balance, I was able to get a few takes of two or three songs, and I took notes about the names and lyrics of each one. I was excited, and when I let him hear through the headphones what he had just played, he became excited too. It was the first time he had ever heard his own recorded music, and the childlike expression on his face as he listened was unforgettable. We agreed to do another recording session after I returned from my travels outside the city. He told me that he always played in front of that same stone wall, and that whenever I was ready, I would find him there. I paid him a good sum for that first recording session, we shook hands, and we said *hasta pronto*.

After traveling with a friend to visit small towns and Inca ruins in the valley of Cusco, I returned to the city, and after a day of rest, I walked up the hill to the ancient stone wall. Sure enough, Leandro was there with his harp, but this time, another blind musician was alongside him, playing *bandolina*, an Andean ten-string mandolin. I approached after they finished their song, and Leandro became excited upon hearing my voice. He said he had been waiting for me to return, and asked if his friend Benjamín could also play on a few tracks for our next session. I was excited about the opportunity to record yet another blind street musician, and we agreed to meet the following day at a *chichería*, a bar that serves *chicha*, or fermented corn beer. That's when I met the harpist's two children, César and Maruja, who arrived there after school to meet their father and guide him home after the recording session. After each song, I asked questions and took notes about the lyrics. I paid both of them for the recording session, and we made a date to record again a few days later. Fortunately, I had begun a friendly relationship with Guillermo, the owner of a small music and souvenir shop in the main plaza, and he introduced me to Manuel and Reynaldo, two members of a professional folk group named *Grupo Expresión*. All of them encouraged me to continue recording the blind musicians known locally as *"los cieguitos,"* and they helped me to translate into Spanish some of the Quechua lyrics of the songs I was recording.

A few days later, when I arrived at the meeting spot for the next recording session, I could hardly believe my eyes. In addition to Leandro and Benjamín, there were two more blind musicians! Leandro explained that sometimes they all played together, and he asked if I would record the whole group that day. I was delighted. We recorded about three or four tunes that day – in various takes because of occasional interruptions from a barking dog, a screaming child or a crowing rooster. The harpist's son, César, was there again, and this time I also met the flute player's son, Basilio. We recorded for a few hours at a *picantería* (a small restaurant), and I paid each of the musicians for the session. The next day, I asked them to sign a recording agreement that I'd prepared with Guillermo's typewriter. The agreement was in Spanish and English, and it stated that after I recovered my expenses, I would pay them sales royalties. I read it to them, and they "signed" it by placing an inked thumbprint on the signature lines.

At the end of the month, I returned to New York feeling content. I'd gathered some good information for my graduate school research, and I'd recorded and documented several hours of good quality field recordings. Back home in my apartment, I mastered the cassettes onto an open reel deck by equalizing the signal and adding a little reverberation. I pitched the album concept to an independent record label in New York City called Lyrichord, one of the only independent labels that specialized in traditional music from around the world. They agreed to release the album, along with my corresponding photos and descriptive notes, and they paid me a small sum, plus a few free LPs. Aside from the home-made cassettes I had already produced for my little company, this was my first commercial recording on an established record label.

The following year, I returned again to the Cusco area, and I made more recordings with Leandro (*arpa* –Andean folk harp); Fidel (*quena* – notched vertical bamboo flute); and Benjamín and Carmen (*bandolinas* –mandolins). I also brought them some royalty money from the LP release and a few of their albums. They didn't have a record player, but they brought it to Guillermo's store on the main square, and he played it for them as they listened. Later that year, I released a cassette on my own label called *Peruvian Harp & Mandolin*, and it was released as a compact disc a few years after that. I returned to Cusco several times over the next eight years with royalty money and boxes of cassettes and CDs, which they sold to tourists as they played on the streets and at small venues. During these trips, I also became a godfather to the harp and flute players' children.

Although all the *cieguitos* are now deceased, I still occasionally return to Cusco, and now it is to spend quality time with my godchildren and with their own children, all of whom know me as "*padrino*." My connections to my *familia* in Cusco have been sustaining and nurturing. All of these beautiful things happened in my life because I somehow found the courage – after being robbed and losing all my belongings – to go right back to Peru the following week. I have remained in touch with my godchildren by video chat and email; they are mentioned in my will and testament; and I feel honored to be able to help them whenever possible. I never had children of my own, but each of them help to fill that void, and the nature of our connection is deep, meaningful and spiritual.

Benjamín (bandolina) and Leandro (harp)

Carmen (bandolina)

Lulu and Richie

One day in the late 1970s, while riding a northbound subway in Manhattan, I spotted a pretty girl standing near the door, holding a handrail. I snaked my way through the other passengers, grabbed hold of the same handrail, and began some casual conversation. We talked about this and that, and I probably asked her where she was getting off, so I knew how to time my move. After a few minutes, I asked if she'd like to get together sometime, and I asked for her phone number. She smiled and gave me her number. Her name was Laura Royster, and her nickname was Lulu.

She was sweet and fun. We were both young, it was the late hippie era, and there was nothing too serious between us. Every so often we'd get together at her apartment in Manhattan, near Central Park, or we'd meet somewhere and go to a concert, or I'd pick her up and take her for a drive in my car to the beach, or back to my apartment in Brooklyn. We dated for a few months, and I don't remember how we faded apart, but it probably had something to do with my travels. I was a school teacher at that time, and since I had my summers free, I would usually leave the country for several months. Although we never saw each other or stayed in contact after that time, I never forgot her, and I always had very nice memories of our brief time as friends.

More than 20 years later, while reading the arts section of the local newspaper, I noticed that Richie Havens was booked to play at The Arts Center in Carrboro, North Carolina, about a ten-minute drive from my home. I jumped at the chance to see this pop legend in an intimate setting. Richard Pierce Havens (1941–2013) was an American singer-songwriter and guitarist who recorded cover versions of many famous songs of the era, and whose music contained elements of folk, soul, and rhythm and blues. He used open tunings on his guitar, played in a strong and rhythmic style that was instantly recognizable, and had a unique and distinctive voice. Richie recorded over twenty albums between 1966 and 2008, and he was the opening act at the world-famous Woodstock festival. In the late seventies, I'd once had the opportunity to meet him while I worked as a stage assistant at a summer music festival in New York. I interacted with him several times during the sound check to make sure that he was happy with the mix. He was a sweet and unpretentious man, and I remember that he made me feel special, even though I was only a stage announcer. A West African artist I was promoting at that time was appearing right before his performance. Richie and I spoke briefly before he walked on stage that day, and I was elated to have met him.

I was excited to see him perform again after so many years. I arrived at the theater a bit early so I could get a good seat, and I brought one of my old Richie Havens albums in the hopes of having him sign it for me. As the crowd settled in and the house lights dimmed, a female announcer pulled back the curtain and walked onto the stage. A spotlight was turned on, and she greeted the audience: "Good evening everyone, and welcome to a wonderful evening of music with the great Richie Havens. My name is Laura Royster, and I'm the new Program Director at The Arts Center..." I heard the name, and as I looked at her face, it took me a few seconds to realize that I was looking at Lulu, the girl I'd dated over twenty years ago. I could hardly believe it! What was she doing in my hometown, and when had she arrived here? She finished her opening announcements, welcomed us once again to the concert, and introduced the star of the show.

The curtains opened and there was Richie, smiling and radiant as I'd remembered him. He played a great first set, the crowd loved him, and we went to intermission. I knew some of the staff at the theater, and I knew I could get backstage during intermission, but I decided to wait until after the show. The second set was as enthralling as the first, and during the course of the evening, Richie sang and played his original songs, as well as some of his most famous cover tunes, including George Harrison's *Here Comes the Sun*, Bob Dylan's *Just Like a Woman*, James Taylor's *Fire and Rain*, and the iconic song *Freedom* that made history when he performed it at Woodstock.

As the show ended, most people left the theater, but a few remained in hopes of meeting the artist. I waited until they had gone, went backstage, and walked to the green room where artists would change clothes, relax and eat snacks. Laura was there, speaking to Richie who was sitting on a couch. I knocked on the open door, Laura turned around, looked at me, and I asked: "Don't you know who I am?" She exclaimed in an excited voice: "Bob!" We hugged and laughed and asked rapid-fire questions of each other, and all along Richie was watching, smiling, and taking it all in.

At one point he asked how we had met each other, and Laura looked at him and replied: "This guy picked me up on the subway. I was headed uptown, and he just walked up to me, struck up a conversation, and asked me for my number."

Richie started laughing and asked: "And how long has it been since you've seen each other?" I replied that it had been since the late 70s. "And you didn't know that you lived in the same town?" he asked. "No," Laura replied, "I just moved here not long ago to take this job." We continued to hug each other, and Richie was laughing really hard now, saying how cool it was that we had gotten reacquainted. Then she turned to him and said: "This is Subway Bob. Even my mother knows about him."

We joked and carried on, and Richie was fully part of our reconnection experience. In fact, his presence and participation made it even more special. After things calmed down with Laura, we agreed to exchange numbers and get together. Then she left the room, and I had a chance to speak to Richie personally. I asked if he would sign my album, and he agreed. As I sat down next to him, he looked deeply in my eyes and asked: "Do I know you from somewhere?"

"Well," I answered, "Once we met at a folk festival and…"

He interrupted: "And you were a stage hand, and you helped me with my sound… yeah, I remember now. You were working with an African musician, right? Wow, man, it's cool to see you again. How've you been?"

I was beyond myself that an internationally-known musician like Richie Havens had remembered a brief conversation that he'd had with a young stage announcer… and that he actually recognized my face after that one brief encounter! That evening was such a joy. I got reacquainted with an old friend that I hadn't seen in many years, and I also had an amazing few moments with the great Richie Havens, a truly beautiful person, and someone who had remembered me from a ten-minute exchange we'd had backstage at a folk festival more than 20 years before.

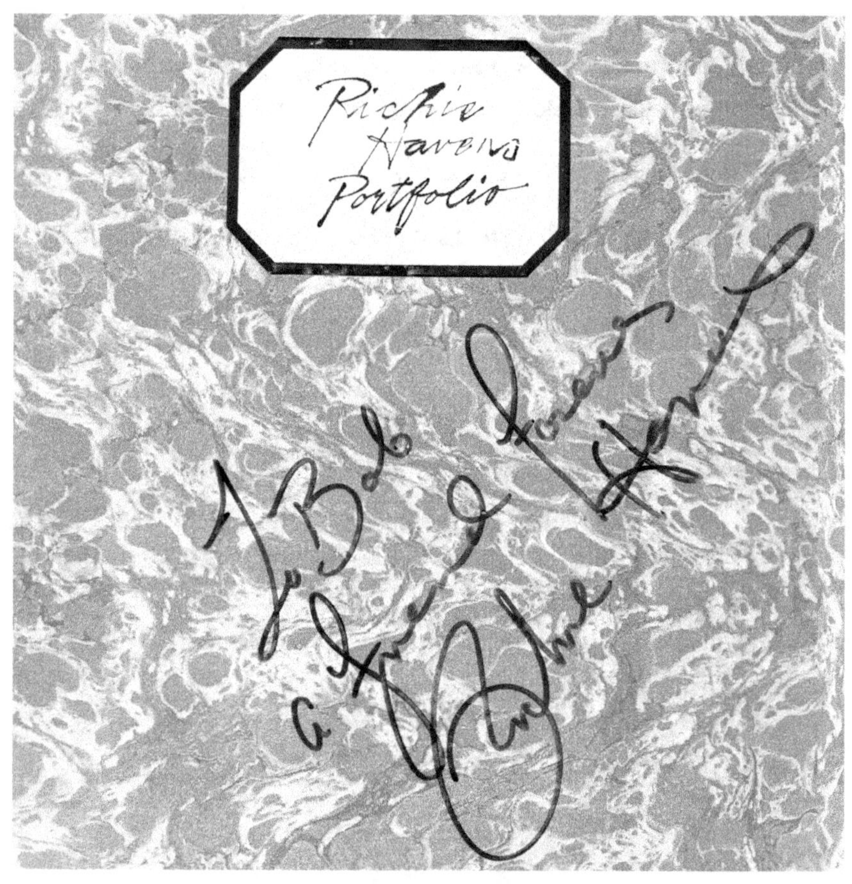

The lp album signed by Richie

Spongy balls

In my late thirties, I moved to North Carolina with my girlfriend. A friend from New York named Philip was finishing an academic residency in the same area, and he and his wife Kinza were preparing to move to the West Coast, where he would begin a new teaching position. One day we planned to meet for dinner at an Indian restaurant that had recently opened at the edge of town. I and the others were no strangers to Indian food. Back in New York, I had many Indian friends. I loved Indian classical music, and I sometimes played percussion with my sitar-playing friend Arooj at an Indian restaurant in Manhattan called Shagorika. After each performance, the owner would feed us lavishly. I loved curries, *kormas*, *biryanis*, *samosas*, *dahls*, and all the delicious homemade breads and condiments... and Indian desserts were amazing too.

We were all excited to share a meal together and have some fun. We entered the restaurant, were seated at a nice table, ordered drinks and appetizers, and began to catch up with each other and enjoy the evening. After an hour or so of lively conversation and good food, our waiter approached the table and asked if we'd like dessert. We all agreed that some Indian sweets and *chai* would be a great way to round off the evening. We asked the waiter what he had for dessert. "Well," he said in a strong Indian accent, "we have rice pudding, mango ice cream, and spongy balls." We giggled when he said that, and I said, "Spongy balls? Do you mean *gulab jamun?*"

"Oh sir," he said excitedly, "you know what is *gulab jamun*? Yes, we have it, and it is very good tonight." *Gulab jamun* are small fried dumplings made of milk solids, flour, sugar and cardamom, usually served warm in a small bowl of rose water and sugar syrup. They have a slightly spongy texture, and that's why he was calling them spongy balls. At that time, in a small town in North Carolina, many people might not have been familiar with *gulab jamun*, but we multicultural city slickers certainly weren't among them.

Several of us were still grinning at the "spongy balls" term he had used, but we proceeded to give him our dessert order. As he cleared the dinner plates and began to leave the table, I said to him, "You know, my friend, before you go, let me tell you, you really shouldn't say 'spongy balls' to the customers. It doesn't sound right. It might give a strange impression to people or make them laugh."

"Oh really?" the waiter answered. "But then what should I say, sir?"

"Well," I answered, "you could just say *gulab jamun*, and then if they ask you what it is, you can describe it and say they are small fritters served in rose water syrup."

"Oh, I see. OK, thank you, sir, I will try it," he said, and he left to return to the kitchen to place our dessert order.

Within a few minutes we were enjoying our desserts and tea, and winding down the evening. At the same time, the table next to ours had just finished eating their main course. A busboy came to clear their table, and upon noticing that, I whispered to my friends: "Let's see what the waiter says when he asks them for dessert." Excited at the thought of eavesdropping, we started giggling again. "Shh, here he comes," someone said. Sure enough, the same waiter approached our neighbors' table and asked if they had enjoyed their dinner. Then he said to them: "Would you like some dessert tonight?"

One of the customers asked: "What do you have?"

"Well," he replied, "we have rice pudding, mango ice cream, and *gulab jamun*."

One of the women at the table said in a strong southern accent: "Gulajamin? What's that?"

We held our breath with anticipation, and the waiter responded ... "spongy balls."

Amazonas

On one of my many journeys to Peru, I met a Spaniard named Don Damián Magro, who owned a cattle ranch in the Amazon rainforest. We were staying in the same guest house in Lima; we exchanged contact information; and he invited me to visit him one day. A month later, after recording music and traveling in the southern Andes, I decided to contact him and ask if I could visit with him. He agreed, and he sent me some very basic information about how to get to his village. My idea was to fly back to Lima, travel into the jungle for about ten days, and then return to the capital to fly onward to my next destination. I had no fixed plans or hotel reservations. I didn't really know how to get there, and I didn't know anyone along the way, but I had a large fold-out map of Peru. The first town on Damián's note, San Ramón, was on the map, but neither the next town nor my final destination were charted. Little did I know what would be in store for me.

The next morning, I took a small bus for ten bumpy hours over the Andes mountains, and then downward to the fertile plains to the east. I arrived at my first stop, the village of San Ramón Chanchamayo, where I stayed at a small hostel. It was green, fertile and humid, and many of the inhabitants were indigenous people who spoke the Campa language. Over dinner that evening, I learned that the best way to my next stop, Puerto Bermúdez, was by small airplane. Damián had also mentioned that, and although it was expensive, I decided to do it. The next morning, I walked a few miles up a hill to a small packed-dirt air strip. I bought a one-way ticket, and as I waited at the landing strip, I heard a radio announcement that blood donors were needed for people who had been critically injured in a recent airplane crash that occurred because of poor visibility. I asked someone where this had happened, and I learned that it was on the very same route to Puerto Bermúdez. Another person confided that in the past month there had been three plane crashes in the area. I began to get very worried. Eventually, when the little six-seater plane arrived, the passengers disembarked and told me that it was a terrible ride and that there was very poor visibility. That's when I decided that I wouldn't be flying, and that even if it took another two days, I would travel overland. I asked for a refund of my one-way fare, and at first the attendant refused, but eventually, he kept a portion of my money and refunded the rest of it to me.

I returned to the little village and began asking people how I could get to Puerto Bermúdez. By a stroke of luck, I met a man named Carlos who told me he was heading in that direction with his two kids, and that he could take me at least half the way in his pickup truck. I offered to pay for his gas, and we had a lovely full day of travel, talking about politics, social welfare, music, agriculture, and life in general. When I learned that he was a cacao cultivator, I mentioned that I had never seen a cacao pod. A few minutes later, he pulled the truck to the side of the road and asked me to follow him into a field. He grabbed a red fruit about the size of a papaya from a small tree trunk, and cracked it open on a rock. Inside were white clusters, similar in shape to cloves of garlic, which contained bright red seeds. He explained how the seeds were removed, toasted and then ground into powder. The fleshy interior smelled like chocolate, and it was a wonderful experience. Toward the end of the day, we arrived at his final destination, the village of San Juan de Cacazú. On a map, the town appeared as a dead end, but the locals assured me there was a dirt road that continued onward. I found lodging, settled in for dinner and a few beers, and chatted with local people. One of them was a man who knew Don Damián, and he told me that local people referred to him as "El Tigre." He said that Damián had once been attacked by a large puma, and that he managed to fight it off.

It poured heavy rain all through the night, and I slept soundly. The next morning, over breakfast, I was lucky to meet a man who had hired a pickup truck to take his family to Puerto Bermúdez, and he invited me to come along. About three hours into the ride, we arrived at the first of several washed-out wooden bridges. The torrential rains and flooding from the night before left lumber and debris all around the bridge, making it impossible for a vehicle to pass. The driver asked us to wade across the river to reduce weight, and then he followed by rushing at full speed through the shallow water to reach the other side. After pushing the vehicle onto the shore from the river bed, we re-boarded the truck and continued onward. About an hour later we arrived at a much higher steel-framed bridge, which was also washed out. This time the driver said he couldn't go any further, and that he would have to leave us there and turn back. My fellow travelers decided that we could walk on the few planks of wood that were haphazardly strewn over the metal girders. They reasoned that once we were on the other side, word would get out, and another vehicle would eventually come to pick us up and take us the rest of the way. The local people were small and nimble, and were able to cautiously balance their weight on the thin wooden boards as they slowly walked to the other side. I was scared at the thought of crossing a washed-out bridge over a rushing river, but I tried to quell my fears, and after everyone else had crossed, I began to slowly make my way on a row of unsecured planks of wood, placed end-to-end over the open steel girders. About 20 feet into my crossing, I caught a glimpse of the rocks and rushing water below, and I froze in my tracks. Realizing that fear was my worst enemy, I took a breath and continued walking slowly until suddenly the left plank gave way and it slipped out of position. For a split second my left foot stepped into thin air. Instinctively, I quickly retracted my leg, fell on my hands and knees, and grabbed hold of one of the steel girders. It was one of the scariest moments of my life. From the other side, people were encouraging me to not be afraid, and to continue walking, but I never stood up again. My backpack was strapped to my back like a tortoise shell, and I slowly crawled on all fours, inch by inch, to the other side of the bridge, much to the amusement of the others.

The villagers were right. A short while after crossing the bridge, a young military man appeared and checked everyone's papers. Later, he used a walkie-talkie to call the next town to request transportation for us. A few hours later, we reached the village of San Ramón, and by the end of the day we arrived in Puerto Bermúdez. It was now the third full day of travel, yet according to my map, I had gone no more than 200 miles since departing from Lima. I checked into the guest house recommended by Don Damián, and I had my first and only personal encounter with a domesticated coati. This sweet coatimundi was the size of a large cat, but had bristly raccoon-like fur, a face like a bear, a pointed snout, and a long and thick prehensile tail. I played with him for quite a while, and eventually, as I began to pet him, he curled up and leaned his body against my leg, as a cat would do. Later, I had dinner with several people I'd just met, and one of them, a young man named Carlos, told me that he was transporting some goods up river the following morning, and that he could drop me off at the village of La Llovera, where Damián's ranch was located. The next afternoon, I got into a large dugout canoe, and we traveled about two hours to the village. When we arrived at La Llovera, Carlos got as close to shore as possible. I thanked him, offered him some money, stepped into a shallow portion of the river, and I made my way to the river's edge, holding my backpack above my head. At the shore, a few Indians dressed in robes pointed me in the direction of the ranch. I slipped and slid up a muddy hill until I arrived at a vast green grazing area. A wooden barn was in the distance, and as I approached, Damián came out of the building, greeted me, and showed me to a small thatched hut (*choza*) with a cot. Later, one of the workers gave me a quick tour of the ranch and its 200 head of Brahman cattle (*cebú* in Spanish). For dinner, I was offered fish soup and squash, and we engaged in light conversation until we retired for the night. I remember that first evening, alone in a tiny hut in the middle of the Amazon rainforest. It was so noisy that I couldn't fall asleep for a long time. All throughout the night, tropical birds, monkeys, cicadas, and the loudest toads imaginable made abrasive and piercing sounds that I had never heard before in my life.

Early the next morning, after interrupted sleep because of the sounds of the jungle, I emerged from my *choza* to the visual delight of colorful macaws and parakeets resting, preening and fluttering in the trees and bushes nearby. As I welcomed the morning and sipped a cup of coffee, I noticed an amazing number of fascinating and colorful insects, including assassin bugs, preying mantises, katydids, and large horned beetles and leafhoppers that seemed like animals from another planet. There were also large numbers of beautiful butterflies whose wing markings distinctly resembled the numbers 88, 89 and 98.

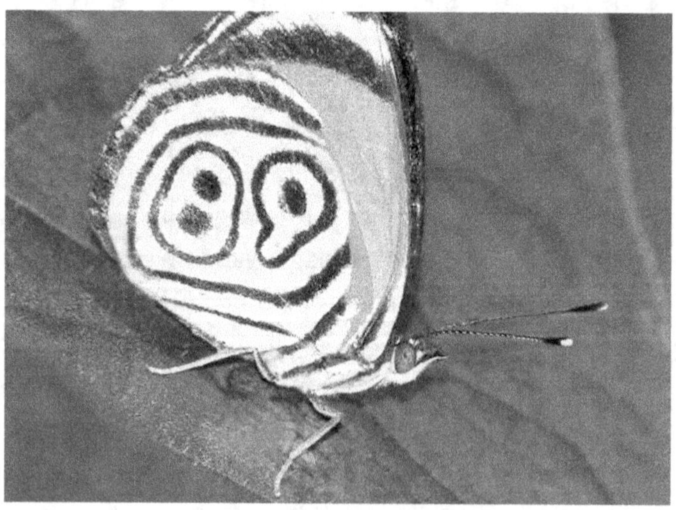

An "89" butterfly near the Pichis River

Campa woman with her daughter

I needed to wash my clothes, and I was told that I could do so in the river, but Damián had already warned me about the *pez raya* (stingrays) that camouflage themselves on the muddy shores. He told me that he'd once been stung by a stingray, was in the hospital for several days, and narrowly escaped having his leg amputated. Though I had unknowingly waded through the river just the day before, there was no way I would step into that river again after the stories I'd been told. Luckily, I was able to kneel on a large rock and bend forward in order to rinse, wash and wring out my pants, shirt, and socks. The sights and sounds of the river that morning were unforgettable. A few Indians were washing clothes, and others were fishing with spears nearby. The birds were squawking, and monkeys and other animals were rustling in the trees. Occasional large canoes floated by, silent except for the faint splashing sound of the wooden poles that propelled them forward. This was the Pichis River, a long and wide tributary of the mighty Amazon.

Over the next few days, I had one unique and new experience after the other. One afternoon, as I was writing in my journal at a small wooden table outdoors, a toucan flew right by me, and then somewhat miraculously turned back and landed on the table. I could hardly believe that a wild toucan had landed right next to me. I stared at it and began to talk to it. It craned its head and seemed to look right into my eyes. Slowly, I held out my hand and it approached, and soon it allowed me to touch its beautiful beak and stroke its head. He didn't seem to be going anywhere, so I picked up my pen to describe the event in my journal, and he immediately hopped closer. He began to gnaw on the pen in my hand, blurring the ink of the words I'd just written with his saliva. I played with him a little longer, and eventually I was able to hold him in my hands against my body. One of the ranch workers passed by, and I asked him to take a photograph.

On another day, a young man named Carlos invited me to visit his village, about 20 minutes upriver. It was his day off from work, and he said we would go in his canoe, and that I could get a ride back to the ranch with one of his friends. He knew that I had brought recording equipment, and suggested that I could record his family and friends singing traditional songs. As we chatted in the canoe, I learned that he wasn't Campa, but rather from the Ashaninka tribe, who live in the Peruvian Amazon and also across the border in Northwest Brazil. He told me that the local native languages were mutually unintelligible and that Indians from different tribes generally spoke to each other in Spanish. First, he brought me to his home, a beautiful and large thatched hut. The bamboo floorboards were suspended over platforms several feet above the jungle floor to stay dry and to keep out snakes and other creatures. I was offered *yuca* (cassava root) and spiced fresh fish that was wrapped in banana leaves and cooked over burning embers. It was so delicious.

Carlos, in his canoe

With the friendly toucan

After recording some local people singing Ashaninka songs, I was invited into the hut of a family that served me *masato*, a type of beer made from cassava root. Similar to *chicha*, which is made from corn, the plant is traditionally chewed among family members who sit together at a table. The masticated roots are spit into a large wooden bowl, mashed with a tool, and then covered with leaves. After a few days, enzymes in the saliva convert the starch to sugar, and the sugar ferments into alcohol. I had drunk machine-made chicha in Cusco before, fermented with sugars and other ingredients, but I knew that the process of chewing and spitting was the norm outside of large urban areas. I was reluctant to drink it, but I realized that they served it to me as part of a welcoming ceremony, and I didn't want to seem rude. Everyone held up their cups, and it was clear that they were waiting for me to join them. I raised the tin cup to my mouth, held my breath, took a sip, and to everyone's delight, I smiled and said: *"Delicioso."*

One of the most jarring and revolting experiences of my life happened one day when I was invited to experience the slaughtering and butchering of a cow. I had stopped eating red meat many years before, and I had no interest in witnessing the event, but Damián requested that I be there, and he was my host, so I felt I should oblige him. To prepare for the butchering, the poor animal was tied up, hung upside down, and lifted into the air with a pulley. The cow began to make bellowing sounds, which were deeply disturbing. Then its throat was slit, and the sounds became unbearable for me to hear – like a mid-pitched human voice screaming in fear and pain. Regardless of the courtesy I wished to extend to my host, I couldn't continue to watch any more, and I turned to walk away. As I exited the barn, the haunting sounds continued only for another few moments, but they unpleasantly remained in my heart's memory for the rest of my life.

There were no bathrooms or running water anywhere in the village, so when people had to relieve themselves, they would walk into the jungle canopy or down to the river bank to find an appropriate place. Then they'd cover up the waste with some dirt or sand, or wash it away with a bucket of water. One day, while I was down by the river, I had the need to defecate, and with no one in sight, I found a comfortable place not far from the shore line. I lowered my pants, crouched down, and began doing my business. As I stared straight ahead, I noticed a large animal foraging directly ahead. It was a peccary, a wild boar (*jabalí*). In this region they grow to about three feet high by four feet long, often weigh over 100 pounds, and have a very developed sense of smell. I'd never really seen a wild boar in a natural setting, and I was enjoying the view until it turned its head and noticed me. Suddenly, it made an aggressive movement with its head, and it began to charge at me from about 50 feet away. I panicked, and hobbled away as fast as possible while struggling to pull up my pants, only to watch the animal dive into a feast of my still-warm excrement.

After four days of strange new experiences, I decided to return to the guest house in Lima where I'd left my baggage, and to move onward to my next destination. I wasn't happy at the thought of taking canoes and pickup trucks just to get out of the dense rainforest, and I was still traumatized by that washed-out bridge. Luckily, Damián said that I could hitch a ride on a plane that was arriving the following day to transport several butchered and quartered cows back to San Ramón. That would save me two days of overland travel! I jumped at this opportunity and offered to pay him something, but Damián refused, saying that he had already contracted the plane. The next afternoon, a two-seater plane landed in the grazing field, and within a few minutes, workers began loading large slabs of beef into the cabin. I said my goodbyes and gave my thanks to everyone, but by the time I was allowed to board, there was no place to sit because large portions of the recently slaughtered cows took up all the available space in the tiny plane. The pilot encouraged me to simply sit wherever I could, so I sprawled over the carcasses for the 25-minute plane ride back to relative civilization. I spent the night in the same little guest-house where I'd been a week before. I took a glorious shower, had a wonderful dinner, and the next day I began the remaining ten-hour bumpy bus journey back to Lima. All of the wild, unusual, and unexpected experiences that occurred on my short but intense trip into the Peruvian Amazon have remained crystal-clear in my memory.

Interspecies miscommunication

Once, after a business trip to Los Angeles, California, I took a few days to explore the area before returning home. My wife and I visited my friends George & Patty nearby, and later we drove to Santa Monica, on the coast. Santa Monica is known for its beach, and a long boardwalk that leads to a pier with stores, a Ferris wheel, and other activities. It was a sunny day, and it was fun to breathe the salty ocean air while strolling past food stalls, souvenir stands, fishermen, and performing musicians.

We stopped near the end of the pier, where there was a view of the expansive ocean and the rock formations that frame the long beach. As I gazed into the Pacific, I heard the shrill noise of a bird and spotted a seagull perched on top of a lamp post about 25 feet high. It was squawking loudly and agitatedly, making sounds I'd never heard from a seagull before: "Pa-PAA, Pa-pa-PAA." There weren't any other seagulls in sight, and I wondered about the motivations behind all that loud noise. It continued to squawk repeatedly, and eventually it became a bit annoying. Other people were distracted too, and they began to point and speak to each other about the raucous seagull on top of the lamp post. After a few moments, I decided to playfully interact with it by making a similar noise, something I've enjoyed doing with other animals from time to time. Whenever I've done this with a bird, a cow, a cat or another animal, it seems to me that they become curious, and it sometimes results in direct eye contact. It's fun to think that somehow I may be engaging in a type of interspecies communication.

I gazed up to the top of the pole and began to imitate the gull's sound. When it made a sound, I responded exactly as I heard it. I tried to match the same timbre and pitch of the call. The bird squealed, and I responded in the same way, looking directly at it. A few seconds later, the bird squawked loudly again, with a rhythmic, pulsing call: "Pa PAA pa PAA pa pa," and I answered exactly in the same way. Some of the people around me began to watch this exchange, giggling and smiling at me, and waiting to see what the bird would do. Sure enough, the bird looked down at me and squawked once again. I looked directly at it and imitated the exact sound and cadence of the call in a loud voice. Then suddenly, the seagull took a full-speed nose dive into the crowd. The people all around me scattered, and a moment later I felt the bird's beak hit my head. Startled, I took a few steps away, and by the time I looked up, the bird had flown high into the sky and was headed down again in my direction. I began to run away from this aerial attack, covering my head with my hands, and leaving my wife behind with the other people. Slam... I felt another direct hit to my head, and this one really hurt. Rubbing my head as I continued to run on the pier toward the beach, I heard the sound of another seagull who decided to join the attack. Now two seagulls flew after me as I ran, and one at a time, they dove toward me and smacked my head with their hard beaks. They hit me two or three more times before they retreated, circled high in the sky, and then flew off to sea.

By this time, many people on the pier were watching and laughing at the whole incident, and after the birds left, some of them came up to me to ask what had happened. As I began to walk back to where the aerial attack had begun, my wife was laughing hysterically, and so were the other people who were right next to us when I'd begun to mimic the gull's sounds. We all had a good laugh together, and fortunately I suffered only minor cuts to my scalp, which healed within a few days.

Ixcatlán and
the mule kick

In my third year of college, I participated in a study abroad program in Mexico City. By that time, I was a more focused student, and my areas of concentration were Latin American Studies and Romance Languages. Some of the American students in the program had limited knowledge of Spanish and were relegated to courses that were taught bilingually. Since I already had an excellent command of Spanish, I was allowed to take courses that were offered to Mexican students who were not part of the study abroad program. One of these was a cultural anthropology course that dealt with the languages, traditions and customs of various indigenous groups in Mexico. I was the only non-Mexican in the class, and I sensed that the professor wasn't particularly happy to have me there, but the administration had allowed me to enroll in the course, and I was excited. A textbook was provided, but we also had to do independent research on a number of topics, and a term paper was required at the end of the course. Many of the students chose to study and write about aspects of culture, language and history of well-known pre-Columbian groups, but I wanted to do something out of the ordinary. As I pored over books in various libraries to get inspiration for my term paper, I read about an indigenous group that lived exclusively in one small village in the mountains of northern Oaxaca. From the little I was able to learn, it was the only place in all of Mexico where the Ixcatec language was spoken, and where several ancient traditions were still practiced. Because of its extremely remote location and tiny population, little research had ever been done about this cultural group. I immediately became excited about the idea of going there, meeting the local people, recording and documenting information, taking photos, and then returning to Mexico City to write my term paper. The village was called Santa María Ixcatlán.

A few days later, I managed to convince a fellow student to come along with me. He was an American named Steve who didn't speak much Spanish, but he was ready for the adventure. The village didn't appear on my personal map of Mexico, but I found it on an ethnographical map in the college library. On the map, Ixcatlán appeared as a small dot in an expanse of mountainous terrain, and there were no roads connecting it to nearby towns. A train ran from Mexico City to Puebla, and then into central Oaxaca, but I had no idea which stop on the railway would be closest to the village. Nevertheless, Steve and I decided to take the journey during a one-week school break. At the train station, we bought tickets to the nearest town on the map that was connected by rail service. The first train took us to Puebla, and there we transferred to another train. The journey took about five hours, and when we disembarked at what appeared to be the closest nearby town, we learned from the station attendant that we would need to travel to another village to get closer to Ixcatlán. He told us where to ask about transport, and we eventually found someone who took us in the back of a pickup truck to the next town, about 30 minutes away. We were tired and hungry after a long day of travel, so we found a place to eat, removed our backpacks, and I began to ask local people how to get to Ixcatlán. Someone told me that the rest of the way would have to be done by foot or pack animal, and that we should speak to a man who rented mules and horses. They told me where to find the stables, so I went there and spoke with the owner. He said it was approximately a two-hour journey by mule to Ixcatlán, and that he would rent me two animals for several days at a reasonable price. It was already late afternoon, and he recommended we leave early the next morning because the trail was more dangerous at night. He said that if we didn't have a place to sleep, we could stay overnight in his stables, and that he'd provide us with blankets and woven straw mats called *petates*. I accepted his kind offer and returned to the restaurant to tell my travel companion. Later, we arrived at the stables with our backpacks, we had dinner nearby, and we spent the night sleeping on straw mats placed over hand-fashioned cushions of hay.

The next morning, the stable owner greeted us, and after breakfast he saddled up our mules. I had been horseback riding before, but I'd never been on a mule. We were assured that the animals knew the way, and that we simply had to follow the trail that was occasionally marked on trees. He said there was only one trail to and from Ixcatlán, and that we might meet other people along the way. He led us to the trailhead on his horse, and Steve and I set out on the last leg of our long journey. About halfway through the trip we arrived at a river crossing. A man on horseback was headed our way through the river, and we decided to wait until he arrived so we could speak with him. He told us to cross the river just as he had done, and he pointed to a flag tied to a tree where the trail continued onward. Ixcatlán was only 40 minutes away, he said. The river bed was lined with large gray stones, and about two feet of clear water flowed slowly downstream. The mules nimbly traversed the river, and after we crossed, we decided to take a short break to rest, and to eat some of the food we'd brought with us. We dismounted, tied the reins to a tree as we'd been shown, and we sat in a small clearing near the river to drink some water and have a snack. A few minutes later, we decided to continue onward, and as we approached the mules, they began to move a little bit. Without thinking and without knowing better, I walked directly behind my mule, and before I knew what happened, I was lying on my back about five feet away. The mule had kicked me in the belly, and the impact hurled me through the air. Lying on the ground, I felt disoriented, and I was in severe pain. Steve rushed over to me and asked if I was alright. We pulled up my shirt to see a swollen bruise on my lower left abdomen, in the fatty area below my rib cage. It hurt like hell, but after the initial shock wore off, we mounted the mules again, and this time I made sure to not approach my animal from behind. We continued on the trail, and a short while later we arrived at the village.

Santa María Ixcatlán, Oaxaca, Mexico

The tiny village of Ixcatlán lies at an elevation of 6,040 feet (1,840 meters), and when I was there, it was inhabited by the only remaining speakers of the Ixcatec language. Several hundred people lived in the town and surrounding hills at that time. Villagers raised subsistence crops such as corn, black beans and wheat. Some people bred and sold goats, cattle, horses and donkeys, and mezcal was also produced. I had no idea how we'd be received when we arrived in the village, but when we rode into town on mules, everyone stopped to take a look. The first people we met were friendly and curious, and they asked us many questions. Where did we come from? Why had we come to their village? How long were we planning to stay? After explaining that we were college students in Mexico City and that I had come to learn more about Ixcatlán and its people, word spread quickly about the two gringos: one was tall with curly hair and a mustache, and the other was a *güero*, a pale-skinned blond-haired boy who spoke very little Spanish. Within minutes of arriving in the town, we were welcomed by many people and offered water and snacks. We tied up the mules at a place recommended by one man, and we set out to find a place where we could spend the night. There were no hotels or guest houses, but after speaking to a few people, one of them said that we could stay in a spare room of his house, and that he would bring us *petates* and blankets. We took a look at the place, and we decided to accept his kind offer. His name was Jobito, and he raised horses and mules. He was a well-known merchant in the village, and he spoke only a few words of Ixcatleco, but his father spoke it fluently. Everyone we met was truly kind to us, and within a few hours, we felt at home. That evening we ate at a food stall nearby, and we chatted with everyone we met. By a stroke of luck, a few boys told us that the following afternoon there would be a ball game of *pelota mixteca* in a neighboring village, and they invited us to come along. I had read about this game, and I was happy that we had been invited to attend. Along with the interviews I would collect during my few days in the village, I was excited that I could also include information about the traditional ball game in my term paper. When we returned to our room for the night, Jobito told us that he was also going to the game, and that we could ride with him in his pickup truck. I didn't sleep well that night. First of all, it was very cold, and I went to sleep wearing all my clothes. Secondly, my stomach was still hurting from the mule kick, and although the swelling hadn't increased, I tossed and turned all night, trying to get into sleeping positions that would be less painful.

The next morning, after breakfast, I conducted short interviews with people of all ages using a small cassette recorder, and I took notes in a spiral notebook. One of the boys took me to the local school, and the teacher asked me to say a few words to her students about where I was from and why I had come to the village. As I collected my information, Steve had made friends with a few kids in the village, and when I returned, he was playing basketball with them in the school-yard. He was considered a superstar by their standards, and despite the language barrier, they had no trouble communicating through sport. Sometime after lunch, we met Jobito at his house, jumped into the back of his pickup truck, and collected five or six more people before heading to the ball game. After about twenty minutes on a bumpy dirt trail, we arrived at a village even smaller than Ixcatlán, and it looked like the whole town had come out to witness the game. The ball court had been prepared with brightly-colored paper streamers tied to the trees; women were selling *tamales*, corn, and drinks; and everyone was staring at the two foreigners. The teams greeted each other, gathered on their respective sides of the court, and the game began.

Pelota mixteca is a team sport played only in a few towns in the Mexican state of Oaxaca. There are five players on each team, and each one wears a large leather glove with a flat striking surface that is studded with nails. The gloves, which can weigh up to ten pounds, are ornately painted and decorated with beads and stones. The game is played on a long, narrow court of compacted dirt, and the balls used at the game I attended were heavy, about six inches in diameter, and made of solid rubber. The rules and scoring are somewhat similar to tennis, but a net is not used. Many anthropologists claim that the game is a direct descendant of a ballgame played by ancient Mesoamerican civilizations thousands of years ago. They point to stone reliefs I once saw at the archaeological site of Dainzú that depict ceremonial players using similar gloves and balls. Needless to say, it was exciting to be able to watch a friendly game between two villages, to socialize with the local people, and to be in a place where very few foreigners had ever been before. After the game, we attended a big feast held under a large tent. Jobito and the other people from Ixcatlán made sure that we were treated to the best food and drink available. After returning to our village, we continued talking and drinking *cervezas* late into the evening.

Ball players with their gloves

The next day, we ate a light breakfast, offered some money to Jobito for his hospitality and friendliness, mounted our mules, and began our journey back across the river and down the mountain. The ride seemed much quicker this time, and we arrived back at the stables without incident. After returning the mules to their owner and paying him, we got a ride to the next village, where we spent the night in a small hostel. The following day, we took the train back to Mexico City and returned to our regular schedule of studies and social activities. By the end of the next week, the pain in my belly had subsided, and the redness and swelling were gone. Over the next few weeks, I began to put together the notes from my journal about the time I spent in Ixcatlán. I wrote what I thought to be an exciting account of the whole journey. I included information from the interviews I'd conducted, some examples of Ixcatec language, a thorough description of the ballgame, and I recounted the fabulous hospitality and friendliness I'd experienced from the local villagers during our short stay. I was sure that my term paper would impress the professor because, unlike the other students who had simply done research in the library, I had actually traveled to the town of the people I was studying. But my professor wasn't very impressed after all, because I received a grade of C+ for the paper. My earlier suspicion that he didn't want a *gringo* in his class may have been the reason. Nevertheless, the whole experience was wonderful and memorable for me, and I'll always remember that long and arduous journey by train, then by truck, and then by mule, to visit a town high in the mountains where very few foreigners had ever been. In addition to those memories, there is also an interesting epilogue to this story.

Over 30 years later, I began to experience an unusual pain in my right upper arm. I hadn't had any recent trauma there, and I couldn't understand its cause. The pain was unusual in that it only appeared after I lifted my arm into a certain position and then released it again to a resting position. Over time, I felt the pain slowly increase whenever I brushed my teeth. There was no discomfort as I lifted the brush to my mouth or while I was brushing my teeth, but every time I lowered my arm from that position, I felt a sharp pain at the lateral aspect of my upper arm. As a massage therapist, I tried to work on the area myself, but I wasn't able to use my other hand to adequately treat it, so I decided to call Joe. My colleague Joe Badstein knew anatomy extremely well, and made amazing correlations between muscle groups, tendons, and fascia, but he was also aware of Eastern perspectives of energy flow and metaphysical aspects of illness. I arrived at his studio after about two weeks of feeling pain in my arm every time I put down the toothbrush. I explained the situation to him and showed him the epicenter of my pain. As usual, he began a light review of my entire body in supine position, checking my legs and abdomen for possible correlating areas of blockage or trauma. After a few moments of exploring my lower abdomen, he asked, "Did you ever suffer a blunt trauma to your abdomen when you were much younger?" I thought for a moment and replied that I couldn't remember any time in my past when I'd had a trauma to my stomach. "OK," he said. "Just keep thinking about it, and let me know if anything comes to mind."

He continued to review my upper body and worked on my arm at the same spot I had worked myself. We talked about how neither of us had sensed any blockage in that area, and yet that was the place where I was feeling the pain. This phenomenon is known as referred pain: a pain perceived at a location other than the site of the stimulus or origin, and often transmitted through interconnecting sensory nerves, or as a result of energetic blockages. Once we determined that my pain was referential, Joe began to explore other areas of my body, and he returned to my stomach. He dug his fingers deep into my abdomen, felt the area with considerable pressure, and said: "So have you remembered any time in your life when you may have suffered blunt force trauma here?" Suddenly, as if my long-term memory were triggered by the combination of his question and his hand pressure, I remembered the mule kick in the mountains of Mexico when I was a college student. "Well," I said, "the only thing that comes to mind is when I was kicked by a mule in Mexico." He giggled at my statement, and as he continued palpating and exploring, I told him the whole story about the journey to Ixcatlán. "Yeah," he responded, "that must be it. What I'm feeling is in the shape of a hoof." Then he sank his fingers much deeper into my abdomen, and I felt deep discomfort. He held on to that spot with prolonged pressure and I said: "Ooh, right there, that hurts." I felt pain as he sank his hand even deeper, but I trusted Joe, and I breathed into his increased pressure.

"OK," he said, holding the spot with deep pressure. "Try brushing your teeth and lowering your arm." I lifted my arm, simulated a brushing motion, and then lowered my arm again, but I felt no pain.

"No pain at all," I said. Our eyes connected excitedly; he removed some of his pressure from that spot, and he asked me to try it again. I did the same motion, lowered my arm, and, owww, the pain was back. He moved his fingers a few inches away and we tried the test again. First, no pain, then pain.

Joe asked me if I was ready, and he warned me that what he was about to do would hurt, and he told me to breathe into the pain as he worked. I asked for a quick moment, took a deep breath and relaxed my stomach muscles under his touch. He sank his fingers firmly into the spot, and began to press into and around my psoas muscle with deep, focused pressure. I began to writhe in pain, but I continued to breathe deeply and surrendered to his therapeutic work. I knew he was on to something, and I wanted to address the source of my arm pain. He worked the area as I squirmed slightly on the massage table, and after a few minutes, he removed his hands from my abdomen and said: "I think we got it. Try brushing your teeth." I simulated the arm lifting and brushing movement, and when I released my arm, the pain was completely gone, and it never returned again.

I'll always remember the excitement and curiosity that led me to journey to a tiny mountain Mexican town where traditional customs were still observed, and where local people warmly welcomed two *gringos* who arrived unannounced on mules. I also won't forget the kick that brought about a mysterious referred pain more than 30 years later.

Paucartambo and
the Panaderos

I first went to the small Andean town of Paucartambo when I was 32 years old. I'd heard about the village from an ethnomusicologist who told me that the annual fiesta held there was the oldest festival known in the Americas, dating back to the Spanish conquest of Peru. I was researching Andean music for my work in graduate school, so I jumped at the opportunity to go there while I was in Peru at the same time of year. Paucartambo lies in the central cordillera of the Peruvian Andes, at an altitude of about 3,000 meters, or 10,000 feet. As the crow flies, it's only about 60 kilometers from Cusco, but it takes over three hours to get there because of the mountainous terrain. Back then, the single lane road that skirts the mountain passes was so narrow and treacherous that traffic was allowed only in one direction on alternate days. You could go there on Monday, Wednesday or Friday, and the return days were Tuesday, Thursday and Saturday. It was best to avoid traveling on Sunday because that was the only day of the week when traffic was allowed in both directions, and as a result, accidents sometimes occurred with vehicles plunging to the depths of the valleys below. Little did I know that this trip would pave the way for many other visits, that I would develop deep and meaningful connections with people who lived there, and that my actions would somehow serve as a source of inspiration for the future of the festival itself.

On that first visit, I made connections with folk dancers and traditional musicians, and I witnessed the spectacular five-day fiesta for the first time. I also met the mask maker of the town, who taught me how to recognize the different dance troupes by the masks and costumes they wore. One of the few other foreigners at the fiesta that year was an older American woman named Shirley. She didn't speak Spanish, but was exceedingly kind and generous to the local children that she met. As a result of that connection, I met some of the children in the village, as well as their parents, and in subsequent years, I would become a godfather to two of them. During my first visit to Paucartambo, I was able to record a few tracks of music from several groups and learn about the origins and practices of the fiesta, but it wasn't until the following year that I decided to produce a commercial recording of the music for my record label.

The *Fiesta de la Mamacha del Carmen* in Paucartambo takes place each year from the 15th to the 19th of July. The festival combines Catholic and traditional Andean beliefs, and is held in honor of the Virgin Mary, the patron saint of the town. However, the Andean earth goddess (*la Pachamama*) is also revered under the surface of the Catholic ceremonies. The *Pachamama* presides over planting and harvesting; she enables fertility; and she sustains life on the planet. The image of the Virgin Mary has been associated with the earth goddess for indigenous groups in the region since the Spanish conquest, when Indians were forced to convert to Catholicism or face death.

The festivities begin with the entrance (*entrada*) of various troupes who sing and dance through the streets of the town throughout the day, and at night there are fireworks (*qonoy*) and a communal singing ceremony in the town's small plaza. For the next few days, dancers, singers and musicians representing about 20 different groups parade through the streets from morning to late night as they dance, sing, and engage in ritual ceremonies. All dancers wear masks made of plaster, metal screening or cloth, and dress in wildly decorated cos-tumes that characterize their particular group. Occasionally, there are performances that simulate the struggle between good and evil, and of course, good always prevails. Every year, each group of dancers and singers is sponsored by a person in the town who assumes the responsibility to provide food and drink, pay for their costumes and masks, and otherwise support the dancers, singers and musicians of that particular group. These sponsors (*carguyoc* in the Quechua language) save money all year in order to carry out their responsibilities, and they sometimes take on extra jobs in order to pay the necessary expenses.

Some of the most well-known dance troupes are the llama herders, devils, jungle Indians, and Black laborers, but there are also troupes that perform parodies of Western doctors and lawyers, Spanish bullfighters, sick and infirm people, Chilean wine merchants, and many more. Each group meanders through the streets of the town from morning till late night, singing several proprietary songs in Spanish and/or Quechua as they dance. Most groups are accompanied by their own acoustic band, which follows them wherever they go, and which may include fiddles, harps, reed flutes, brass, accordions, strings, drums and percussion.

The *Qhapaq Qolla* descend into the village from the hills with herds of llamas, and represent itinerant merchants and llama herders. They wear large rectangular hats crowned with fringe, and their faces are covered with cloth masks. The stillborn baby llamas they carry on their backs bring good fortune and are often buried in the foundations of new homes and other structures to ward off evil spirits. They are one of the troupes who honor the *Mamacha* (Blessed Mother/ Earth Mother) with their cheerful songs and coordinated dance steps. The colorful characters known as *Saqra* (devil in Quechua) are general troublemakers and adversaries of the *Mamacha*. They taunt other troupe members and the general public by scaring them, climbing roofs to throw things onto the streets, and engaging in other mischief. They constantly seek control and power, but they lose the battle on the final day's war ritual, and pile their "dead" troupe members onto wagons as they retreat to the underworld. The *Qhapaq Chuncho* represent Indian tribes of the Peruvian jungle. They are easily recognized by their painted screen masks and spears, and by their ornate headdresses of brightly colored feathers. They participate in the final warfare ritual alongside the *Qhapaq Qolla.* With crests that adorn their robes and gold accents on their costumes, the *Qhapaq Negro* pay homage to the African slaves who were sent across the Atlantic and were forced to work in the gold and silver mines of the Andes. They sing lively songs and perform coordinated dance steps, and it is said that their costumes have remained relatively unchanged since Colonial times.

I was overwhelmed and overjoyed during my first visit to the fiesta of Paucartambo. In addition to this feast for the senses, I was lucky enough to meet a number of local people who invited me into their homes, offered me food, helped me to understand more about the fiesta, and asked me to return the following year. I felt so privileged to be one of the only foreigners there, and as an amateur ethnomusicologist and owner of a small record label, there was no doubt in my mind that I would continue to document the music of the fiesta. I returned to Paucartambo the following July, and this time I arrived several days before the beginning of the festivities so I could get settled and develop a plan to make field recordings. I was welcomed by the people I'd met the previous year, and I was given permission to march along with various troupes as they paraded through the streets. Sometimes I held my omnidirectional microphones aloft and taped to a stick. Private recordings in courtyards and practice rooms also took place, and whenever possible, I made small donations to the groups, and I bought them drinks in partial gratitude for allowing me to record them. Word had spread that I was planning to make a commercial recording of the music of the fiesta, and I was encouraged to record as much as possible. By the end of the fiesta,

I had made new friends, recorded music of the major dance groups, and conducted interviews with troupe sponsors, dancers, musicians, costume designers and mask makers. I was also able to obtain a copy of a locally-made book about the history of the fiesta.

During the following year, I put together master tapes of what would become the ninth release on my label, entitled *Paucartambo: Festival of the Andes*. It had a fold-out paper insert that included as much information as possible about the festival. As with other titles I'd released, it was sold to retail stores and through distributors in the United States, Canada and Europe, and promoted through advertisements and reviews in music and travel magazines. The next year, I returned again to the village, this time with my friends Paul and Martha. We met with the American woman Shirley, her friend Verna, and a number of other people from Europe and Latin America whom I'd met during previous visits. This time, the goal was to raise money for the town. I'd brought about 100 cassettes with me, and in coordination with the *Qolla* troupe, a makeshift booth was set up in the plaza, and a few volunteers sold cassettes to the visitors who came each day in tour buses to witness the festival. By the third day of the fiesta, we had raised a considerable sum of money, and now we had to decide how to give it back to the town. That night, several members of the *Qollas* arranged a meeting at someone's home so we could decide how to allocate the funds. We sat around a candlelit table and each person made suggestions about what could be done with the money. The church steeple needed repair, and several of the men thought that the money should be given to the church in order to make those repairs. A few other people made suggestions, and after a brief moment of silence, one of them asked me what I thought should be done with the money. I answered that it would be wonderful if the money could be given to a dance troupe that was in financial need. This sparked a conversation about the various dance groups, until someone suggested that we use the money to revive a group that was no longer active in the fiesta: the *Panaderos*, or bread bakers. Excitedly, we all agreed that we would use the money for that purpose. At the end of the meeting, some words in Quechua were solemnly recited, and we toasted each other with alcohol, which sealed the agreement that had been reached. The next day, several women villagers said they remembered the costumes worn by the *Panaderos*, and they agreed to create them for the following year's fiesta. The money was delivered to the town council that afternoon in the presence of the *alcalde* (mayor) and several dance troupe leaders. On one of the remaining days of my visit, I was asked to be the godfather of two teenagers, Franco and Carmen, and I agreed. A ceremony was held in which I was asked to cut locks of their hair, and I offered a small amount of money to their parents as a sign of my commitment to help care for the children if their parents were unable to do so.

About eight years passed without much contact except for an occasional letter, since most homes didn't have telephones, and email wasn't yet widely available in the village. I was busy growing my business, paying the mortgage on my home, and navigating life, and I couldn't easily return to Peru for a few weeks. One day I received a letter from Shirley, saying she had just returned from Paucartambo and that the *Panaderos* dance was alive and well. She sent me a photo of that year's troupe, and it touched my heart. A few months later, I received a letter from the mother of my godson saying that some of the children I'd known were now dancing in the troupe. She said that they all missed me, and that I should try my best to return for the next fiesta. As soon as I read that letter, I knew that I would be going back the following July. The following year I returned once again to get reacquainted with friends and to bring more cassettes (and now compact discs) for the town to sell to the international tourists attending the fiesta. Also, I would meet for the first time the singers and dancers of a troupe that I'd helped to revive many years before.

I made an additional donation of money to continue the efforts of the *Panaderos*, and I learned about the costumes and dances of the bread bakers. On my last night in the village, I was invited to the town council building, where the Mayor held an honoring ceremony for "El Señor Roberto" and awarded me a printed proclamation of gratitude stamped with the official town seal.

Twenty years later I returned once again to the fiesta. This time, several people I knew had passed away, my goddaughter had a teenage daughter of her own, and there was internet and cell phone service everywhere. But aside from those changes, the fiesta was as vibrant and traditional as ever. Word spread that I was in town, and I was able to meet the young dancers and singers of the troupe, as well as their organizers, who invited me to their special festivities and private gatherings. At the traditional ancestor honoring ceremony at the cemetery, the parish priest gave a speech to the *Panaderos*, acknowledged me as the co-founder, and asked me to address the young singers and dancers who were gathered in a semicircle around me. Needless to say, it was a profound and spiritual experience for me because I could never have imagined how my simple actions, based on my own interests and passions more than thirty years before, could have affected so many people.

Since its rebirth, the *Panaderos* dance has continued to play a major role in the fiesta. They are one of the official dance groups in the fiesta, listed in festival programs, acknowledged by the local government, and even mentioned on the Wikipedia website. The reappearance of the group in the fiesta, as well as my name, has been referenced in academic papers and books on social anthropology and ethnomusicology. I have been rewarded beyond imagination, and I remain humbled and honored for having shared such wonderful, deep, and meaningful experiences with the beautiful people of Paucartambo, Peru.

A bread baker in costume

Revival of the *Panaderos*, 1989

The troupe, almost 30 years later

A connection
of ecstasy

During my years as a music producer, I would often solicit and book concerts at various venues around the United States for the musicians on my label. Sometimes they would occur around the same time that studio recordings were made, and at other times the gigs would simply help the musicians to earn more money and promote their recordings as they toured and performed in the area. It was always an honor for me to help the artists who had inspired me so much during my career.

One such event happened during a USA tour of Purna Das Baul, the most well-known Baul performer of Bengal, India. The Bauls descend from a lineage of wandering troubadours who believe in simplicity in life and pure love, and they share many beliefs common in Sufism and Buddhism. They believe that pure love can emancipate us from the dominance of self, and they strive to remain unattached to the pleasures of life. Bauls believe we are all interpreters of divine power, that the body is a temple, and that ecstatic music and singing is the way to connect to that power. A common Baul instrument (and the one that Purna Das played) is the one-stringed *ektara*, carved from a gourd, with bamboo handles, a tuning peg, and a resonating chamber covered in goatskin. Baul lyrics convey a deep sense of mysticism, integrate metaphysical and esoteric topics, and stress a longing for oneness with the divine. Purna Das knew and had performed with the likes of Bob Dylan, Mick Jagger, George Harrison, and the beat poet Alan Ginsburg. I first met him in the 1980s and recorded and hosted him in New York in subsequent years. On this trip, he and his troupe were coming to perform several concerts in the Triangle area of North Carolina, and I was their host and presenter. It was a great honor for me, and I was excited to once again be with him, his wife Manju Das, his son Bapi Das, and my old friend, the wonderful *tabla* player Badal Roy.

One of the venues on this tour was at The Silk Road Tea House, a laid-back bohemian cafe with floor cushions and low tables, delicious teas, coffees and snacks, and beautiful Turkish carpets arranged on the floor and walls. The Tea House was *the* place to go in town, and you could stay for hours to read, socialize, eat, and listen to a great selection of recorded music. Owned by Cem Williford, a Turkish-American, he and his brother Demir sponsored events such as Sufi *zikirs* (ritual prayer and dance ceremonies). They also hosted The Rumi Festival, which presented music, dance and poetry of Jelaluddin Rumi, a 13th century poet, philosopher and mystic who lived in Iran and Turkey. A Sufi spiritual teacher named Sherif Baba was living in my area during those years, and I was attracted to his magnetism, charm and penetrating smile, and also to his teachings of unconditional love and non-attachment. I enjoyed hearing him speak and make presentations, most of the time through an interpreter. Sheikh Sherif Baba Çatalkaya was born in Istanbul, trained in Islam, and attended an Islamic seminary at the age of 17. Around 30, he felt a need for a larger, more encompassing perspective on spirituality, and he found it in the spiritual teachings of Sufism. When I knew him, he was lecturing on spirituality at universities and conferences throughout North America. I was reading a lot of Rumi's poetry at that time, and I was attracted to the basic tenets of Sufism. When I proposed to Cem and Demir that Purna Das and his troupe would be visiting with me and were willing to perform there, they jumped at the opportunity, and we began to make preparations for the concert.

My staff and I arrived early that day to set up the stage area and to put microphones and a sound system in place. I arrived with the musicians about a half-hour before the show, and there was a line of people outside waiting for the doors to open. I noticed that Sherif Baba was already in the room, and we smiled and greeted each other by placing our right hands over our hearts. I did a quick sound check with the musicians, left the instruments in place on the stage, and we went downstairs to a private area. By the time we went on stage, the place was packed. The first set went flawlessly. Purna Das sang with his inimitable voice as he danced and gestured with one hand and played his instrument with the other hand. The three accompanists played *dotara* (another stringed instrument), *harmonium* (hand-pumped keyboard), finger cymbals, percussion, and Indian *tabla* drums.

After the musicians left the stage for a long intermission, Sherif Baba approached and asked me if I would introduce him to Purna Das after the show was over, and of course I agreed. The second set also went well, and there was a standing ovation. I escorted the musicians past a crowd of appreciative fans, and we retreated to the private room downstairs. After about ten minutes, we returned to the main area to relax, have a drink and eat some snacks. I noticed Baba was there, and I remembered what he had asked of me. I gestured to him to wait there, and I went to Purna Das and told him that someone I knew wanted to meet him. Purna got up from his chair and followed me to the center of the room, where I had left Sherif Baba standing. As they came closer together to each other, I said, "Purna Das, this is Sherif Baba. Sherif Baba, this is Purna Das Baul."

What happened next is something I'll remember for as long as I live. They both remained there, no more than two feet away from each other, and said nothing. Standing motionless, they simply gazed into each other's eyes for what seemed to me a very long time, at least for 30 or 40 seconds. I had never witnessed such an eerie silence and lack of verbal communication when two people met each other for the first time. After a few moments, I began to feel awkward, and I took a step backward to get out of their way so they could do whatever it was that they were doing. Another long period of time passed without moving their bodies or saying anything. I may have taken another small step backward, but I kept watching, mesmerized. Then a few sounds could be heard. They were sounds of pleasure, short moans, sounds you might hear from a person receiving a massage, or between two lovers as they engage in sexual intimacy: "mmmm... oahhh... hmmm." They stood motionless through all of this, with laser-locked eyes on each other, and as they emitted these sounds of pleasure and affirmation, only their facial expressions changed slightly. Then, after about 90 seconds, Sherif Baba placed his right hand on his heart and bowed; Purna Das made a *namasté* gesture and bowed; and they backed away from each other before turning their backs and walking away.

Purna Das returned to his table, and a few moments later, Sherif Baba came to me and said: "Thank you, Bob, for introducing me to Purna Das. I look in his eyes and I see his big heart. So beautiful. Thank you."

Later, as we prepared to leave the Teahouse, Purna Das took me aside and said to me: "That teacher, he is a real Sufi. I look in his eyes and I can see his soul... very deep... a real Sufi."

We all take away different things from life experiences. What I learned from this experience is that often in life, words are overrated and not always necessary for deep and meaningful communication. At least in some cases, it may be better to not say anything at all, and instead to take a deep and deliberate look inside; to seek refuge and repose in another person's heart; to give love and compassion; and to bare your soul for the world to see, without ever saying a single word.

Purna Das Baul

Sherif Baba Çatalkaya

Spirit in the rice field

Do you believe in spirits, and in their ability to influence and even inhabit human beings? I do. No one could ever convince me otherwise, because I've witnessed spirit possession and intercession in others, and I've also been visited by and inhabited by spirits. I personally observed a spirit possession of a musician in the recording studio, and a ritual I once carried out in northern India brought about an unexplainable physical manifestation in my body. I saw a green wave of energy come out of my mother's head right after she died, and months later I heard her voice in my living room. An apparition of my father visited my living room on the night before he died, and my teacher in Thailand was able to sense and interpret information about an event in my life before it happened. These stories are recounted elsewhere in this book.

Spirit intervention is often thought of in negative ways. We've all seen movies or read novels about demonic possessions that turn people into savage creatures, but I've experienced in my life (and I have been part of) spirit possessions that are benign and even beneficial in nature. The concept of spirit intervention exists in many cultures and religions, including Buddhism, Christianity, Hinduism, Islam, and African-derived and syncretic traditions such as *voudou*, *santería* and *candomblé*. Depending on the cause, source, and cultural context in which it appears, spirit possession may be voluntary or involuntary, and although it can sometimes have detrimental effects on the host, it is more often insightful and positively transformational. Throughout many parts of the world, spirit altars are commonly found in public areas. In Southeast Asia, they can be found in front of homes and commercial buildings, including shopping malls, hotels, stores and restaurants. The spirits are "fed" daily by placing fresh water, fruit, flowers, candles, incense and other objects on the altar. Passersby stop, bow, and say brief prayers to the spirits so they continue to inhabit and protect the place and its people.

One year, shortly after arriving in Chiang Mai, Thailand for my yearly residency, I began teaching courses, writing a book, and meeting with students and friends. My mind was a bit cluttered, and I wanted to be more grounded and settled before I paid a visit to my mentor, Ajahn Pichest. He had a strong connection to the spirit world, and over the years I'd shared experiences with him that are difficult to believe. After my busy work schedule subsided and I had some free time, I made a plan to spend the morning at his home and classroom in Hang Dong, south of the city. I took public transportation to the southern part of what was once an ancient walled kingdom, and then I boarded another vehicle for a 25-minute ride to the intersection of the street that led to his home. I was happy to be visiting with him after many months, and I was looking forward to chanting, meditating and reconnecting with him. I stepped out of the vehicle, paid the driver, walked to the corner, and turned left onto the alley that leads to his home. I always enjoyed walking on this street, and that morning it was very peaceful and pleasing to the eyes. The narrow winding road borders a vast field that is usually planted in rice, and the sea of green shoots bursting through the soaked soil is accented by flowering trees, an occasional circling bird, and a vast expanse of blue sky. This last segment of the journey to his home was always gratifying: it provided me with a time of self-reflection, and it allowed me to feel content and at peace before a day of therapeutic practice.

That day, just a few meters into my walk alongside the rice field, I began to feel an unusual type of happiness. I was feeling content with my work and my accomplishments, but not in an ego-laden way. I reflected on the many years I had returned to Thailand to study traditional healing arts, and I acknowledged the respect and gratitude that I felt for my main teacher. Memories of previous experiences with him flashed through my brain, and the view of the rice field, trees and birds was particularly striking. As I walked, feelings of strength and happiness continued to fill my consciousness. At one point, I even spoke aloud to myself: "Oh, I am so happy today." I thought about how wonderful it would be to spend some meaningful time with Pichest, and I imagined that he would be very happy to see me. It's hard to explain how I was transformed that morning. I felt like I was being filled and fortified by an outside energy of some kind, and that I was absorbing that energy through my senses, my visual perception, my memories, and from the air I was breathing. With every step I took, I felt stronger, more invulnerable, and extremely happy: almost as if I were being sustained by an outside force of some kind. I'd never felt this particular way before in my life. I imagined myself as a beautiful, strong, peace-filled, loving person with a big heart, and I felt unusually excited about visiting with my teacher and being in his presence that morning. I could never have imagined what was about to happen.

The rice field in Hang Dong, Thailand

I continued down the last section of the road and entered the courtyard of his home. Students had already assembled in the classroom; the opening prayers had begun; and everyone was facing the altar. I removed my shoes, quietly slipped to the back of the room, did the customary prostrations, and joined the group in chanting and prayer. I continued to feel unusually fortified and content. After several minutes of prayer and recitation of a traditional mantra, the teacher customarily turns to the students and delivers a *dharma* talk before beginning the lessons for the day. Pichest abluted his face and head with holy water, and as he turned around to begin speaking to the students, he spotted me at the back of the room. Instead of happily greeting me aloud, saying my name, or telling the other students about me as he sometimes did, this time he just stared at me with an expressionless gaze. As I sat cross-legged at the back of the room, I smiled deeply at him, but then his facial expression changed to a scowl. Without saying a word, he looked at me as if he were looking through me and trying to read or decipher some information. The room fell quiet, and the students remained still, waiting for him to begin class. He continued staring at me, however, without speaking a word. Then I greeted him aloud with an honorific term in the Thai language, and I asked how he was doing, but he didn't answer. Instead, his scowl grew bigger and meaner. I had no idea why he seemed so angry, but for some reason I wasn't bothered or offended by his state. My response to his apparent displeasure at seeing me was to smile at him even harder. Then he exploded. While looking directly at me, he began to speak in an agitated voice: "Why you do this? Why? Why you come here?" He lowered his head, spoke some words in Thai language, and then he looked at me again. As he screamed toward the back of the room and over the heads of the students seated in front of me, I remained immobile, smiling back at him. I remember thinking to myself that I didn't know what the problem was, but that I was sure it had nothing to do with me. I had come to show him my respect, and I hadn't done anything wrong.

Sitting in a meditation position at the back of the room, I continued to smile widely and directly at him as he yelled, and this seemed to agitate him even more. I remember feeling inviolable and resolute, but filled with compassion as I looked directly into his eyes.

After he finished his rant, he stood up and left the room. The students whispered nervously to each other, trying to understand what had just happened, and some of them looked back at me. We all remained in the room until the teacher returned, and then the class began as usual. Several students in the class knew who I was, and asked me for guidance as they practiced techniques. Ajahn Pichest never acknowledged or greeted me that morning, but for some reason I wasn't at all offended. We worked until around noon; I went to lunch with some of the students; and then I decided to return to the city for the rest of the day. As the students got settled in the classroom for the afternoon session, I peered through the window, and with my hands in prayer position, I offered my teacher a goodbye greeting. He looked at me and nodded his head slightly in response. I left his home, walked alongside the beautiful rice field to the busy avenue ahead, and I boarded the next public vehicle. All throughout the journey, I was filled with a strange and elevated sense of happiness and fulfillment. I wondered why he had been so angry, but I didn't understand why he was looking directly at me as he yelled and screamed. Yet somehow, none of it mattered.

I returned to my apartment, sat down at my desk, and continued the work I was preparing for an upcoming course I was about to teach. Around 5 p.m. I received a call from one of the students in the class that day, someone who knew me and had my local phone number. She said that for the entire afternoon session, Pichest continually talked to the class about a spirit that had entered the room that morning, and that was why he had become so agitated. He'd told the students that the spirit's name was Bapu, and that he had come to the classroom that morning to transmit some important information, something that was confrontational but also enlightening. As my colleague told this to me on the phone, I began to consider for the first time that I had probably been inhabited by a spirit as I walked past the rice field that morning. That would explain why I felt so elevated and unreasonably strong and happy. She continued: "Bob, you were the only person who left after the morning session, and it sure looked like he was screaming right at you. Do you know anything about this? Have you heard of this spirit before?" Without divulging very much, I told her that I hadn't known about Bapu before, but that I had a feeling that somehow I was connected to what had happened that morning. I thanked her for calling me and telling me what Pichest had said to the class after I left.

A few weeks later, I called Ajahn Pichest and asked if I could visit with him. As usual, he seemed happy to hear from me, and we agreed that I'd come the next morning before his class started, so we could have time to chat, have a cup of tea, and catch up with each other. I took the same route from my apartment, but this time, as I approached the rice field, I spoke out loud: "Bapu, if you are here, please don't come into me." Immediately after I said this, I began to chuckle at the thought that I was attempting to communicate with a spirit. Nevertheless, I tried to shield myself against outside influences by transmitting nonverbal messages of peace and harmony to the spirits in the field. Reaching the end of the alley, I entered Pichest's home, and he greeted me excitedly as he always did. We chatted for a while about his work and about my teaching and travels. He wanted to know all about me, how long I would be in the area, and if I was still teaching courses at the same school in Chiang Mai. Then we chatted about his family, and about a few people that we knew mutually. I hoped to be able to segue into a conversation about what had happened a few weeks earlier, but he said nothing about it.

Finally, as the first of the students drifted in, I became emboldened. "Ajahn," I said, "Can I ask you a question?" He nodded his head, and I continued: "A few weeks ago, when I came to see you, I think a spirit came into me. Is that correct?" "Yes," he confirmed. Then I asked: "And who is this spirit?" He looked at me first with a grin, and then with pursed lips that seemed to convey disappointment. He stood up from his chair and said: "Why you ask a question like this? You already know who is he. He come inside you! Why you ask me this question, Bob?" Then he laughed sarcastically: "Haha, why you ask this question? You know who!" I didn't know what to say or do, so I just looked at him and smiled, and he turned and walked away. I had no idea what kind of message Bapu delivered to him through me that morning, but I was sure it was something very personal.

Ajahn Pichest Boonthumme

The students continued arriving; morning chanting and prayers took place; and from time to time during the day, Pichest asked me to help the students as they practiced their techniques and postures. "You teach today," he said several times. In the years since that event, he and I talked about some of the amazing spiritual experiences that we shared over the years, but we never spoke again about that day. In subsequent years, when I returned to visit him, he would often greet me with a big smile, and then announce to the students: "Ah, everybody, this is Bob. He have some good stories."

"Oh, nothing much."

During my career in the healing arts, I studied with a wide variety of teachers in Thailand, Europe and the United States. Once, I enrolled in a course in medicinal herbs in Charlottesville, a hip college town in the mountains of Virginia. One day after class, I returned to the hotel, rested for a while, and decided to take myself out for a drink before heading to dinner. I found a nice pub nearby the hotel, and I sat at the large wraparound bar and ordered a beer. Seated not far from me was an interesting-looking man with a sparkle in his eyes. We smiled and greeted each other, and within a few minutes we were engaged in lively conversation. He asked if I lived in town, and I told him that I was visiting and attending a course nearby. I asked where he lived, and he replied that he had been in the area for a number of years.

I'm usually pretty good at guessing people's ethnicity, especially as it relates to a person's spoken accent, but this man had me stumped. He was Asian, but he didn't look or sound Chinese, and his English had a slight Indian accent. After a few minutes of conversation, I asked him about it, and he told me he was from Tibet. "Tibet?" I said, "What's a guy from Tibet doing in a small town in Virginia?"

"Oh, nothing much," he replied, and then he immediately asked about my ethnicity and my interests and passions. He was such an interesting and engaging person, and I was having a wonderful time getting to know this guy at the bar. I remember at one point I told him a few jokes, and I poked his arm with my elbow as he laughed at the punch lines. We continued talking about common interests, and I mentioned that on my upcoming two-month stay in Thailand, I'd planned to visit Nepal for about ten days. I'd always wanted to go there, and it was a relatively short plane ride from Bangkok. He told me that he often traveled to Nepal, and when I told him the dates I'd be in Kathmandu, he said he would also be there at that time, and he offered to meet me there. He mentioned that if I hadn't already made hotel reservations, he'd be staying at the Nirvana Garden Hotel, and that he highly recommended it. He said that when I arrived from the Kathmandu airport, he'd be at the hotel to greet me. I couldn't believe my luck! First of all, I had met this cool guy named Tenzin from Tibet, and I was having a great time with him at the bar. In addition, he'd given me a hotel recommendation in Kathmandu and had offered to show me around town when I arrived.

We continued to chat for a little while, and then he excused himself, saying he had to go. He wrote his name (Tenzin Wangyal) and his contact information on a napkin, and said that we would stay in touch. I gave him a hug, affectionately tapped my hand on his back a few times, and thanked him for his company and his kindness. I also told him I would contact him after I finalized hotel arrangements in Kathmandu. The following week, I bought my ticket to Kathmandu from Bangkok, and made a reservation for the first few days at the Nirvana Garden Hotel. The next day, I emailed my new friend to say that I'd made my arrangements as planned. He wrote back a few days later saying that he enjoyed meeting me, and that it would be good to see me in Kathmandu in a few months.

My study in Thailand went well, as usual. At that point in my career, I was treating clients at my home studio for about nine months a year, and living and studying in Thailand for the other three months. I'd scheduled the trip to Nepal as a break after my first month of study, and I was excited in the days leading up to my departure. I flew the familiar route from Chiang Mai to Bangkok, and then took a flight to Kathmandu. The air was still and thin, and I was happy to be in Nepal, and excited to be meeting with Tenzin at the hotel. Maybe we'd have a chance to have dinner together that evening. I arrived at the hotel, a lovely place with a large lobby, outdoor seating in a beautiful garden, and close to major attractions in Thamel, the tourist zone of Kathmandu. I was greeted by a smiling receptionist who recognized my name on the guest register. As he gave me the key to my room, he said with a smile and a seeming air of deference that "the Rinpoche" had left a note for me. He handed me a sealed envelope, and I proceeded to my room with the key, the envelope, and my luggage. Once inside my room, I sat down and opened the envelope. The note was from Tenzin, apologizing that he couldn't greet me on my arrival because he had to leave unexpectedly. He wished me a pleasant journey, said that it was nice to have met me, and that he hoped our paths would cross again. I was a bit disappointed, but I was also excited to begin exploring Kathmandu. I quickly washed my face and hands, locked the door behind me, and set out to explore the general area. As soon as I exited the hotel, someone on the other side of the street signaled to me. It was a friendly and curious young man selling local handicrafts at an outdoor kiosk. I took a look at his wares, and we began a lively conversation. Before we said goodbye, he asked me to promise that I would come back and visit him, and he said that he would be there every day around the same time. Sure enough, over the next week I continued to spend time with this man, Arjun Tamang, as well as other street vendors that he introduced to me. Whenever I walked past the hotel, Arjun would call me by name and invite me to have tea with him. I was enraptured by the Kathmandu valley. The colors, clothing, smells, sounds, ceremonies and people captivated me, and the temples and historical monuments were enchanting.

After a wonderful visit to Nepal, I returned to Thailand, and then a few weeks later, I went back to the United States. Over the next week, as my body adjusted to the time difference, I began to write thank you notes to the people I'd met along the way. I got in touch with Arjun easily by email. I also wanted to contact Tenzin, but I only had his USA phone number, so I tried to search for him on the internet, and when I did, I was astounded at what I found. Tenzin Wangyal was an esteemed and revered teacher and meditation master of the Bön Tibetan Buddhist tradition. As I read information about him on the internet, I suddenly remembered what the hotel receptionist had said to me, that "the Rinpoche" had left me a note.

Geshe Tenzin Wangyal Rinpoche founded the Ligmincha Institute, and developed centers of learning in the United States, and also in Mexico, Europe, and India. I learned that he was the author of over ten books on the topics of mindfulness, lucid dreaming, energy healing, and a book about the human mind, with a foreword by the Dalai Lama. Trained as a Bön Buddhist monk, he lived a secular life, which allowed him to more fully relate to the needs and concerns of his students in over 25 countries worldwide. The friendly guy that I'd met at a bar – to whom I told slightly off-color jokes, poked with my elbow, and slapped on the back in a parting hug – was one of the most esteemed and accomplished scholars and masters of the Tibetan Buddhist tradition, and someone who personally knew the Dalai Lama. Yet when I asked him what he did, he quickly and modestly replied: "Oh, nothing much."

I eventually found his email address, wrote to him, and thanked him for his help and friendliness. I told him that after a long time of not knowing, I had finally learned his true identity and that, in my opinion, what he was doing with his life was far more than "nothing much." In addition to this lovely experience, and as a result of his hotel recommendation in Kathmandu, I met Arjun and his wife and son, with whom I've shared a beautiful friendship for many years.

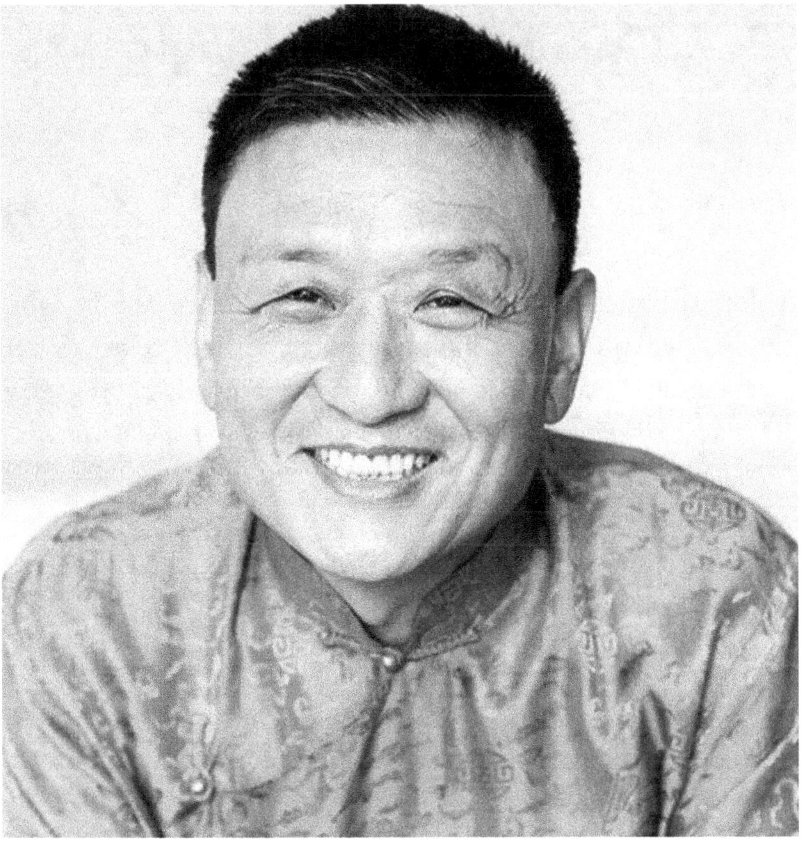

Tenzin Wangyal Rinpoche

The unexpected magic
of Thai massage

After a divorce that left me emotionally drained and in debt, I struggled to keep my composure and try to plot a course into the future. Luckily, I was able to sell the master recordings of my record label to a pioneering audio streaming platform. My financial woes were over, but I was left without a clue of what to do next in my life. After a few months of considering other types of jobs and pondering possible new careers, I still had no clear way forward, so I decided to take some time off to travel and to "find myself." Travel always worked well for me when I didn't know what to do, and this time I decided to go to parts of the world where I had never been before.

I started my adventure in the Philippines and then went to Bali, where I settled for a month as I journaled, witnessed syncretic Hindu rituals, performed with local musicians in a jazz club, watched traditional dance performances, listened to *gamelan* (gong) orchestras, and pondered my past, present and future. The spirituality, ritual and sweetness that I experienced on this small, beautiful island was grounding and fulfilling, and it fueled my desire to return again in the years to come. From Bali, I flew to Bangkok, Thailand, where I met a friend and her son. We spent a few days visiting temples and tourist sites, and then I flew to the northern city of Chiang Mai, a place that would unknowingly play a long and meaningful role in my life. Chiang Mai seemed magical to me, and the large number of Buddhist temples enticed me to explore my spirituality on a deeper level and to begin a meditation practice. This helped to calm my mind and prepare the groundwork for whatever was to come.

As I explored the city, I was solicited by people who offered massages to locals and tourists. "Massage? You want massage, mister?" I had never experienced a complete Thai massage session, so I decided to try one. In the hands of an experienced therapist, a 90-minute massage seemed to relieve my stress, tone my body, and calm my mind. I continued to receive a few more treatments from men and women in Chiang Mai, and I languished in the positive effects that I felt after each session. I became so curious about Thai massage that I decided to take a beginners' course at one of the only schools at that time that taught foreigners in the English language. My fellow students were from all over the world, and as part of our study, we had to practice with each other as we followed the teachers who guided us through the techniques and routines presented in our student manuals.

In Thailand, massage (*nuad*) belongs to one of the branches of the Thai traditional medicine system, and is influenced by early Buddhist and Indian Ayurvedic medicine. The theoretical basis for healing is rooted in the belief that all forms of life are sustained by a vital force (*lom*) that is carried along *sen* – the muscles, nerves, ligaments, tendons and channels that run through our bodies. This life-force is extracted from air, water, food and other natural elements, and it is believed that dysfunction and disease (dis-ease) come about when blockages occur along these pathways. The goal is to free trapped energy, to stimulate the natural flow of life-force, and to maintain a general balance of wellness. Traditional Thai massage combines elements of focused acupressure, compression, stretching, assisted yoga postures, and the stimulation of *sen* lines. It differs greatly from Western massage because treatments take place on a comfortable floor mat, not on a massage table, and because the receiver wears loose-fitting clothing. The muscle-rubbing and kneading techniques found in Western massage are mostly absent in Thai massage, and creams and oils aren't used. Therapists may use their feet, knees, elbows, forearms, hands or fingers to relax muscles and stimulate energy in the body. Although the client's physical body is moved, stretched and manipulated, the ultimate goal is to bring holistic balance and harmony to the receiver, and to encourage a process of self-healing. The practice is also a spiritual discipline since it incorporates the Buddhist principles of mindfulness (breath awareness) and loving kindness (focused compassion).

After my time in Thailand, I returned home and continued practicing the techniques and sequences I'd learned. I asked some of my friends if they'd allow me to practice on them, and I had no shortage of volunteers. As I slowly came to the conclusion that this could become my next career, I studied with a few teachers in my own country who offered short courses in Thai massage, and I continued to practice on friends and acquaintances from a spare room in my home. After a few months, some of them began to leave money on a table near the door, but I still wasn't ready to open a professional practice. I knew that I needed to study much more, and I also wanted to find a mentor.

At that time, the only books about Thai massage in the English language were written by a German-born yoga practitioner named Harald Brust, who lived in northern Thailand and was known by the spiritual name of Asokananda. I learned that he would be teaching a one-week advanced course in southeastern Spain, and I saw this as an opportunity to study with him. I registered by paying a deposit to the organizer of the workshop, and a few days later I received an email from the teacher. He thanked me for my registration, and said that since this was an advanced course, he wanted to know more about my previous study. I answered his email, explaining that I had taken a two-week basic course in Thailand, and that I had also studied with two other teachers in the United States. A few days later, he emailed to say that, based on my limited previous experience, he was unable to accept me into his advanced class. He sent his best wishes for my continued study and practice, and said that my registration fee would be returned. I immediately wrote him another email explaining that I had been following his work, that I had read his books, that I knew in my heart that I needed to study with him, and that I was certain that he would be an important catalyst for me to deepen my practice. I asked him to reconsider, and to kindly accept me into his class in Spain. Several days passed until an email finally appeared in my inbox. It said that after meditating on the issue, he came to the conclusion that it was clear I was passionate about Thai massage, and that he had decided to accept me into the course. I was overjoyed, and when we finally met in person a few months later, we had an immediate and deep connection with each other. He and I were about the same age, and we related to each other in a different way than the younger students in the class.

Several months after the course in Spain, I returned to Thailand for additional study, and I visited Asokananda in the hilltribe village where he lived and taught. On that trip he introduced me to several masters of the tradition, including herbalist Mama Lek Chaiya and two of his own teachers, one of whom became my mentor throughout the rest of my career in Thai healing arts. By the time I returned home, I felt ready to open a professional practice. I began to advertise my massage services in local newspapers and networked with health-care and wellness providers In my area. Rather than rent a commercial office downtown, I decided to build an addition to my home to use as a client treatment space. As my professional practice grew, I began to teach weekend introductory courses and offer presentations at yoga studios, public venues, and massage schools.

I returned to Thailand every year for more study, and after a few more years, I began to teach longer courses and workshops throughout the United States, Canada, Europe, Latin America, and eventually at one of the major schools in Chiang Mai, Thailand. In the years to come, I authored two books on the subject of traditional Thai massage, founded an international association for Thai healing arts, maintained a regular client practice, and taught advanced courses to students and therapists from all around the world.

I'm very grateful to my teachers, students and clients for their inspiration and guidance. My personal life, career, and social connections for more than 20 years were completely and positively transformed as a result of that first trip to Southeast Asia. After an 18-year career in the music industry, I had jumped into the unknown in order to explore new horizons, and once again, the Universe had taken control. I could never have imagined the transformative, fulfilling and magical effect that traditional Thai massage – along with my teachers, students and colleagues around the world – would have on my life.

Buddhism, suffering, and animals

Over many years of living and studying in Thailand, and through my connections with friends and teachers there, I've become aware of the ways that many Buddhists view the concepts of suffering and compassion, as contrasted to the cultural beliefs and proclivities of other groups, particularly Judeo-Christian Westerners. In Buddhist thought, suffering is the true nature of all existence. It seems that in modern Western civilization, rather than accepting and trying to understand suffering, many people are inclined to disavow or disregard it, or to run away from it rather than internalize it and face it directly.

In Buddhist doctrine, suffering (*dukkha*) exists; it has a cause; it has an end; and there are ways to minimize it. Three types of suffering are generally distinguished. These result from pain, such as old age, sickness, and death, from pleasure that often changes into pain, and from the fact that, because of the law of impermanence, all beings are susceptible to change and pain at any moment. Compassion is a valuable tool to address suffering, and genuine compassion must also have wisdom and loving-kindness. According to Buddhist thought, compassion is an aspiration, an active state of mind, and an ongoing desire for others to be free from suffering. Compassion isn't passive, and it's not merely empathy. It is an empathetic altruism that recognizes and accepts suffering, and actively strives to free others from it.

I've experienced two incidents of suffering in animals that involved compassionate human interaction in Thailand. One happened in front of the Pansook apartment building in Chiang Mai, where I lived every winter for many years. One day, I took the elevator to the lobby and said my usual hellos to the office staff and the doorman. As I walked down the front steps, I saw three people, their bodies bent forward, facing the lowest step near the curb. Changing my angle of descent to stay out of their way, I turned around when I reached the bottom, and I saw an extremely large rat. It was trembling, hunched over, and seemingly unable to move. Its hair was frizzed, and it looked as if it were very sick. Now, most people I know have a natural aversion to street rats. They scavenge and eat garbage, and they carry diseases that can be transmitted to humans. In many parts of the world, if a trembling rat were found on the steps of a person's residence, the animal would be feared and despised. It would be shooed away with a broom or a shovel, or prodded with a stick, and in some cases killed. Yet what I saw that day was something quite different. My Thai neighbors, including a young girl about twelve years old, were trying to help the suffering rodent. They were actively engaging in the rat's suffering and seeking ways to minimize its pain. Someone had lit a small candle and put it at the base of the steps as if to pray for it. Another person slid a small plastic lid of rice toward the animal, and all of them were crouched down on the sidewalk, actively concerned about the rat's welfare, and bearing witness to its suffering.

I also wanted to participate, but I didn't know what to do. I looked at the woman who had offered food to the rat and said: "*Mai yak kin.*" (It doesn't want to eat.) She acknowledged my words with a nod and a sad expression. We remained there for a few moments, observing the poor rat's suffering. By this time, the doorman from the apartment building had also joined the group on the sidewalk. Finally, an idea occurred to me. If I could somehow scoop up the rat and carry it over to the open field near the apartment building, at least it would be more safe and free from harm. A few days earlier, in my Thai language lessons, I had learned the word for cardboard, which translates literally into English as "hard paper" (*kradat khaeng*), so I asked the doorman if he had any cardboard (*Khun mee kradat khaeng?*) He responded that he didn't know, but he immediately left to go inside the building, and a few minutes later he emerged with a metal dust pan attached to a long wooden handle. He offered it to me, and while the others stayed near, I attempted to scoop the animal into the pan. The first few attempts weren't successful, as the rat jumped slightly every time the metal lip touched its body, but on the third try I was successful. I lifted the dust pan, the rat slid backward onto the metal tray, and I quickly walked about 50 feet to a small open field near the corner of the street. Once there, I placed the pan on the soil, and the rat quickly jumped out and hid under a nearby bush. Delighted, I turned around and began to walk back to the apartment building, and the neighbors, including some other onlookers, cheered me and thanked me with applause and big smiles, some with their hands placed in prayer position.

Another, perhaps more spiritually profound experience happened on Bumrungrad Road, on the east side of the Ping River in Chiang Mai. From my apartment it was an easy ride on public transport, and I'd go there whenever I wanted to relax, meet with friends, sunbathe, and swim at the large pool at the Eco Resort. One day, after getting off the red bus on the corner, I began my usual walk, and about a hundred feet ahead, I noticed a man standing in the street a few feet from the sidewalk, staring at something on the ground. As I approached, I could see it was a wounded animal. Traffic was flowing in both directions, but the man's position was encouraging ongoing cars to veer slightly away from the edge of the street as they passed. I walked up to him and looked down to see a severely wounded cat. It was a terrible sight. Blood was slowly oozing out of its head and ears, and its eyes were prolapsed and dangling out of its skull, almost like something you would see in a cartoon.

I looked at the poor cat, and I looked up to the man and asked: "*Tam arai?*" (What should we do?) He answered in a soft voice that he didn't know (*mai roo*). We both felt helpless, not knowing how any intervention on our part could alleviate the poor cat's suffering. Its condition seemed too serious to be addressed by a veterinarian, and besides, it wasn't realistic to think we could transport it without causing more harm. Knowing that it was hurting so badly, we couldn't simply walk away either. As cars and motorbikes passed by, the man and I remained frozen and silent. Suddenly, without thinking, I bent down, extended my left hand, and held it gently against the cat's lower body. I don't know why I did this; it just came naturally. Upon seeing me do this, my new friend also bent down and placed his right hand a few inches higher on the cat's upper body. We remained motionless for about ten seconds, and then the cat twitched several times; the tension in its body relaxed, and it died. Shocked by what had just happened but not really surprised, we slowly stood up, faced each other, and placed our hands in the prayer position known as *wai*. With our heads slightly bowed, we looked deeply into each other's eyes. After a few seconds of reflection, we thanked each other and backed away. I turned and slowly walked in one direction, and he went the other way.

I'll never forget the day when two strangers met on a street curb, and by wishing for a wounded cat to be free from suffering, we somehow facilitated its passing.

Intuition, premonition, apparition

In July 1997, I traveled to a little town in southern Peru named Paucartambo. It was there, over repeated visits in the 1980s, that I'd carried out music research and made recordings of traditional music from the region. After almost ten years, I was returning once again to get reacquainted with friends, and to raise additional funds for the town. Also, for the first time, I would meet the singers and dancers of a festival troupe that I'd helped to revive many years before. After a connection in Lima, I arrived in Cusco, a place that felt as comfortable to me as home. I spent several days visiting friends there and getting adjusted to the altitude. On the designated day, I climbed into the back of a pickup truck, and we traveled on the narrow road to Paucartambo. Once there, I found a place to stay, dropped off my bags, and set out to get reconnected with my friends and contacts. Email wasn't available yet, and most homes didn't have telephone lines, so no one knew I would be coming.

The opening ceremonies of the fiesta were as wonderful as always, and I was able to meet the young dancers and singers of my adopted troupe, as well as the organizers who invited me to special festivities and ceremonies. On the evening of the second day, Mariano, a friend who danced in another troupe, invited me to his home for some tea and a chat. A short while later, he asked me to join him in chewing some coca leaves, and after a short opening ceremony, we began to chew. He told me that word had spread quickly that I'd returned to the town, and that the mayor had decided to hold a reception in my honor the following evening. Being there once again was a very spiritual experience for me. I felt like I was helping to make a small difference in the world, and there in the high Andes, I felt in tune with the energy of the universe.

The next day, I attended various celebrations in which I was requested to walk at the head of the group of dancers and singers, and to accompany them to the church and to the cemetery to honor the ancestors, as is customary in this town. Later that evening, I spent some time at the home of my *compadres* (my godson's parents), and it was then that I began to feel unsettled about something. I didn't know what it was, but I was beginning to think that I should leave the town before the end of the festivities. I had originally planned to spend about a week there, but something was telling me that I should leave as soon as possible. I reasoned that I needed to stay at least through the next evening in order to attend the mayor's ceremony and surrender the donations I'd collected and brought. When I woke up the next morning, I felt even more convinced that I would leave the following day, return to Cusco, and then fly on to Lima as soon as possible. My friends in the village begged me to stay until the end of the festival, but I told them I had to leave the next day. I didn't exactly know why, but an unexplainable intuition was urging me to do so. I rationalized that my work had been done, that I'd seen the people I needed to see, and that I should be moving on. I mentioned the change of plans to my godson Franco, then already in his mid-twenties, and he told me that if I was leaving the following day, he would accompany me back to Cusco, where he was living at the time. The rest of the day went well, saying goodbye to many people and attending the ceremony at which the mayor read a proclamation about my contribution to the town and offered me a handmade figurine of one of the dance groups as a memento. I had planned to take the first mini bus to Cusco the next morning.

I woke up to my alarm clock feeling sick with a headache, congestion and chills. I grabbed my bags, exited the small room, walked onto the outside porch, and clambered over drunken revelers asleep from the night before, their ponchos and hats covering everything but their mouths and noses. A few blocks away on the main road, I boarded the vehicle that would take me back to Cusco. A few minutes later, my godson Franco arrived, and he came aboard and sat next to me. It was a freezing cold Andean winter morning on Saturday July 18th, and we were wearing gloves, hats and scarves made of llama and alpaca wool. The road out of Paucartambo was as beautiful as always, curving around terraced fields with expansive views of mountain peaks, valleys, and a winding river below. The three-hour bumpy ride went fairly quickly, and as we approached Cusco, my godson and I made plans to meet for dinner at 6 p.m. at the Plaza de Armas, in front of my friend Guillermo's "Mini Shop." The statue that was given to me at the mayor's ceremony was encased in glass, and I asked Franco if he could bring it to someone who could remove the glass for me so I could travel with it more easily. I gave him some money, and we agreed to meet that evening for dinner.

I walked to the hotel where I'd left my bags locked in the lobby until my return, and fortunately I was able to check into my room a few days early. I retrieved my bags, left them in my room, and immediately went to the Aero Perú airline office to try to change my air ticket to an earlier day. As the agent checked her computer, she said there was nothing available to Lima in the coming days, but I persisted, and after a few moments, she said that the only seat she could find was on a 6:50 a.m. flight the next morning. It wasn't ideal, and I would have preferred to leave a few days later, but I impulsively agreed, paid the change fee, and bought the ticket. Now I had to explain to all my friends in Cusco that I couldn't go out with them over the weekend as planned. They were preparing a picnic and music gathering for the following day. Everyone was disappointed when I told them that I was leaving the next morning. "*Pero ¿por qué?*" they all asked. My only response was that I needed to return home as soon as possible.

I returned to my hotel, exhausted and still dirty from the road. My head was aching, and I had an unsettling feeling. I took a glorious shower with the first hot water I'd felt in days, and I decided to nap for a few hours before meeting Franco again for dinner. I fell off into a light sleep, but moments later I awoke with a very unsettling feeling, a sensation that something was wrong, that something bad had happened. The feeling was about my parents. Something was wrong with my parents. I reminded myself that I was tired and that I needed to sleep. I repositioned myself under the covers, and again I nodded off, but moments later I was awakened by a deep trembling in my body. It was more like an electric shock that ran up my spine and rattled my neck, head and face. It jolted me into a sitting position in bed, and suddenly I had another very strong sensation that something bad – something dangerous – had happened to my parents. I couldn't tell if it was about my mother, my father, or both of them. But something had definitely happened. It was the strongest premonition I've ever experienced in my life. Nothing was wrong with my wife, my brothers, or their families. It wasn't about my personal friends or co-workers or business partners. This upsetting, horrible feeling was pointing directly to my parents. I sat there for a moment, wondering how I should react. I somehow found the energy to pull myself out of bed, add another layer of clothing, put my coat on, and leave the hotel. The only thing that came to mind was to walk over to the Mini Shop and see if any messages had been left for me. In the days before mobile phones, the shop's phone number was the only emergency contact I had given to my wife and my family. I walked briskly to the plaza about three blocks away, and I entered the shop. The owner wasn't there, and his employee Rosita was minding the store. I greeted her and asked if there had been any messages for me. She looked at papers on her desk near the telephone, and she checked the fax machine. "*No Señor Roberto, no hay nada,*" she said. "*¿Está esperando algo?*" I answered that I wasn't completely certain, but that yes, I was expecting something. I walked around the plaza, feeling disoriented and trying to understand the strange feeling swelling inside me. I said a few quick and emotional goodbyes to some of my musician friends, and I eventually met with Franco for dinner. The whole time we were together, and as hard as I tried to be in the present moment, I couldn't disconnect from that terrible feeling. I was sure that something was wrong with my parents.

After dinner, I asked Franco to accompany me to my hotel so I could give him some clothing and money that I'd brought. On the way, I decided to stop and return to the Mini Shop to ask Rosita once again if there had been any messages for me. From inside the store, she saw me approach, and she rushed to the door with a piece of paper in her hand and said emotionally: "*Su esposa llamó. Su papá está muy enfermo y está en el hospital. Tiene que llamar este número.*" My wife had called. My father was critically ill and in the hospital, and I needed to call the number written on the paper.

Franco and I immediately walked a few blocks to the public telephone office so I could make long distance calls. I spoke with my wife, who was visiting friends far away from home while I was in Peru, and she told me that my father was on his deathbed, and that the family was gathering in Brooklyn. We spoke about how best to coordinate our flights so we could meet there in the next day or two. I then called my brother, who told me that Dad was in a coma, connected to a respirator, in critical condition, and expected to pass soon.

I had originally planned to spend a few days in Lima, visiting friends there, but now I needed to get to New York as soon as possible. Because of the unsettling feeling I experienced in the village, I'd already bought the last ticket on the first flight to Lima the following morning. I arranged for a taxi to the airport at 5 a.m., and I asked for a wakeup call. I tossed and turned all night, but I arrived at the airport in time to board my flight. I landed in Lima at about 8:30 a.m., and now I had to find a way to get to the United States. I went to the American Airlines desk since my original return ticket was for the following week on that airline. I explained my situation and asked them to find me a flight to anywhere in the USA that was leaving immediately. They told me there were no seats available on any of their flights to the mainland for the next two days. One ticket agent after another told me the same story: some sort of holiday rush was affecting all departing flights from Lima to North America. I tried Continental Airlines to see if I could catch the next flight to Houston, and it was fully booked. I tried for the next flight on Aero Perú to Miami... and it was also fully booked. *"Es una emergencia. Mi papá está muriéndose y tengo que regresar hoy mismo."* (It's an emergency. My father is dying, and I have to get home today.) *"Lo siento señor,"* was the answer. *"No hay campo hasta mañana por la noche."* (I'm sorry, sir. There's no availability until tomorrow evening.)

I was devastated and defeated, lost and confused. I remember walking back and forth from one ticket counter to another, loaded with my baggage on both shoulders and practically begging to buy a one-way ticket to anywhere in the United States. I kept checking the departure boards, and I noticed that Aero Perú had a flight to Miami that was boarding within a few minutes. As a last-ditch attempt, I closely eyed the three or four ticket agents behind the desk, and I tried to pick the right person to whom I would plead my case. I caught the eye of a compassionate-looking young woman, and I approached her. I told her that my father was dying and that I desperately needed to get on the flight that was now boarding to Miami. *"Señor, no tengo nada,"* she said, as her fingers moved over her keyboard. Everything was full, she said, as she continued to look at her screen. *"Todos los vuelos están llenos y no hay..."* No sooner had she said there was nothing available when a wide-eyed expression suddenly came over her face, and she told me that she had found a single seat in the smoking section on the flight that was currently boarding to Miami. She couldn't honor my American Airlines ticket, but I could have that seat for the price of a one-way fare. I had my charge card on the counter before she could finish her sentence, and within a minute I was running to the departure gate with all my luggage. As I ran, I could hear my name on the loudspeaker, urging me to board immediately. I finally got there, walked down the metal steps to the tarmac, and continued running toward someone who was signaling to me at a waiting plane about 100 yards away. The door was shut behind me as soon as I boarded, and I took my seat in the last row of the plane, wedged between two older women in the smoking section. I was happy to be heading home, but I was deeply worried and saddened about the whole situation. Six hours later, I arrived in Miami – tired, sad, confused, and not knowing what to do next. Should I try to fly straight to New York? Should I go home to North Carolina first? Would American Airlines honor my ticket five days early? I looked at the departure board, checked all possible flight options, and asked about availability. There was nothing available to either destination. There were flights, but they were all overbooked, and there were no confirmed seats on any northbound flight until the following evening. Finally, in desperation, I decided to take my chances on the waiting list for a flight to Raleigh, my home airport. The ticket agent did as I requested, but told me that I was number 32 on the standby list, and that my chances of boarding were next to impossible. I had about two hours to wait, so I ate some food, made a few phone calls to family members to say that I was on the mainland, and then I walked to the departure gate.

A sign at the gate confirmed that the flight was full, and that there was a long waiting list. After a while, as people began to get in line to board the flight, they posted the standby list, and I noticed that my name was indeed at the very end. How could there be more than thirty people hoping to fly on standby? I walked up toward the front of the line, where a woman was setting up the podium at the entrance to the gate, and I began to make light conversation with her. I asked how long she had been in the industry, if she was based in Miami or elsewhere, and if she normally flew domestic or international routes. After a minute or two of this small talk, I came closer to her and said: "Listen, you've got to help me." I explained that my father was lying critically ill in a hospital in New York, that I'd just returned from a small village in Peru against all odds, and that I desperately needed to get on this flight. She looked at my name on the ticket, glanced at the standby list, and said, "But you're number 32." Then she looked deeply into my eyes, asked for my ticket, wrote on it and stamped it, and gave it back to me as she said: "Here, 19B. Go ahead and board. I'm so sorry about your father." It was miraculous. Two hours later, I arrived at my home airport. I'd made a call from the plane to ask my friend John if he could pick me up, and he was waiting for me in the terminal. Once home, I bought a ticket to fly to New York, where I would rendezvous with my wife the following day, and I called my family to tell them that I'd be there by late afternoon.

I still had dirt in my shoes from hiking in the Andean village only two days earlier, and I was exhausted after waking up at 5 a.m. and taking three planes to get home. To compose myself and ponder what was to come, I took off my jacket and sat down at the kitchen table. After a minute or so, with my elbows braced on the table, holding my head in my hands, I began to wonder if I would make it to the hospital before my father passed. My mind ran through all the plans I'd made with my family, and the logistics involved in getting to New York to meet those who had already arrived there. I began to think about my father, almost in an attempt to communicate with him on a meta-physical level and send him my love. I closed my eyes and tried to get him in focus. I remember speaking aloud, telling him that I was trying to reach him. His image slowly began to appear in my mind's eye, but it was moving and wavering, going in and out of focus for a few moments. Suddenly, I felt something pull me out of my motionless pose. I lifted my head and opened my eyes toward the living room area, and I was shocked by what I saw. There, in the far corner of the room, suspended in the air, was my father's body. He was lying on his back, his eyes were closed, and his hands were folded on his chest. I stared at the apparition in disbelief, adjusted my gaze to another place in the room, and then looked at it again to be sure it wasn't a momentary illusion. After a few moments, in awe at the idea that I had somehow been able to summon his energetic body, I began to speak to him aloud in a soft voice. "Did you know that I had a feeling in Peru that something was wrong?" He nodded his head ever so slightly. Tears started rolling down my face. "And were you calling for me?" Again, a slight nod. I asked if he was in a lot of pain, and he shook his head. "Dad, I love you very much," I said emotionally. With that, he turned his head slightly toward me. He seemed to strain as he opened his eyes slightly to offer me a faint smile, and then he slowly returned his head to its original position and closed his eyes. He continued listening to me as I spoke in a loud whisper, urging him not to wait until I arrived, and that I wanted him to let go and to be at peace. As I watched him through my tears, his image completely dissolved. After I composed myself a bit, I went to the liquor cabinet, poured myself a stiff glass of rum, and remained shocked and bereft for the rest of the night until I fell asleep.

The next day I arrived in New York, met my wife at the airport, and we drove a rented car to my parents' home in Brooklyn. Sitting outside on the steps of the house were my nephews and nieces. They told me that my father had passed away that morning and that they had just returned from the hospital. We entered, I hugged and kissed my mother, we consoled each other, and we began discussing plans for a wake and a funeral. It was already late in the afternoon, and my mother, in true form, began to prepare food for everyone. After dinner and conversation, some of us began to head back to our hotels for the evening. Before we said goodbye for the night, I decided to go downstairs to the basement, where my father often spent time by himself, reading, paying bills, doing crossword puzzles, or playing cards. I walked down the two small flights of steps into the kitchenette and dining area of the finished basement, and I turned on the light. Directly ahead, a white tablecloth covered with a clear plastic liner was draped over the round table where he often sat. On top of the table was a deck of cards arranged in an unfinished game of solitaire. His gray-rimmed reading glasses were within arm's reach of the blue-green padded chair where he always sat. His watch was there too, a silvery-gray Timex with a black leather band. I stood there motionless, looking at that sight, and I realized that he had been sitting there just a few hours before falling asleep in his bed for the very last time. I became emotional, re-living the premonition I'd had in Cusco a few days before, and then communicating with the apparition of his levitated image in my living room. As tears bubbled from my eyes, I thought that I would ask my mother if I could have his watch as a memento. I reached for it with one hand and placed it in the palm of my other hand, and as I watched the thin second hand move around the face of the watch, it suddenly stopped. The watch stopped right before my eyes! I shook it several times and tapped the crystal with my fingers, but my father's watch died at that very moment, in the palm of my hand, as I was looking at it. I now keep it on my altar, and its hands are still frozen at 9:44 p.m.

About a month after his death, I had a session with Sherrie Dillard, a powerful, intuitive medium, and someone I'd known and worked with in the past. I had requested a session with her because she had an amazing ability to contact the spirits of deceased people and interpret their energies, and I wanted to connect with my father once again. The only thing she knew was that I wanted to communicate with my father, who had passed away. Never at any time did I disclose information about the circumstances of his death: when he died, where I was at the time, or about the apparition I'd witnessed in my home. In other words, all she knew was that I wanted to contact my father in the afterlife. Before we began, she asked if there was anything in particular that I wanted to ask of him. I responded that I only wanted to know that he was at peace, and to tell him that I loved him. She asked my father's name, and we started with a generic prayer of supplication to all the gods, deities and spirit guides, and then we both closed our eyes. Within a few moments, she said that she had made contact with him, and a few moments later, she said in a soft voice: "Your father says that you were far away when he became ill. Somewhere... somewhere in the south. Is that right?"

"Uh-huh," I answered.

She continued: "And that he somehow communicated with you while you were there, and that you made some last-minute changes, or something like that... that you changed your plans. Does that make any sense to you?"

"Yes, that's exactly what happened," I answered.

Then there were a few moments of silence, and she said: "He also is telling me that he took up residence in your home before he died, and that you both had an encounter right before he passed."

Stunned, I began to explain what had happened, but she stopped me from explaining further. She asked if there was anything else I wanted to ask, and I requested that she transmit to him that I loved and respected him very much, and that I was grateful for all he did for me, and for all the sacrifices he made for me in my life. After a few more seconds of silence, she acknowledged that he understood that, and we proceeded to end the session. Afterward, I told her exactly what had happened; that I was, in fact, very far "south," in

South America; that I'd had a premonition, changed my travel plans, and bought new airline tickets without exactly knowing why. Then I told her about the apparition when I returned home the night before he passed away.

It is so miraculous that I was somehow guided to leave the village early, to return to Cusco, and to change my air ticket for the next morning on the only available seat... all without knowing why. The electric shock that woke me from my sleep left me with the feeling that something was wrong with my parents, and I'd returned to my friend's shop a second time to get the message that my father was critically ill in the hospital. Then the flood gates opened from one magical airline connection to the next, and my father passed away the morning after his ethereal apparition in my home. I'll never forget how his watch stopped in my hand, and how the psychic knew what had happened even though I hadn't disclosed any information to her.

I know in my heart that my father summoned me, high in the Andes and thousands of miles away, so we could have one final and deep connection together before he left his body.

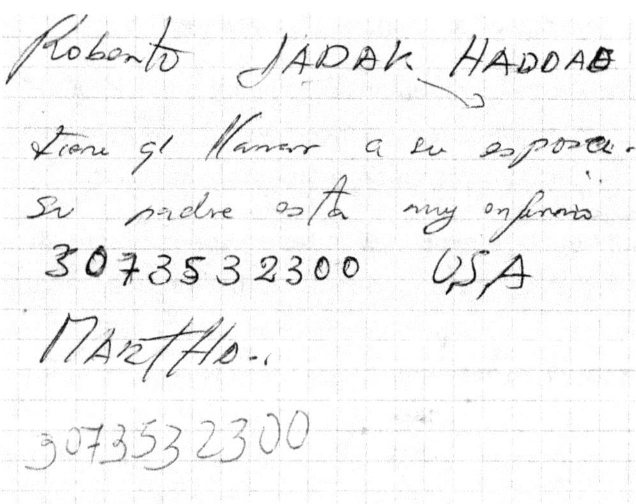

The note from Rosita at the Mini Shop

John (Chakib) Haddad

"From your passport, of course."

One year, after three months of teaching, researching and living in Thailand, I decided to take a few weeks to explore Indonesia. I'd been going through a lot of inner work, and I was looking forward to being alone on the road and continuing my personal explorations. Part of the trip would coincide with my birthday, and I'd decided to spend a week in Bali during that time. I felt very much at home there, and I wanted to be in a comfortable and spiritual place. No one would know that it was my birthday, and I could treat it as just another day in my life. I flew from Chiang Mai to Penang, Malaysia, and had a wonderful time on that beautiful island. From there I headed to Singapore, where my friend Richard joined me for a few days of fun and travel. After that, I went on to Bali for a final week of rest before flying onward from Kuala Lumpur to Europe.

I'd been to Bali several times before, and this time I wanted to avoid the more touristy places, so I chose to return to the small town of Sanur and stay once again at a hotel I'd known from a previous visit. It was a lovely place, with a central courtyard filled with orchids and intoxicating frangipani trees. They gave me a room on the third floor with a partial view of the sea and a small balcony. Three young women with warm smiles worked there, and the friendly doorman wore a snappy suit and cap. I arrived in the late afternoon, and that evening, I took myself out for a drink and dinner, followed by a good night's sleep. The next morning, I awoke to the awareness that it was my birthday, but I quickly pushed that thought back into my subconscious. I had wanted so much to not "celebrate" my birthday that year – I wanted to simply experience it as another new day in the continuum of my life. I had a wonderful time riding a hotel bicycle to the downtown area, shopping for some snacks, walking along the beach, listening to an outdoor rehearsal of a *gamelan* orchestra, and chatting with school children in their uniforms. I rode the bike back to the hotel at about 5 p.m., settled into my room, and took a shower. I thought I'd rest for an hour or so, and then take myself out for dinner at one of the lovely restaurants within walking distance.

Around 6 p.m., the phone rang. It was the voice of the always-smiling manager at the reception desk, and she said that there was a visitor for me in the lobby. "Someone is here from the USA to visit you," she said. I told her that I didn't know any Americans in Sanur, and that nobody knew that I was in Bali or staying at this hotel. But she insisted it was someone that I knew. "He knows you," she said. When I asked his name, she said, "I think it is Mister Alex."

"Mr. Alex?" I responded. "I don't know anyone named Alex." Then she asked me to hold on, and with her voice pointing away from the telephone, she said something in the Bahasa Indonesia language. Then she spoke to me: "Yes, his name is Alex, and he is here for you in the lobby. Can you please come down to see him?" After a few more comments of disbelief, I thanked her, and I told her I would be there In a few minutes.

Giggling to myself and wondering who this person could be, I put on more presentable clothes and went down to the lobby, but as the elevator doors opened, I found the ground floor completely empty. No one was behind the registration desk, and even the porter wasn't at the door. I slowly walked through the empty lobby, calling out, "Hello, hello," but no one came out or responded. "Hello," I called again as I slowly walked toward the main door of the hotel. I opened the front door, looked outside, and when I turned around to come back into the lobby, I saw the entire hotel staff, including the door-man, walking toward me. They were holding a cake with lit candles, and they began to sing "Happy Birthday to You." I could hardly believe it. After they finished singing, they told me to take the cake back to my room, but I insisted that we all share it, so we sat down at one of the tables in the dining area, and we all ate some cake together for a few minutes. It was an impromptu and unexpected birthday party. When I asked how they knew it was my birthday, one of the girls said: "From your passport, of course."

This simple and thoughtful gesture brought tears of gratitude as I rode the elevator back to my room with a large piece of birthday cake in my hands. I had wanted to play down my birthday that year, to be alone and to treat it just like any other day, but the Universe had other plans. Through the kindness and playfulness of the Balinese people, I was reminded that my birthday is indeed a special day.

How old was I when this happened? Look at the photo of the cake, at top left. It was my "62th" birthday!

My "62th" birthday cake

Hotel workers in Sanur, Bali

Thai Healing Alliance International

About five years into my study and practice of traditional Thai massage, I began to notice that most students weren't being adequately trained. Many of them seemed somewhat careless and flamboyant in the way they practiced, and this ran contrary to the sensitive and compassionate attributes that were constantly stressed by my main teachers in Thailand. At that time, there was no way for students to stay connected to their Thailand-based teachers after they returned to their respective countries, nor was there an international support system for students and practitioners of Thai massage. I began to think of forming an organization that would offer these services to serious students and massage therapists. One day after class in Hang Dong, Thailand, I asked two of my fellow students, James and D'vorah, if they would give me their opinions about this concept. We met at a small restaurant, and based on our discussion, I scribbled some notes on a napkin, which I later expanded on my computer. Within a few days, I created a structural overview and a flow chart for an international organization that would endorse and assist students and practitioners of traditional Thai massage. I then sent it to my teacher, Asokananda, to ask for his feedback and guidance. He wrote back to me and said that he felt it would be a difficult, if not insurmountable task, and that although it was a great idea, he sensed that many people might not be interested in joining a global effort. I was disappointed, and when I returned home, I completely abandoned the idea, and I resumed my growing practice with clients.

A few months later, I received an email from Asokananda asking if I had continued with my idea to form an international organization for Thai massage. I answered that based on his feedback, I had already abandoned the idea. He responded that he'd recently had a lucid dream about this concept, and that it had become clear to him that what I was proposing was extremely important for the world of healing arts. Furthermore, he believed that I was the only person who would be able to bring it to fruition. He said that he would give me his complete endorsement, and that he'd help to spread news about the new organization to his students in Thailand and around the world. I became re-energized, and I contacted several of my colleagues in the USA to ask for their help and involvement. After a few months, and with several people on board as volunteers, I expanded my original proposal for the organization, hired a graphic artist to create a logo, and consulted an attorney about beginning a non-profit organization. A few months later, Thai Healing Alliance International (THAI) was born. I invested a large amount of my own money based on a promissory note, opened a business bank account, created a website, and recruited volunteers and members from around the world to join the effort. There were various levels of membership, small annual fees, quarterly newsletters, guidelines for the study and practice of traditional Thai massage, and a code of ethics for safe and effective practice. An online library containing articles and information about Thai healing arts was created; several international colleagues became Board Members and Advisors; and a membership committee reviewed applications of those who wished to be recognized as Registered Thai Therapists (RTT) or registered Instructors.

I put all my energy into working for the alliance by answering emails, preparing and sending newsletters, approving applications, and overseeing the operation of the organization. After several years of hard work, THAI had several thousand members in more than 15 countries, but I was beginning to realize that most everything depended on me. Although people were joining from all over the world, and the organization was offering great benefits to its members, I was doing almost all the work... and without pay.

One year, I returned to Thailand specifically to create a member benefits program. I'd made appointments to meet with healthcare providers, dentists, hotels, and merchandisers in Bangkok and Chiang Mai, who agreed to give discounts to THAI members who came to study and travel in Thailand. One day, during a week of busy meetings in Chiang Mai to bring Thailand businesses onboard, I took a few hours to visit my main teacher. He greeted me in the usual friendly way, invited me to sit down, and asked me when I had arrived and what I was doing. I told him that I was establishing scholarship and discount programs for members of the organization, and as I spoke, he gazed at me deeply, reading my energy. Then, after a few seconds of silence, he quietly said to me: "Bob, you already do many things for organization, but now I think you need to separate." He continued, saying in a soft voice that I needed to regain my freedom, and that if I didn't change things, I'd be creating more *dukkha* (suffering or hardship) for myself. "Now is good time," he said. "Make change and separate."

I'd already been feeling overwhelmed with all the work I was doing. The volunteers and Board Members were helpful and had good intentions, but none of them were assuming true leadership positions. I knew in my heart that my teacher was assessing the situation and reading the energy correctly, and I listened to him without interruption as he expressed his compassionate concern for me. After he finished speaking, he called me to his altar for a blessing. He tied a *sai sin* (cotton wristband) to my arm, blew on it with his breath, and chanted in the Pali language. I remained silent with my head bowed and my hands in prayer position until he was finished. When I opened my eyes, he looked at me and said the word "separate" once again. I thanked him, we said goodbye, and I left.

My next appointment was with the director of the school at the Old Medicine Hospital, but instead of taking public transport all the way, I got off a few blocks early so I could contemplate what had just happened. As I walked toward the school, I thought about how I could transform the organization and step back from the unpaid work that had begun to consume me. Just as I turned onto a long alley leading to the school entrance, a motorbike came from behind and stopped in front of me. A woman got off the bike, took off her helmet, and said to me: "I remember you. You come here long time ago and you work hard for Thai massage. I never forget you in my heart." She said she was very happy to see me again, and that she wanted to give me a massage right away. I told her that I had an appointment with the school's director, and that I didn't have time to receive a massage. But she continued: "But you need to receive massage now; I know this in my heart. You can have meeting later." With that, she took a pen from behind her ear, stretched open the palm of my left hand, and wrote her name on it: Tasithorn. She said: "Come now, OK?" and then she put on her helmet, mounted her bike, and rode ahead to the clinic. I didn't clearly remember having met her previously, but I couldn't resist the opportunity to get a massage, especially when it had been handed to me in such a mysterious way and at such a fortuitous time. As I approached the school office, the director greeted me, and he also encouraged me to receive a massage before our meeting. Tasithorn worked on me in a deep and methodical way, and the session was transformational. In casual conversation as she was working, she told me that she had recently gone through a difficult period in her life, and that she had begun to re-invent herself. At one point, while I was lying on my stomach, she directed her bodyweight onto my back with her feet, and began to walk on my back while supporting her balance with a bamboo cane. As she stepped and pressed with incremental pressure, the tension eased from my body and mind with every exhalation. I felt myself being transported into a state of repose and thoughtless relaxation, something I had needed during recent days. Then I heard her say: "You know, sometime I think we have to separate so we can see. You know what I mean? We have to separate." I was astounded by what she had just said to me. The word "separate" had been directed to me twice within a short period of time and under very interesting circumstances. After the massage was over, I remained on the floor mat for some time to gain composure, and by the time I exited the treatment room, I was convinced that a change was due for my relationship with the organization.

I said goodbye to Tasithorn, had a brief meeting with the director about the member benefits program, and I left him with brochures and membership stickers. I made my way down the alley to the main street, and I hopped on a *tuk-tuk* to take me across town to the Chiang Mai Dental Hospital. The hospital had already agreed to offer discounts to THAI members for fillings, bridges and crowns, but that day I was receiving some dental work. Dr. Kraivit, a sensitive and compassionate man who meditated daily, had been my dentist for a number of years. Still in a daze from the deep therapeutic massage, and the way that the massage therapist's words echoed those of my teacher, I opened the door of the dental clinic and approached the counter. Dr. Kraivit exited his room with a smile on his face, came up to me, looked at me deeply, and asked: "What happened to you?" Surprised that he could tell from my expression that something had just occurred, I told him that I'd had a deep experience with my teacher earlier that day. "Oh," he said, "so before we start with your teeth, come and sit down and tell me what happened." He led me to a couch in the waiting area, and I began to tell him the whole story. He listened attentively as I described that I had been doing almost all the work for the organization, that my teacher had told me to separate, and how later, while receiving a massage, the massage therapist used that very same word to me. I don't remember the extent of our conversation, but I do remember that the stress continued to drain out of me as I sat there speaking to my dentist. At one point he looked at me deeply and said: "Your teacher loves you very much, and he worries about you. Maybe he knows." "Yes," I answered. "Maybe he knows."

A few months later, I began to plan for a change in the structure of the Thai Healing Alliance. Over the following five years, the organization slowly began to evolve from its original member-endorsing structure into what it eventually became: an online platform for the dissemination of information about traditional Thai massage & Thai healing arts. After more than 17 years of directing the organization, the non-profit corporation was dissolved, and the custodianship of the website was shared via written agreement and a joint bank account with several colleagues. Today, thaihealingalliance.com contains the largest online library in the world about traditional Thai healing arts. There are more than 800 items in the THAI archives, ranging from short articles to academic dissertations and clinical trial studies. Over 20 categories feature entries about Thai massage, Thai herbal medicine, techniques for study and practice, Buddhist spirituality, academic research, comparative studies between Western and Eastern medicine systems, Thai language, customs and spiritual beliefs, and many other interesting topics. The THAI Archives are open-access and are completely free to the general public.

Thai Healing Alliance International

"I know you."

My father was an immigrant from Aleppo (Halab), Syria, and he came to the United States as a seven-year-old boy after a three-month journey on a steamboat. His name was Chakib Haddad, and when he arrived at Ellis Island without papers, a customs official asked his name. Wanting to sound as American as possible, he answered, "Jack." The customs agent replied that Jack was a nickname for John, and then asked: "Your name is John, right?" The young boy nodded his head, and his first name was changed to John right there at the Statue of Liberty. My father spent the rest of his life in Brooklyn, New York, and after he retired, I thought of taking him back to Syria for a visit, but every time I brought it up, he had one excuse or another: "Nobody knows me there; my Arabic isn't very good anymore." After he passed away, I was sad that I'd missed an opportunity to share that experience with him, so a few years later, on the exact day of his death, I left for Syria on a pilgrimage in his honor. I brought a photo of him so we could be there together after all. A few years earlier at a music convention in Cannes, France, I'd met a French-born performer of traditional Arab music named Julien Weiss. Julien lived in Aleppo, where he played the *kanun* (Middle Eastern zither) and directed a well-known touring ensemble called *Al-Kindi*. He knew of my record label, and when we met each other in France, he told me that if I ever came to Aleppo, I should visit with him. We had been in touch by email, and he knew I was coming to Aleppo that week, but I didn't know how to find him. I only had his phone number.

I flew to Istanbul first, and met with some musicians I knew there. A few days later I traveled to visit another musician friend named Latif in the southern city of Mersin. After a few lovely days with him and his family, I took a bus to Antakya, near the Syrian border, and toured the area. Of special interest there was one of the earliest Christian churches in the world. The chapel was built entirely within a cave during a time shortly after the death of Christ when worshippers prayed clandestinely in order to avoid persecution. The following day, I boarded another bus to the Syrian border, passed through immigration, and continued onward to Aleppo, about four hours away. During the bus ride, word had spread that I was an American whose father was born in Syria, and despite the language barrier, several of my fellow passengers were friendly, welcoming and encouraging to me. I spoke in broken French to one of them, and in Spanish to someone else. Another man named Soheil Midiwan spoke English, and he took a particular interest in me. At one point, he moved from his seat to an empty one next to me, and we began a lively conversation. He wanted to know all about my father, and he asked me many questions, some of which I couldn't answer. Did I know where my grandparents had lived in Aleppo? Did I know my great-grandfather's name? Was I planning to search for my father's birth records? Did I know of any remaining relatives that still lived in Aleppo?

Much like others on the bus who had familiar-looking faces, Soheil looked like he could be one of my cousins, and by the time we arrived, I felt like I'd known him for years. As we pulled into the bus terminal, he asked at which hotel I would be staying. I told him that I hadn't yet made hotel reservations, and that I was simply planning to walk around and find a place that looked nice. Hearing that, he kindly offered to show me some hotels in the central part of town. I thanked him for his help, and said that I would be fine on my own, but he wouldn't hear of it: he insisted on accompanying me until I found a hotel to my liking. "How much you want to pay? Ten dollar? Twenty dollar? I show you first one hotel. If you not like, then we go to differ-ent hotel." Before I knew it, he had told his wife to return home with the children, and that he would join them after he got me settled in a hotel. I was so impressed with his concern and cordiality, and I found it hard to refuse his offer. We walked down the street to a hotel, and I was shown a room that was a bit dingy. When I returned to the lobby, Soheil noticed my expression and said: "OK, you don't like, we see other one." We walked a few more blocks and arrived at a stately old place with lots of character, and I decided to get a room there. After I registered and got my room key, he said he would return the next day at 5 p.m. to take me to the main Melkite Christian church so I could try to find records of my father's birth and learn about my ancestors. I told him that I didn't really need to do that, but he insisted that we should try to find some records about my family's origin. Once again, I found it hard to resist his offer.

I spent the next morning touring the beautiful historic center of Aleppo, and then I climbed up to a hilltop fortress known in English as the Citadel. The current structure is from the 12th century, but an earlier settlement was first occupied by the Seleucids around 300 BC. Back down at street level, I wandered around and took in the sights and smells. Beautiful children played in schoolyards, and colorful street vendors sold everything imaginable. I returned back to the hotel for a shower and a nap, and then I phoned Julien. He was excited to hear from me, and he invited me to dinner with his friends that same evening. He asked me to call him again in a few hours so we could make arrangements to meet at his home later that evening.

Around 5 p.m. I came down to the hotel lobby to see Soheil wait-ing for me. We greeted each other with double-cheek kisses, and we set off on a long walk, up and around and up again, until we finally arrived at a street called Sharia Talal, where the Melkite church was located. We entered the church, and a service was in progress, so we sat down in a pew. I remember enjoying the choral singing set in a distinctly Arabic style. After a few minutes, we entered an office where a short man with a sweet face and a twinkle in his eye was sitting behind a desk. His name was Abo Aboud, and when he looked at me, I felt an immediate connection. Soheil explained in Arabic that he had brought me there to see if we could locate records of my father's family. He told him that my father was born in Aleppo in 1910, and that if possible, we would like to trace all the Haddads in the city at that time to try to uncover some information about my ancestors. Abo Aboud explained to me in English that a service was in progress, and he asked if we could return in about 30 minutes. We agreed, and before we left, he took my father's name and his birthdate.

Soheil and I exited the building, and we went to a fruit juice stand nearby to have a frosty tamarind drink. It was getting late, and I had to phone Julien again to make dinner arrangements. I still didn't know where he lived, but he said he would give me the address when I called, and then I could take a taxi to his home. After our cold drink, we returned to the church office and were greeted once again by the smiling office manager Abo Aboud. I sat down at his desk to fill out a request form for birth records, and when I was finished, he looked deeply into my eyes, and he said: "I know you." He also looked familiar to me, but we couldn't have possibly met before, so I joked with him that maybe we had known each other in a previous life. But he repeated: "No, I know you." His words and his strong gaze affected me deeply, and just a few moments later, an amazing thing happened. I asked if I could use the telephone because I had made plans to be somewhere that evening at 8 p.m. He agreed, and he asked me for the number I wanted to call.

I took a piece of paper from my pocket with Julien's information, and while he held the receiver to his ear, I read the phone number aloud to him. Abo Aboud looked at me and said: "I know this number. Who do you want to speak to?" I explained that it was a man named Julien. He hung up the phone, looked at me and said: "Julien, you know Julien?"

"Yes," I answered. Then Abo Aboud asked a string of inquisitive and somewhat amusing questions: "How do you know Julien?" "Is he your friend?" "When did you meet him?" "Are you absolutely sure that he knows who you are?" "Is he expecting a phone call from you?" Finally, and after satisfying his curiosity with my answers, he explained that he worked at Julien's home several days a week as a cook and as an organizer for his musical activities. Abo Aboud and I stared at each other in surprise, but Soheil began to giggle at the thought that we both knew the same person. "You have connection," he said, smiling.

Abo Aboud picked up the phone and dialed the number from memory. He spoke with Julien in French and English, and he confirmed that I was with him at the church, and that he would personally deliver me to his home. Soheil and I said goodbye until the next evening, when he would meet me at my hotel and bring me to his home to have dinner with his wife and children. A few minutes later, Abo Aboud and I traversed an area of maze-like streets and alleys without access to modern vehicles. It seemed as if we'd stepped back in time. This part of old Aleppo had buildings that date back over a thousand years, and the smells, sounds and sights were stimulating and evocative. There were men in flowing *jalabiya* robes, veiled women, horse carts, and children playing in the alleyways. We finally arrived at a large wooden door, struck it with an ornate metal knocker, and when it opened, Julien and I greeted each other with kisses and big smiles. I was led to a large living room where several people were socializing, drinking whiskey, and eating snacks. I became reacquainted with Julien's girlfriend, Sabine, whom I'd met at the music convention in France. I also met Leila Haddad, a well-known belly dancer, and she and I called each other "cousin" for the rest of the evening. Her boyfriend Raheem was visiting from Senegal, and after a few minutes of chatting about my love of West African music, we discovered that we both knew personally the same Senegalese musician from Dakar. How could all of this be coincidence?

At about 9 p.m., we all left to go to dinner, but on the way, we stopped at the residence of one of Julien's friends who would be joining us for dinner. It was at this moment when the cycle of already hard-to-believe connective events came to a closed circuit. Julien knocked on the door; his friend exited and joined us, and we continued our walk to the restaurant. Along the way, Julien introduced me, and he explained that it was my first visit to Aleppo; that my father had been born here; and that Abo Aboud, whom I'd coincidentally met earlier that day, had brought me directly to his house. When he heard this, the man – with a beautiful face, white hair, and a big round belly – looked at me and said: "Weren't you at the church today?" When I nodded confusedly, he said that he had noticed me when I entered the church and sat down in the pew. He was the priest who performed the religious service earlier in the day, and in the afternoon he had begun to review the church records to see if he could uncover any information about my relatives.

To this day, so many years later, I am convinced that I was one part of an intertwined, cosmic, spiritual experience, and that none of this was happenstance, serendipity or mere coincidence. I had gone to Aleppo to celebrate the life and death of my father, and while riding a bus from Turkey, I met a man who brought me directly to someone who knew the person I was supposed to visit that same evening. Once there, I met a woman with my same surname and a man from Africa who personally knew someone that I also knew. Finally, the priest who had begun to review my request for genealogical information had already been invited to join all of us for dinner that same evening.

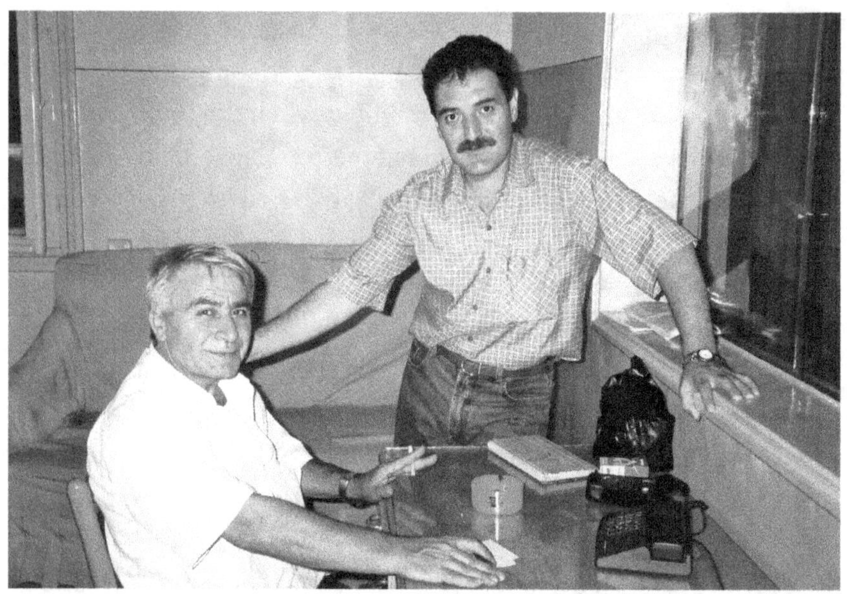

Abo Aboud (seated), and Soheil Midiwan

At dinner with the priest, Julien Weiss, and Leila Haddad

Maha Shivaratri
in Kathmandu

On one of my trips to Southeast Asia, I decided to visit Nepal for about ten days. I was excited to do some exploring, visit temples, hike in the mountains, and meet local people. The flight from Thailand took us northwest over Burma and Bangladesh, and then to the foothills of the Himalayas. The views from the airplane were stunning, especially as we flew over the Kathmandu Valley, where snowcapped peaks completely filled my field of view. I arrived in the late morning of February 18th, which, to me, was simply the day I'd decided to begin my journey. Little did I know the significance of that day to the local people, or what I was about to experience.

I took a taxi from the airport to a hotel in the Thamel district of Kathmandu. Weary from the journey, I decided to take a shower and catch a nap before I ventured out to explore the city. When I finally emerged from the hotel lobby a few hours later, I was pleasantly surprised to see many people, some dressed in traditional garb, dancing, singing, and processing down the street. "Some kind of ceremony," I thought to myself, and I sat there for a few minutes, just watching until the procession passed. I wanted to cross the street, but more people were coming from different directions, laughing, singing, and dancing. Some were playing drums, cymbals, and wind instruments. There were hundreds of people gathered on that one corner. What was going on?

I began to walk alongside the dense group of people and tried to make my way through the crowd when, all of a sudden, someone came up to me, and with a big smile on his face, asked me where I was from. I told him about myself, and that I had just arrived in Nepal. "Oh, that is great," he said. "Today is big festival. You will have good time." I thanked him, and I excused myself so I could continue walking to the other side of the street, but halfway through the crowd I was stopped again by another person.

"Welcome, welcome, where are you from?" This person was a bit wobbly, and he looked and sounded drunk. As I began to explain a little about myself, he invited me to his house. "Come, come, I will take you now." I told him that I appreciated the offer, but that I had just arrived and I wanted to walk around and then get something to eat. I excused myself, and I continued walking up a long street that was completely filled with people. Chanting was pouring out from a loudspeaker somewhere, and that spiritual sound clashed with the other noises and sights that were dominating my senses. Further ahead, I saw a cross street that looked less crowded, and as I pushed my way through throngs of people, many of them greeted me happily with "*Namasté*, hello hello," and "Where are you from?" I had never seen such a large gathering of people in one place that seemed so happy, wild and loose. Nepali people seemed so friendly and welcoming.

I ducked into a small alley to get away from the noise and the crowds, and about halfway down the road, I saw an entrance to a small Hindu temple. I cautiously walked inside, since I wasn't sure if it was permissible to be there. In one chamber, I saw a *sadhu*, or Hindu priest, passed out on the floor, lying on his side, his head resting on a small pillow. The little room had a dank smell, and I felt like I didn't belong there so I left immediately, but not before snapping a quick photo. I made my way outside toward a nearby street, and among the throngs of people, I saw other *sadhus* sitting on reed mats, behind bowls of fruit and other offerings. Their hair was braided in long strands, and some had it tied in coiled buns atop their heads. Their foreheads were painted in bright colors; their faces were covered in white ash; their necks were draped in strands of prayer beads; and the whole place smelled like marijuana. One of them summoned me, blessed me with a prayer, and applied a *bindi* to my third eye. *Bindi* is a decorative dot made of sandalwood paste that is believed to retain spiritual energy and strengthen concentration. As I looked around the room, I noticed one of them smoking pot from a clay pipe. I would never have imagined that priests in Nepal would smoke marijuana. I thanked them with a "*Namasté* thank you," and I left the temple area.

After receiving a blessing from a *sadhu*

More confused than before, I walked back to the main street so I wouldn't lose my bearings, and I turned onto a smaller street, away from the intersection where the hotel was located. Again, more and more people were stopping me, smiling and laughing, some of them offering me drinks and food. I continued a little further on this street until I reached a courtyard where small groups of people were sitting outside their homes. Night was falling, and some of them were sitting around small fires they had built, chatting and laughing. Pots filled with *dal bhat* (lentils mixed with rice) and kettles of spiced tea were hot and ready to serve at any time. I walked by slowly, and I smiled and sometimes responded *namasté* to their greetings. Suddenly, a man came up to me. He was wearing a red t-shirt and a bright blue brimmed hat that had the words "sea horse" embroidered in red thread. "*Namasté, namasté*. Where are you from?" he asked. We began a conversation, but he seemed drunk or stoned or both. "Come to my house. Come have some *chai*, and to meet my family. We play music together." I began to excuse myself, but he wasn't having it. He shouted out some Nepali words, and behind him a few people came out to greet me, all bouncy and smiley. "Hello, hello, come, come." I followed them into their house, and inside I saw several people eating and laughing. Some of the men were also smoking *ganja*. "We can play music for you," the man said as he signaled others to join. I was offered food, tea, and *ganja*, and then the man and a few others began to sing and dance and play drums. I and the others cheered them on and clapped in unison. I got high very quickly. How could it be that almost all the people I'd seen that night (except for the children and some women) were all so stoned? What the hell kind of a festival was this?

A *sadhu* smoking ganja from a *chillum*

The partying continued, with me as the guest of honor, taking photos with family members, being introduced to the neighbors, some of whom spoke English very well. We continued eating, drinking and smoking from small clay pipes (*chillum*) and encouraging the musicians, especially my quirky older friend in the red t-shirt. I lasted another hour or so until I realized that I'd be in big trouble unless I left immediately. It was dark outside, and I didn't know where I was or how to get back to my hotel. I was very stoned and a bit drunk, and I still didn't know what this festival was all about, only that it was called *Shivaratri*. I began to say my goodbyes, but they wouldn't let me leave without a final cup of tea for the road. Somehow, I made it back to the hotel that I had checked into earlier that day. It was already late at night, the party had apparently just begun, and it would continue into part of the following day... but I needed to crawl into a bed.

Later, I learned that *Maha Shivaratri*, held on the 13th night and 14th day of the waning moon, is a festival dedicated to Lord Shiva. According to Hindu mythology, it marks the day he saved the universe from darkness and married the goddess Parvati. It's a time when people can break bad habits and behaviors and make vows to bring about positive change. Legend says that deities (*devas*) and monsters (*rakshasas*) once stirred up the oceans in search of a sip of immortality (*amrita*). Due to the constant churning however, a lethal poison was released (*halahala*) that threatened all of creation. To protect everyone from this danger, Shiva drank the poison and succumbed to illness and great pain. In order to soothe the pain, he consumed large amounts of cannabis leaves and seeds (*bhang*). In commemoration, the festival of *Shivaratri* has a reputation for wild and quirky behavior, and widespread consumption of cannabis. Although marijuana is technically illegal in Nepal, law enforcement authorities look the other way on that day, and even partake in the celebration.

How is it possible that I unknowingly had the great fortune of arriving in Kathmandu on the very day of the grandest, wildest and most raucous festival in the whole country? Thank you, Shiva.

Stoned people in the street during Shivaratri

My host (with drum), and his friend

The Bedouins near Aleppo

A few years after my father's death, I decided to travel to his home town of Aleppo (Halab), Syria, to get reacquainted with my roots. It was an unforgettable experience in many ways.

After the first few days of touring the city, a hotel employee asked if I would like a half-day excursion outside the city to visit the ancient ruins of the Christian church of Saint Simeon (*Q'alat Siman*), dating back to the 5th century. He wasn't working at the hotel the following day, and he offered to drive me in his car. I could tour the ruins, we'd have lunch, and then we'd return. The price was very reasonable, and the man seemed very nice, so I agreed. Wahib, my bubbly guide, picked me up in front of the hotel the following morning, and we got in his car, a 1955 Studebaker. A few miles out of town, he asked me if I liked his car, and I replied that it was fantastic. I remember his facial expression and thick Arabic accent when he said: "This car, if you want to buy from me, even you give me ten thousand dollar I do not sell it."

Along the way we engaged in lively conversation about many things, and he was particularly excited to know that my father had been born in Aleppo, and that this was my first visit here. As we made our way to the outskirts of the city, buildings became sparser and the ground was more parched by the sun. We turned onto a smaller road and headed northwest out of the city and into the desert. Sheep, goats and camels were grazing everywhere. In the distance, long walls made of stacked stones marked the boundaries of parcels of land, and stone-paved entrances led to smaller roads. About halfway through the journey, on a flat stretch of desert land, Wahib lowered his window and honked the car's old-style horn. In the distance, across a deep field, I saw a large tent, and a few people in white cotton robes (*jalabiya*) waved their hands in response.

"Who is that?" I asked.

"These are Bedouin people," he replied. "They come and go, stay for few month, then take animals and everything, and go away and come back later."

"And you know them?" I asked.

"Yes of course, they are my friends. Sometime I go have tea with them, and for talking, and eat some food." I remained with that image in my mind – that someone who lived in the city and worked at a hotel knew real Bedouins, and that he sometimes drove here to socialize with them. His voice interrupted my ruminations: "You would like to meet them?"

I answered quickly and without hesitation, "Yes, that would be wonderful."

"OK, so maybe after we finish tour, when we come back, we stop there and see them."

"OK," I said, smiling inwardly.

About ten minutes later, we arrived at the ancient ruins, a UNESCO World Heritage site. It was a complex of high stone arches supported by large columns with ornamental capitals. Walled courtyards housed four different basilicas, and beautifully-carved stone fragments lay toppled on the ground. It didn't seem entirely Roman or Hellenic in style, and it wasn't Egyptian either, but it was very beautiful. I spent about half an hour wandering around the complex while Wahib waited under the shade of a tree. The ancient church was set amidst patches of green against swirls of brown sandy soil, and I enjoyed the experience of being there. Afterward, we walked to a small outdoor restaurant adjacent to the ruins, and we had a light meal together before beginning the drive back to the city.

On the return trip, I remember gazing out the car window at the buildings, people and animals we passed, and imagining that this was the birthplace of my ancestors. About 20 minutes into the journey, Wahib said: "So, you want to see the Bedouins?"

"Yes, of course," I replied.

"OK, we go," he said.

For a moment I wondered if maybe this would be a tourist trap of some kind. I didn't want to walk into something that I wasn't sure of, so I said: "Wahib, is this for tourists?"

"No, not for tourist!" he answered emphatically. "These are my friends. So we go for visit, OK?"

"Yes, thank you," I said.

I was getting excited about my first encounter with real nomadic people of the desert, but aside from a few phrases, names of foods and curse words, I didn't speak Arabic. I began to wonder how I should behave, if there were any customs or cultural *faux pas* I should know about, and how it would all go. The next thing I knew, the car slowed down, and we made a right turn off the road and onto a nondescript patch of hardened sand. We bumped and bounced along at a very slow speed as we approached the tent, and once or twice the car bottomed out against the sand. He honked his horn a few times, and sure enough, someone came out of the tent and waved back.

It was a beautiful tent, the size of which I would never have imagined. The car moved slowly onto a patch of dried grass to the left of the tent, and just ahead I could see a large herd of sheep and a few camels. By then, two men were standing outside, wearing *jalabiyas* and cloth head coverings. "*Salaam alaikum, merhaba, merhaba,*" one of them said as we got out of the car.

"*Alaikum salaam, shukran,*" I managed to say. We began to walk toward the tent. "So OK, here we go... yes, take off my shoes first... keep smiling Bob... keep my head bent downward out of respect. Should I put my right hand on my heart? What should I do?" I asked myself all these questions as I followed Wahib into an amazing tent in the desert. It was rectangular in shape, and it seemed to be at least 50 feet in length. Other people inside were now greeting us – another man, three or four women, and a few young children, all smiling, all welcoming us in Arabic. The larger and rounder man seemed very happy to see Wahib. A small fire was sparkling in a hearth to the right, with a perfectly placed flue right above it for ventilation, and one of the women was there, preparing some food. In the distance, against the far corners of the tent, was a sleeping area, and closer to the entrance was a long rectangular coffee table surrounded by pillows. The interior was covered with handcrafted carpets that hung against the walls from beams of wood and cane that framed the ceiling. The floor was covered with gorgeous rugs too, and the stuffed pillows and seat cushions looked almost too nice to sit on. The women were dressed beautifully, wearing partial head coverings over their long braided hair, embroidered sleeve cuffs, and hammered bracelets and anklets.

A few of the women went scurrying toward the kitchen, and we were invited to sit on the floor at the dining table. I guessed that the nomads were asking about me, and perhaps happy that their friend had been working with a tourist on his day off from the hotel. The larger man said something and Wahib answered, and then he turned to me and said, "He ask me where you from and if you speak Arabic, because you look Arabic. I tell him your father born in Halab."

"Yes, yes, my father from Halab," I said with a big smile. He smiled back and motioned to me to sit down. The kids were playing in another part of the tent. Within a few minutes, the women brought a pot of tea, some pistachios and other snacks, and they sat down on the other side of the table. Tea was poured for me by one of the women, and I smiled in thanks. Not knowing what to say or do, I listened to the happy exchange between the men, sometimes interrupted by bursts of laughter. I tried to keep smiling as much as possible as I sipped my tea and kept a low profile.

Wahib was to my left, occasionally translating for me. The tall and round man was seated across from us. His forearms, hands and even his fingers were covered in decorative tattoos, and he also wore bracelets. Directly to my right was another Bedouin who reminded me of one of my father's brothers, Uncle Eddie. He had the same type of long face, with pronounced cheekbones and a graying mustache that seemed to be growing from inside his nose. He had hairy ears and a deep gaze, and he stared at me with a penetrating expression and a constant smile. It seemed that his face was only about one foot away from mine. He passed me a plastic bag filled with tobacco and a pack of rolling papers. "Cigarette?" he said. I didn't want to say that I didn't smoke, so I thanked him and began to roll something that looked much more like a joint than a cigarette. He lit it for me, and I did my best to smoke it and to seem pleased.

They were speaking in Arabic now, and there was more verbal banter back and forth. I was trying to seem as inconspicuous as possible as I sipped my tea and smoked a funny little cigarette. Then the round tattooed man started speaking in Arabic in a slightly louder voice. He went on and on, and the others said nothing, but sometimes they nodded or gave very short answers. He spoke nonstop for at least one minute while the others listened attentively. After he stopped speaking, there was complete silence for about 15 seconds, which made me feel awkward. Then he uttered a short phrase in a clear voice, and immediately Wahib turned to me and said, "He ask where you born."

"In New York," I replied, "but my father was born in Halab, and he came to America when he was seven years old."

Wahib translated, and the Bedouin made a sound as if he understood. Then came other questions and translations: "He say he want to know if you are married." I didn't know if divorce was taboo among Bedouins, so I answered: "No, my wife died."

"*Aou, an-aasif*" (Oh, I'm sorry) was the reply.

There was another uncomfortable moment of silence until he spoke a few sentences again in a clear voice. Wahib turned to me and said: "He say he is sorry your wife die, and that every man must have wife, and he feel bad for you. He say he have three wife, and he can give to you one wife, and you can pay a little bit money, not very much, just little bit, and you can take one his wife to America, OK?" At that very moment, the three women got up from their seats and assumed standing positions with broad smiles on their faces. The nomad to my right was just inches away from my face, staring at me with his increasingly irritating fixed smile. My host spoke another short sentence, and Wahib translated: "He say which one you like?" The women started winking at me and tilting their heads with flirtatious looks. One of them made a finger-walking gesture against her palm and then quickly pointed first to herself and then to me, as if to say, "You and me, we go together?" When I saw that, I lowered my face into my cup of tea again, not knowing at all what to say or do.

My mind was racing, and I was desperate. "What can I say that won't be offensive to them? Is it a custom of nomads to share their wives like this? Should I say that I don't have enough money? Or that Syrians can't come to America without a visa? That I don't want a wife now? That I have a girlfriend waiting for me back home?" Time stopped, and what seemed like 30 seconds was probably only four or five. I picked up my head from my cup of tea, still not knowing what to say, but knowing that I had to say something. Just as I opened my mouth, the tattooed man spoke again, and Wahib translated: "He say also you can have one children, because wife without children no good." Oh Allah, what could I say now? How would I get out of this? I needed to say something – anything at all – to get me out of this dilemma. I lifted my head once again, and before I could say one word, everyone in the room started laughing. The women began to cackle, and the tattooed man grinned at me with his chin angled upward and his eyes looking straight at me, as if to say, "Did you really think I was going to give you one of my wives?"

Another round of tea and snacks began, a hookah with several hoses was passed around, and the laughter continued every few seconds for a few minutes. When I'd first arrived, I thought I'd be visiting with poor nomads who lived in difficult conditions and who had to move every few months and sell their animals for slaughter to make enough money to survive. And here I was in the most elegant tent, with the most wonderful hospitable people, surrounded by gorgeous rugs and furnishings... and the joke was on me!

Camels near Aleppo

"Oh madame, please don't say this word."

Each time I've been to the island of Bali in Indonesia, I've had a wonderful adventure, full of personal and spiritual insights. The magnificent views of the sea, the cloud-touched mountains, and the occasionally active volcanoes are a treat for the eyes. As the only Hindu island in the entire Indonesian archipelago, a certain charm and beauty is felt and seen in the way people dress, carry themselves, and practice spiritual rituals.

On my second visit there, I spent some of my time in the coastal town of Sanur, where I knew some local musicians that performed at a venue nearby. One day, I decided to take a journey to the holy temple known as Besakih, at the foothills of a range of mountains that include the sacred cone-shaped Agung volcano. I made arrangements with a local taxi driver to take me there. As we drove along a beautiful coastal road, we passed terraced rice paddies, people fishing with nets in the sea, flowering frangipani trees, children playing in front of their homes, men plowing the fields with water buffaloes... all so peaceful and easy on the eyes. My driver was friendly, curious and informative, and we had no trouble engaging in lively conversation along the way. About halfway into the 75-minute drive, we saw someone up ahead waving her arms. The driver asked if we could stop, and I agreed. It was a female tourist in her forties, and she explained that she was trying to find a way to visit Besakih Temple, and she asked which way we were headed. The driver politely said that he was headed there, but that he already had a customer. I then mentioned that if she wanted to join us, we could share the carfare to the temple. She eagerly agreed, and as I slid over to the left side of the back seat, she took her place beside me and closed the door.

We continued driving with the windows open to get the best views, but also to feel the balmy breeze on our faces and breathe the beautifully scented air. A little further down the road a large insect entered my rear window, and it landed on the left shoulder of the woman beside me. It was a large beetle, like a scarab, and it rested on her shirt sleeve as if it truly belonged there. As a longtime admirer of unusual-looking insects, I became transfixed and moved my face closer to admire and examine this creature of beauty. There were no large pincers protruding from its head, and never for a minute did I think it would be dangerous or even capable of biting me. It was simply a beautiful beetle that unknowingly got swept by an air current into the taxi. But my fellow passenger didn't react as I did, and she immediately began to scream: "Get it off me. Aghh... get it off!"

I replied that I would remove it but that she shouldn't worry because it wasn't dangerous and it wouldn't bite her. I could see the driver smile at me through the rear-view mirror when I said that. I continued to stare in awe at this beautiful creature. It was greenish black in color, with brightly-colored fluorescent accents, and its legs were moving independently of each other. But the lady next to me wasn't appreciating my slow response to remove it from her sleeve. I began to entice the beautiful creature to walk into my open palm. "Take it off me now, please," she said again. "Aghh, please hurry... it's so ugly."

Upon hearing that, the driver spoke up from the front of the cab: "Oh madame, please don't say this word."

"What do you mean?" she said. "It's ugly."

"No," he quickly responded. "No, it is not ugly."

"Well," she said, "you must have a word in your language for ugly. How do you say ugly in your language?"

With that, he responded resolutely, but with a sweet smile through the rear-view mirror: "In Bali, we say not beautiful."

I never forgot that simple and sensitive lexical distinction, and to this day, when I hear people refer to other living things as "ugly," I sometimes relate this story, or I just say that they're not ugly to another animal or insect. Sometimes, to drive a point home with humor, I might also say that if reincarnation is true, one day you might be reborn as something you thought was ugly in a previous life, and someone who thinks you are ugly might hurt you.

Besakih Temple, at the Agung volcano

"Be careful when you go. Be careful."

In the initial years of my Thai massage training, I would return to study in Thailand once or twice a year. I had been studying with my mentor Ajahn Pichest Boonthumme, who was helping me to understand how important it was to be still, to meditate, and to use sensing, intuition, and good body mechanics as I worked. After several years of study and practice, I was refining my ability to feel and dissipate blockages in the human energy system with my hands, and I was being guided by a master who sometimes didn't even have to touch someone in order to detect a blockage.

During my second Thailand trip in the same year, and after a month of study with Pichest and other teachers, my friend Della was planning to meet me in Chiang Mai in late December. We had made plans to vacation together on the beautiful islands of southern Thailand over the end-of-year holidays. We would spend a few days in Chiang Mai so she could rest from jet lag as I showed her around the city. Then we would fly to the southern town of Krabi and take a ferry from there to the Phi Phi islands for a beach vacation in the Andaman Sea. All the travel arrangements were made, including flights, ferries and hotels, but a day before she was to arrive, I learned that her flight from Los Angeles had been cancelled because of technical difficulties, and that she would be arriving one day late. When I heard this news, I changed all our travel arrangements to one day later than originally planned, since it takes several days to adjust to the time difference.

Instead of departing to Krabi on a Saturday, we would now be leaving on Sunday.

My teacher knew of my travel plans, and before I left for the south, I wanted to say goodbye to him and ask for his blessings. I decided to visit Pichest on Friday for morning prayers before he began class that day. Della had arrived the day before, so I told her that I would be back in a few hours, but she asked if she could also come along. She had heard about my teacher, and she wanted to meet him, so I agreed to take her. We took the bus to his home and arrived before the beginning of class so I could speak with him for a few minutes, tell him my plans for travel, and say goodbye.

After prayers and chanting, Ajahn Pichest turned around from the altar to speak to the group, but he remained motionless and silent for quite some time. Then he looked straight at me, called my name, and asked if I was leaving the next day for southern Thailand. I replied that no; I was leaving on Sunday. "Morning or afternoon?" he asked.

"Morning," I said.

He became visibly upset upon hearing my answer, and he quickly summoned me to his altar. "Come here, come here for blessing." I approached him and knelt before the altar with my hands in prayer position, and he began to bless me and recite prayers over me while tying a knotted string bracelet around my wrist. Every once in a while, he would look up at me and say, "Be careful when you go... be careful," and then he would return to the prayers in Pali language.

I had received blessings from him before, but never in such a deep way, at an unexpected time, or for such an extended period... and he'd certainly never told me to be careful before. He continued the prayers and blessings for another few minutes, and when he finally stopped, he looked at me with great concern, and he told me once again that I needed to be very careful on my journey. I thanked him, bowed to him and to the altar, and I slowly backed away on my knees. As I turned around and faced the other students in class, I made an eye signal to Della that it was time for us to go.

As she bowed and began to stand up to leave the room, he said: "Oh, you with Bob? Come here," and he motioned to her with his hand. She knelt at the altar, and he also began to bless her, occasionally saying, "Be careful with Bob when you go. Be careful." After his blessing, he took a white object from a box nearby, placed it in her open hand, then closed her hand around it and said a final prayer. He had given her a tiny statue of Jivaka Kumarabhaccha, the spirit guide of traditional Thai medicine. She offered a final bow of thanks, and we left the classroom to begin our 20-minute bus journey back to the city. On the way home, my friend was elated at having been blessed by my teacher. She went on and on about how wonderful it was to meet a true master and to be blessed by him, but I was very worried about what had just happened. Why was he so concerned about my safety on this upcoming trip? He'd never done this type of thing before or told me that he was concerned for my safety. What did all of those blessings mean? What should I be careful about?

For the rest of the day and evening, feelings of concern and uncertainty lingered with me. We spent part of Christmas Day, a Saturday, preparing for an early departure the following morning. The next day – December 26, 2004 – we took an early morning flight from Chiang Mai to Bangkok, and after landing, we walked to another gate, and got our boarding passes for the flight to Krabi. A few minutes later, as we stood in line waiting to board the plane, pandemonium broke out at the airport, and people suddenly began screaming and running through the terminal. The noise level rose dramatically, and some people were holding each other and crying hysterically. Most people were shouting in Thai language, and we had no idea what was going on. I asked some people nearby what had happened, and they simply said, "Look at television," so we rushed to a TV monitor in the departure lounge. What we saw would become forever etched in my mind. A natural disaster had occurred in southern Thailand. We stood with our mouths open as we watched a news flash. A broadcaster was speaking Thai, and on the bottom of the screen were English words describing that thousands were feared dead on the southwestern coast, especially around Krabi and on the Phi Phi islands.

I stared transfixed at the TV screen and read the word Krabi once again. Then I looked at the boarding pass in my hand and saw the very same word. I was stunned. People were still running around the terminal, speaking loudly and emotionally to others, and some were getting in lines to change their air tickets. As we continued to watch the TV monitors, we saw live images of towering waves, and boats, homes and wreckage being swept to sea. The islands had taken a direct hit from a giant tsunami, and a ferry bound from Krabi to the Phi Phi islands had been sucked into the ocean. The tsunami was sweeping over the entire southern Thai coastline, and was also devastating areas in India, Sri Lanka, Myanmar, Indonesia and Malaysia. We were paralyzed by the images on the screen, but there was so much noise and commotion all around us that we decided to leave the boarding area. We walked away from the monitor to a quieter place so we could discuss options to change our travel plans. After entering a glass-enclosed restaurant in the terminal, we ordered some coffee, and then suddenly, we both realized why Pichest had been so worried. This was why he had told me to be so careful, why he had blessed me for so long, tied a protection bracelet on my wrist, and gave the statuette to Della. He had sensed the coastal danger zone that I was entering after leaving the safety of the hills of northern Thailand. That realization was almost as shocking as the news of the tsunami.

Within a few seconds, I knew that I had to call him. If he had known that I was heading into danger, then he surely would be worrying about me right now. It was a time before the widespread use of cell phones, so I went to a public phone nearby, put coins into the slot, and called him. "Ajahn, this is Bob."

"Ah, Bob," he replied, "you OK?"

I told him I was fine, and that we were just about to board the plane to Krabi when the tsunami struck. "Tsunami very strong energy," he replied. We spoke for only another few seconds, I thanked him, and I told him that I'd be in touch with him again soon.

We were in shock, and everyone we met along the way was visibly upset. The news coverage was nonstop, and the images, video coverage and death estimates were looking worse. Nearly 230,000 people were killed in the 2004 Indian Ocean earthquake and tsunami, making it one of the deadliest disasters in modern history. With waves traveling at 500 mph, the death toll in southern Thailand was approximately 5,400, including over 2,000 tourists.

If Della hadn't arrived one day late because of a flight cancellation, and if I hadn't changed all the travel plans to one day later, we probably would have been aboard the ferry that was consumed by the ocean in the tsunami. In any case, we would certainly have already been on the beaches of Krabi at the very time the tsunami struck. And somehow, two days before all of this happened, my teacher had sensed that I was headed straight into danger.

A most exquisite morsel

One of the most exciting cultural and culinary experiences of my life happened on my first evening in Syria. After arriving from southern Turkey, I checked into the Baron Hotel. Once the premier hotel of the entire region, it was a bit tired after 100 years of continuous operation, but it still exuded charm with its high ceilings, carved woodwork, and marble steps and pillars. Famous people like Lawrence of Arabia, Kemal Atatürk, Charles Lindbergh, and Theodore Roosevelt slept here, and Agatha Christie retreated to the hotel to write the first part of her classic novel *Murder on the Orient Express*.

Lobby of the Baron Hotel, Aleppo

After settling into my room around 6 p.m., I was curious and excited to walk around the city of Aleppo ... and I was also very hungry. The manager, Samir, a warm man with a twinkle in his eye, suggested that I try a restaurant just a few blocks away, but when I got there, it seemed quiet, formal and unappealing, and there were very few people inside. I continued walking around, delighting in the street activities, observing the vendors and the shops bursting with trays of fragrant multicolored spices, dried fruits, and nuts. There were people grinding coffee, serving tea out of large hammered-metal tanks, and selling fruits and vegetables on sidewalks and street corners. I walked down one block, and then another, delighting in the visual, auditory, and olfactory stimulation. Then, somewhere in the distance, I heard belly dance music. As I got closer to the source of the sound, I realized that it was recorded music amplified through loudspeakers. I followed my ears to the end of the block, then walked another block to the right, and then to the left, until I arrived at a large courtyard, and there on the corner was a vibrantly wild outdoor restaurant. It was truly the most exciting place I could have ever imagined, and it was exactly where I wanted to be.

I stood there for a minute, transfixed, watching the social activity, and imbibing the semitones and syncopated rhythms of the music that served as a perfect cultural backdrop. On the sidewalk close to where I was standing, twenty or more people were circling around a long metal table, helping themselves to mounds of fresh spearmint leaves, pickled peppers, garlic, onions, parsley, pickled turnips, chili peppers, and many other sauces and condiments. It was a *falafel* restaurant! All around me, another twenty or thirty people were standing or leaning against the walls as they enjoyed their falafel wrapped in fresh pita bread, or on a platter with *tabbouleh* salad. Directly ahead, about 30 feet away, four cooks stood on a long elevated platform as they went about their work. There were two sandwich makers and another young man whose only job was to scoop small amounts of the fresh mixture into a giant cauldron of boiling oil. A fourth man made sure that the tender falafel balls were cooked to perfection by rotating them in the oil with a large metal skimmer. When they were just right, he'd scoop them out and place them onto a large slotted tray to drain, and from time to time, the tray would be brought to the preparation area.

After a few minutes of taking in the whole scene, I began to wonder how I'd be able to order some food. I couldn't read the Arabic script describing the photographs of various items posted on the wall. What was I to do? I couldn't ask basic questions in Arabic, and I had no idea if anyone there spoke English. How would I get my falafel? Not knowing what to do, and with the music blaring and all the activity buzzing around me, my eye caught a gesture from one of the cooks far ahead on the platform. He looked straight at me, and bent his head backward while raising his eyelids. Was he signaling to me? I gestured back to him by pointing my index finger to my chest and raising my own eyebrows. His response was to extend his arm and quickly flap four fingers downward and upward. I could hardly believe that he was calling to me, but I made my way through the mass of people ahead, and I approached the platform. He looked at me for a second – as if to make sure he had my attention – and then he grabbed a falafel ball from the large tray with a pair of tongs. He gracefully swirled some *tahini* on it, delicately placed a single leaf of parsley on top, wound his wrist in the air as if he were performing a magic trick, and reached down to offer it to me. I tasted it, and I was in heaven. It had a light texture and a slight crunch. The taste of the perfectly blended chickpeas, fava beans, herbs, seeds and spices lingered for a while after each swallow, just like a fine wine. He watched me intently with a smile as I ate it. To convey my delight and gratitude, I placed an open palm on my chest as I rolled my eyes a bit. He laughed. I then gestured to him by placing an index finger in the air as I raised my eyebrows and quickly nodded my head. "I'll take one, please," is what I meant to convey. He understood, and he pointed his nose in the direction of a small booth to the side of the serving area.

A large man seated at a small desk was taking money from customers in return for colored tokens. That's when I finally understood the ordering process. The signs posted on the wall showed photographs of various configurations of meals, and each one was associated with a color, but I still couldn't read the prices. Easy enough, I thought: I'll just use hand signals.

Alfaihaa falafel business card

I walked over to the man selling tokens, pointed at the photo of a falafel pita, and gestured "one" with my index finger in the air. I also ordered an *aryan* yogurt drink. I took a bill out of my pocket and offered it to him in my open hand. He delicately retrieved it, gestured with his open hand for me to wait, counted out my change, and placed it in my hand. He gave me the bottle of *aryan*, he handed me the token, and he pointed back to the serving platform as he uttered something in Arabic. "*Shukran lakum*," I said with a smile, and he replied with several words which I assume meant "you're welcome."

As soon as I turned around, the observant and friendly cook signaled me back to the platform, where he took my token and then prepared my pita sandwich. After the pita was stuffed with falafel, chopped cucumbers, tomatoes and parsley, he drizzled some fresh *tahini* into the pocket, and then, making sure I was watching, he put an extra falafel ball inside before passing it down to me. "*Shukran habibi,*" was all I could think to say. "*Shukran, shukran,*" I said again as I turned around and headed to the condiments table. Once there, I did just as the others, stuffing my pita with more goodies. I remember how the fresh spearmint complimented all the other ingredients to perfection.

That evening I was in sensorial ecstasy. The sights, tastes, smells and sounds all combined to make me feel that I had arrived home – home to the land of my ancestors.

"Get me the hell
out of here!"

As my mother began to decline in health during the last few months before her passing, she stayed at different healthcare facilities based on her changing conditions. At one point she was in hospice for about two weeks, but then got discharged because her condition wasn't acute enough. For the last three years of her life, I was her sole caretaker. It was a heavy responsibility, and I was there for her every step along the way, but I also had to prepare for the inevitable fact that she would soon pass. Her dementia had worsened in the last months of her life, and her short-term memory was severely affected. It was both a curse and a blessing. It made things more difficult for me as her caregiver, but her life seemed a little easier, since because of her failing memory, she was less aware of the problems and her general state of decline. I had been involved in a local dementia caretaker's group, and the guidance I was receiving from the counselors was extremely helpful. One of the things we learned in our support group was how to avoid confrontation or condescending or frustrated speech that could remind the patient that they were losing their memory. That type of behavior could unnecessarily foment a decreased sense of self-worth in the patient, which wouldn't be productive or helpful. I was very grateful for the guidance that helped me to remain as mindful as possible about how best to take care of my dear mother.

I would visit her once or twice each day in the hospice and spend several hours at a time. It was a nice facility and she had a great room with a balcony overlooking a beautiful meadow. I'd always bring food that I knew she liked, and encourage her to get out of bed and move around. I'd take her for a walk or a wheelchair ride, make her laugh, and give her a lot of love. One day I opened the door to her room, and a nurse was making her bed, cleaning up the room, and chatting with her. After a lively exchange, the nurse left the room, and I asked my mom if she wanted to get up and sit outside on the balcony with me. It was a lovely day, the sun was out, and I thought it would be good for her to be outside and breathe some fresh air. I also wanted to distract her a bit, change up the energy, and brighten her mood.

She agreed that it would be nice to sit outside, so I helped her to get in the wheelchair, draped something around her shoulders, and wheeled her out to the balcony. I sat next to her in a rocking chair, and we chatted and reminisced. She was particularly taken by a bright red cardinal that flew past the balcony and stopped on a nearby tree. She thought it was delicate and beautiful, and she mentioned that she hadn't seen many cardinals before she moved to North Carolina. At one point there was a lull in the conversation, and after a few moments of silence, she turned to me and asked: "Hon, are we at your house right now?" My dementia training helped me to understand that in order to avoid lengthy explanations that could bring about more confusion, it was sometimes best to answer questions with a simple yes or no. So, I replied that no, we weren't at my house. She then said that she knew we weren't in my "regular" house, the one with the garden and the tall trees. She remembered my house, and she knew that we weren't there.

"Uh-huh," I replied, but then she added: "I just thought that maybe this was another house that you owned." I thought carefully about what to say next, something that wouldn't encourage another train of thought.

"No, Mom," I answered, "this isn't my house."

"Oh," she replied. She turned her head to face forward, and another ten seconds passed. Then she looked at me again and said with a sweet smile and a glint in her eye, "Is this a new apartment that you got for me?"

Her excitement was hard to witness, knowing that I would have to deflate it, so I reached over and held her hand as I said gently: "Well, Mom, you know that this isn't your apartment, right?"

And she answered, "Oh, of course. I know this isn't my old apartment, the one down by the market in Carrboro. I just thought that maybe you had gotten me a new apartment here for a while, that's all."

"No, Mom, I didn't," I answered softly.

Another few seconds passed as I tried to imagine a strategy for completely changing the topic, but before I could say anything, she continued: "But this isn't the hospital, right?"

"No, Mom, remember that the hospital was…"

And she interrupted, "Oh yeah, I remember the hospital. The room was different, and there was a long hallway, and lots of doctors and nurses always came in to visit me. Everybody was so nice there."

I tried to brace myself for her next question. I wanted to avoid a conversation about the fact that she was in a hospice, facing imminent death. Where was that beautiful red cardinal when I needed a good distraction? But before I could devise a strategy, she looked at me and said with a confused expression: "So then, if this isn't your house, and you didn't get a new apartment for me, and I'm not in the hospital, where am I?"

I couldn't dance around the truth anymore, so I simply replied: "Well, Mom, you're in a hospice."

"A hospice?" she asked. "Isn't that where people go when they're getting ready to die?" I simply nodded my head, and then she blurted out in an agitated voice: "Well then, get me the hell out of here! Get me *out* of here, honey!"

Her expression of consternation contrasted so sharply with the comical effect of her words that I began to laugh. She saw me laughing, and then she also began to laugh. We hugged each other as we continued to laugh hysterically, and the tears from our laughter turned into tears of sadness and then back to laughter again. I kissed her and held her for a long time, and I told her that everything was going to be alright.

Grace in hospice

Shona spirits

My work as a world music producer and amateur ethnomusicologist brought me many personal, professional and spiritual rewards. I remember that I was mesmerized when I first heard the *mbira*, a traditional instrument used by the Shona people of Zimbabwe and others in neighboring regions. The instrument consists of a wooden board made of African teak, and an array of tunable metal tines, which are held in place by an iron bar and plucked with the thumbs and forefingers. When the prongs are plucked, they create overtones because adjacent keys produce secondary vibrations. The instrument is sometimes played inside a resonating chamber made of a calabash. Pieces of metal, bottle caps, and other objects are often fastened to the instrument or to the outside of the gourd, and these create a characteristic buzzing sound. Several types of *mbira* are used for different purposes, and there are also various tunings. You may know of the smaller, more modern instrument known as the *kalimba* (or thumb piano), but if you're not familiar with the traditional larger *mbira*, take a good listen one day.

I was lucky to know and record two of the greatest contemporary masters of the *mbira*, Ephat Mujuru and Dumisani (Dumi) Maraire. I first met Ephat during his early performances in the United States. I was a sponge for non-Western music then, and Ephat was a source of inspiration. I remember intimate concerts during which his mesmerizing rhythms and charming storytelling riveted the attention of the audience for hours on end. Dumi and I first met at the Hudson

River Revival, an annual summer festival in Upstate New York that attracted a wide variety of international performers. I was a stage announcer, and Dumi and I hit it off one day in backstage conversation. I later produced his first commercial recordings on compact disc, and I helped to get him concerts at various venues across the United States for several years.

I knew there were different lineages of *mbira* music, and that some styles were more suited for entertainment while others were used for the purpose of communicating with ancestor spirits at spirit possession ceremonies. Ephat's grandfather, Muchatera Mujuru, was one of the most important spirit mediums of his time, and he channeled one of the most revered ancestor spirits in Shona cosmology, Chaminuka.

Naturally, Dumi and Ephat knew each other, but for many years they hadn't been in touch, and they'd never performed or recorded together. Something had happened in the past that brought about hard feelings between them. I supported them individually in their careers, but I really wanted to bring these two masters together for a recording. Some of my colleagues told me it would be impossible to do, but I was determined to take up the challenge.

I invited each of them separately to record a new album at a recording studio owned by a friend in my hometown. I promised to pay them well, buy their air tickets, and put them up at a nice hotel for the few days we would be recording... but neither of them knew that I had invited the other, or that they'd be arriving by plane from different airports within about 40 minutes of each other. Needless to say, they were both shocked when they saw each other.

It was a quiet and tense ride from the airport to downtown. Shortly after arriving at the hotel, they had a big argument, and they refused to speak to each other for the rest of the day. Dumi was angry at me for having tricked him into recording with Ephat. Although Ephat was open to the idea, I decided to change my plans for the sessions. I told them we would record individually in the studio on separate days. I hoped that if I could soften things a bit and bring them together, I could convince them to record a few duet tunes on the third day. To my delight, that is exactly what happened. On the second day of sessions, they began to speak to each other, and that evening we had a nice dinner together at my home, with a few drinks beforehand to soften the mood. By the end of the evening, they were laughing and joking with each other in Shona and English.

The recording sessions were full of wonderful spontaneous experiences. On the third day, after the last of the planned tunes was recorded, we finished our work, said goodbye to the engineer, and we headed to the photography studio to take promo shots for the cover design and press release. At the photo session, they were both holding their *mbiras* and playing gently while posing for the camera, but the two instruments weren't tuned alike. I randomly picked out some other *mbiras* that I thought would look best for the photo shoot, and I asked the musicians to pose with them. They had never played with these two instruments before, and they sounded fantastic together. Both of them wished they had tried this particular combination of *mbiras* for their duet recordings, but Dumi had to be at the airport in a few hours. I immediately made phone arrangements with the studio for a quick return, and the photographer hurried to finish the shoot. As we drove back to the recording studio, they played and sang a traditional tune non-stop with big smiles on their faces. Not a word was uttered. The engineer was ready to go as soon as we walked through the door, and the track *Mawuya Mawuya* was done live in one take – flawless in its integrity, yet wholly improvised.

The most amazing experience happened on the second night of the recording sessions, while Ephat was performing solo on the *mbira dza vadzimu*, considered a sacred instrument by the Shona people. It was after midnight, and Ephat was about to record the last solo piece of the evening. He called it *Mucheka*, the Shona word for cloth, and explained that the song was inspired by the reciprocal value of woven cloth in society. "When children are young, it's the parents' responsibility to provide clothing. But when parents get old, then the children must give them clothing." It was an entrancing cyclical melody played mostly in the mid-range keys, but punctuated with bursts of bass notes, sometimes in unexpected places. Ephat had his eyes closed, and as the song progressed, he began to move his body as he sat in a chair behind the microphones. In the control room, I also closed my eyes so I could focus on listening. The engineer, my friend Randy, was sitting a few feet away from me at the mixing board. Soon I began to hear humming sounds. When I opened my eyes, I saw that Ephat had begun to shake his body, and he now had a strained expression on his face. I rationalized that the humming sound was the result of overtones created by the metal keys, but as the song progressed, the humming increased, and as I watched him through the soundproof glass wall, vowel sounds like "ahhh" and "ohhhh" began to drift into the control room monitors. There was a choral quality to the sounds, very much like human voices, but Ephat's mouth was completely closed. His body shook uncontrollably, beads of sweat began to run down his face, and he now seemed to be in a deep state of trance. As the voices continued, the only conclusion I could reach was that spirits had entered the studio, or were manifesting through Ephat as a medium. Just then, Randy said to me in an alarming voice: "Where are those voices coming from?"

"Shh," I whispered. "I think spirits are in the room. Can you turn down the lights a bit?"

He looked at me with his eyes wider than I'd ever seen them before, and he dimmed the lights in both rooms. "What do you mean spirits?" he asked softly.

"I'll tell you later," was my reply. We both sat there transfixed, listening to the rhythm and texture of the *mbira*, hearing the dissonant humming and the wispy vocal sounds, and watching Ephat shake and tremble as he played.

A little after six minutes into the track, he slowed down a bit, and then he played a final note. His eyes were closed, his hands and head were trembling, and his face and neck were streaked with perspiration. I stood up, opened the door of the control room, walked a few steps to the door of the recording room, and opened it. As I watched him trembling there, he slowly opened his eyes a bit to acknowledge me, and I said: "Ephat, did you hear...?" and before I could finish my sentence, he said ... "the voices?" "Oh yes, I was asking the spirits for their blessing about this recording, and they were telling me it is a very good thing you are doing for me and Dumi to make this CD together. They were saying it is a very good thing."

I didn't know what to say, so I asked if he wanted a drink of water. "Yes, please," was his reply. I quickly left the room, filled a glass with water, grabbed some paper towels, and returned to the recording room so he could dry his face and neck and have a drink. He had stopped trembling, but he still looked a bit stunned. Not knowing if my presence was a help or a hindrance, I told him that we were finished for the night, and that whenever he was ready, we could pack up and go. He thanked me, and I returned to the control room, but there was nothing to say to the engineer because he had heard our conversation through the monitors. We just looked at each other, and I think he said, "This is almost unbelievable." For years afterward, we talked about the day when African spirits visited his studio.

The Shona Spirit CD went on to win several awards, and it received outstanding reviews in major music magazines. Perhaps more importantly, it brought together two great masters of the tradition after many years of discord and non-communication, and the whole experience was in some way connected to the spirit realm. If you listen hard enough to the song *Mucheka*, you can hear some of the harmonic overtones and humming sounds, but of course, those Shona spirits were smart enough to not to allow their voices to be recorded.

Ephat Mujuru

Dumi and Ephat on the last day of the recording sessions

"Photo for your mother."

I traveled to Indonesia for the first time during a period of turmoil and change. I was so stressed and overloaded that I decided to take a six-week period of reflection and exploration in Java and Bali. It was a good decision, because by the time I returned home, I was charged with new energies that eventually led to transformation on many levels.

During the first few weeks, I visited Ubud, the cultural capital of Bali. I especially enjoyed hearing *gamelan* performances featuring bronze gongs, percussion, vocals and dance. I also took side trips to visit Balinese temples, where I sometimes prayed and reflected on my life for long periods. On one of these trips, I hired a guide to take me in his car to various villages and tourist sites. One of the stops along the way was the small village of Tenganan, inhabited by the Bali Aga people. The Bali Aga are the indigenous people of Bali, who live in a number of traditional villages, predominantly in the mountainous areas of the eastern portion of the island. The main language is Balinese, but each of the Bali Aga areas of the island uses different dialects that are often not mutually understood. The Bali Aga are ardent preservers of their traditions, and rituals, ceremonies, community norms, human rights, and even architecture are all codified in community rules called *awig-awig*. All houses, for example, must be built using a mixture of certain types of stone, and roofs must be thatched with leaves from a certain tree which have a water-resistant quality. In order to preserve traditions, Bali Aga generally do not marry residents from outside their villages. If two people from different villages fall in love and decide to get married, they must abandon their villages and families and live elsewhere.

Upon arriving at Tenganan, I was escorted to a guard house at the entrance to the village, where my documents were inspected and the rules for outsiders were explained to me. My guide Wayan had taken me to Tenganan that day to witness a ceremony honoring a large group of recently-circumcised young boys, and to commemorate their rite of passage with parades, food, music and dance. The boys were dressed in white shirts and sarongs with golden sequins, and they wore pointy miters on their heads. Their faces were painted in red makeup, and they even wore lipstick. Nearby, under a thatched area, young virgin girls alongside their mothers had the best view, and all the while, an incredible gamelan ensemble of about twenty men played amazing melodies to accompany the procession. I was so happy to have come here to witness such a beautiful ceremony. A few hours later, and after the ceremonies ended, I struck up a conversation with a few local young men who told me that there would be a ritual fighting and bloodletting ceremony several weeks later. They encouraged me to attend, and said that if I did, they would be happy to spend time with me. I decided right then that I would return!

Later that month, I hired a car and driver to take me back to Tenganan. I went through the formalities of showing my passport at the entrance to the village, and I was escorted by a young man to the center of town, where the ceremony would soon begin. I learned that *Perang pandan* is a holiday during which the *makare-kare* fighting ritual is held to honor deities and ancestors. It is held only in this village, once a year on the full moon in late June or early July, and participation is compulsory for young males. While walking around the central part of the village, I felt like I'd gone back in time. Aside from a few telephone poles on the outskirts of town, I didn't notice any t-shirts, sneakers, pants, watches, television antennas, or any other Western-influenced items. Food was being cooked on open fires and over smoking embers arranged within circles of stones on the ground. Traditional live music was being performed on a stage under a thatched roof. The recently circumcised teenage boys were there again, strategically placed in the center of all activity, and the young girls were lined up at the central building, within view of the ritual battle area.

Bells were rung, an announcement was made, participants drank palm wine in cups made of banana leaves, and then the fighting ceremony began. Groups of two men would face off, dance around each other like boxers, jostle for the best approach of attack, and then strike. The weapons are made by tying *pandan* shoots together to form a small club. Pandan is a palm-like shrub or tree, and many of the leaves are edged with small, sharp thorns. The fighting techniques I witnessed included swinging strikes and scratching movements, particularly on the opponent's back and arms. Participants competed shirtless, wearing only a sarong and a traditional headdress, and they carried round shields made of rattan. Each fight lasted for only a few minutes, and after each combat, the contestants' wounds were treated by applying a liquid made of rice wine or vinegar, turmeric, and galangal. These men were clearly having fun, and some were laughing, but they were also subjecting themselves to considerable pain and bloodshed. The ceremonial battles went on for quite some time, and then everyone shared in food and drink.

At one point, the young men I'd met on my previous visit recognized me and called me over to their side of the fighting area. We spent a considerable amount of time together, and when they weren't engaged in battle, they told me all about the ceremony. A few minutes later, one of them came up to me and said with a serious face: "You also can fight now, OK?"

"Me?" I answered. "No, I cannot fight. I am not from here, and I don't want to fight."

"But you try, OK? Don't worry, you try. We don't hurt you."

At this point, I could see the other boys smiling and laughing, so I laughed too, and I realized that he was only joking. Then he said to me: "Come on, you already have sarong, so only take off your shirt, and we take a photo. Photo for your mother."

My time in Tenganan was soulful, spiritual, and insightful. I was one of only a few outsiders in a traditional village, which is usually closed to tourists – and even to people from neighboring tribal areas. I feel honored to have visited the beautiful village of Tenganan, Bali.

Ceremonial fighters at Tenganan

"Photo for your mother"

"Two, please..."

On my first trip to the Middle East, I combined visiting my father's hometown in northern Syria with other places of interest in the general area. After some wonderful experiences in Aleppo, I visited Homs, the town of ancient wooden water wheels, and then I continued south to Damascus. While visiting the spectacular Umayyad Mosque, I overheard two men speaking in an Arabic that was sometimes speckled with English words. This piqued my curiosity and eventually I greeted them and asked if they both spoke English. They answered affirmatively and asked if I spoke Arabic. I explained that I only knew a few words, but that I'd heard them use some English words as they were speaking Arabic to each other. They laughed and acknowledged that it was sometimes easier to use English words to describe certain things.

They had both lived in the United States for periods of time, and we began a lively conversation. They asked what I was doing in Damascus, and where I was heading next. When I responded that I didn't have a firm plan in mind, they told me that they lived in Beirut, Lebanon, and that if I came to Beirut, they'd be happy to show me around the city. They also suggested that if I wanted to take a side trip for a few days, I should consider visiting the town of Baalbek, where the best-preserved Roman ruins outside of Italy were located. They said it was a beautiful town with great food and nice people, and that I would enjoy a visit there before continuing onward to Beirut. We exchanged information, I thanked them for their kindness, and we said goodbye with kisses on both cheeks. That same evening, I began to make plans to visit the town of Baalbek for a few days and then to travel onward to Beirut.

Within the first few days of arriving in the Middle East, I realized I had a big problem. I had traveled around the world for many years, but I'd never been in a place where I couldn't read the numbers! I didn't speak Arabic, and I couldn't read the value of bills and coins, or the prices associated with food and other items. I had no choice but to force myself to memorize the shapes of Arabic numbers from 0 to 9. Some were fairly easy to recognize: 1 looked like the Roman numeral for 1; 2 looked like a 1 with a little hook on the top; and 0 was a small dark diamond. But others were tricky: Arabic 5 looked like a Roman 0; 6 reminded me of 7; and 7 was a V. After a few days of constant practice, I was able to read Arabic numbers, and after a few weeks I had also learned some very basic Arabic. Once I could read and pronounce numbers, use greetings, and ask basic questions, my life became a lot easier, and interactions with people became more fun.

My Lebanese friends were right – Baalbek was a very lovely town. I arrived from Damascus in the afternoon, found a small hotel just a few blocks from the ruins, and set out to explore the area. A few hours later, I enjoyed an early dinner at an outdoor restaurant. After dinner, I took a leisurely walk back to the hotel, but on the way, I was distracted by a storefront window. Right there in front of me was the most amazing array of Middle Eastern pastries I'd ever seen in my life. My father's family all made their own desserts, and Atlantic Avenue in Brooklyn had some pretty impressive Arabic bakeries... but this one took the prize. It was the mother of all pastry shops! I stared transfixed at the array of pies, tarts, cakes and cookies on the other side of the glass storefront. Inside, there were several counters and displays with even more sweets. With my face pressed up against the glass, I felt as excited as a little boy about to ask his mommy to buy him a treat. For a brief moment I thought about how I would communicate with the man behind the counter. How would I know what to ask for? My mind quickly scanned the Arabic words for hello, goodbye, please, thank you, delicious, how much, this, yes, no... and of course, now I could read the numbers. For some reason, I decided to challenge myself by trying my best to not use any English during this particular conversation. I wanted to earn my pastries!

I composed myself, took a breath, and opened the front door to the sound of a tinkling bell. *Salaam aleikum*, I said. *Aleikum salaam*, the man responded. "Ah," I said, "*lehdidon*" (delicious). "*Lehdidon*," he replied with a smile. My eyes darted all around the showcases. I saw various types of *baklava* (we called it "*batlaweh*") of walnut and pistachio. I recognized the *kunefe* that I loved so much as a young-ster – a pastry made with shredded wheat, sugar syrup, rosewater, honey, nuts and sometimes melted cheese. I saw tarts filled with almonds, walnuts, apricots and other fruits, and sesame seed cookies just like my father's family used to make. As my eyes scanned the glass showcases, my senses were stimulated by smells, tastes and memories. Everything looked so good, but I had to make a decision, and I didn't want to speak any English this time. What should I get? What should I... And then suddenly I saw them: cookies made with semolina flour, milk, sugar and butter, filled with crushed dates and date paste, and sprinkled with powdered sugar. My relatives called them *kaak b'ajwe*, also known as *mamoul*. These were the crumbly, chewy, slightly gritty cookies that I loved most of all!

Excited, I raised my head to find the patiently waiting baker smil-ing right at me. "OK, Bob, no English this time," I said to myself. "*Marhaban*," (Hello) I said. Then I pointed to the cookies and asked: "*Hadidh kaak?*" (Is this *kaak?*)

"*Naam*," (Yes) he answered, still smiling at me.

"*Kaak b'ajwe?*" I asked again.

"*Naam, bel-ajwe*," (Yes, with dates) he replied.

I then asked for two (*isnaan*) while holding up two fingers. He seemed to look right through me with that big grin of his, as if he knew that I was struggling with my Arabic. As he began to wrap my cookies in wax paper and place them in a small bag, I looked at the price that was printed on a card in front of the tray. I recognized the price for one cookie, and I offered him twice as much in my open palm.

"*Shukran lakum,*" (Thank you) he said, as he took the coins from my hand.

"*Shukran lakum,*" I answered, feeling somewhat proud of myself. Then, as I turned to walk out of the store, I said in a sing-song way: "*Ma asalama*" (Goodbye).

"*Ma asalamati, shukran lakum,*" he called out to me, giggling.

Date *mamoul – Kaak b'ajwe*

A Gambian
praise song

In my late twenties, as I became bored with Western pop music and began listening to traditional music from around the world, one of the first genres that attracted me was West African kora music. The kora is a 21-string harp-lute. The resonating chamber is made of a large calabash gourd which is cut approximately in half, and then covered in animal skin, usually cowhide. A long neck and two small handles are fixed to the inner shell and protrude from the top of the calabash. A notched free-standing bridge rests on the surface of the skin. Nylon strings are attached to a long round neck, usually made of rosewood. By raising or lowering leather tuning rings on the neck, each string can be adjusted to the correct pitch.

Dating back many centuries in West African society, troubadours and oral historians known as *griots* had the primary responsibility of preserving the genealogies and oral traditions of their people. As extensions of Royal Courts, they traveled from town to town to spread the news of the day through narrated songs about deaths, births, marriages, and other current events. They also performed at child naming ceremonies, weddings, circumcisions, and other celebrations. This hereditary profession is an integral part of West African culture, and praise songs, composed specifically for ceremonial occasions and famous or wealthy patrons, play an important part of the *griot's* repertoire. In addition to their work as troubadours, *griots* also served as advisors and diplomats to Kings. Over the centuries, their advisory and diplomatic duties diminished, and their roles as performing musicians became more widespread.

I first learned of the kora through a friend who arranged concerts in New York City for several West African *griots*, also known as *jalolu* in Mandinka language. At that time, the most famous of them was Alhaji Bai Konte, a master of the tradition from Brikama, Gambia. His sons, Dembo Konte and Malamini Jobarteh, would often accompany him on concert tours in the West, and when they performed in New York, I sometimes served as their hospitality contact. I helped them set up for their performances at concerts and folk festivals, and escorted them to and from their gigs. They began to call me "Babou" when they stayed at my home in Brooklyn on one tour. As my work in music production continued, I met and recorded other *griots* from Gambia and Senegal, and my love for the kora praise song tradition deepened even further.

Many years later, and after I left the recording business, I finally had a chance to go to West Africa. A *griot* friend, Papa Susso, had recently returned to the Gambia from New York, and he reconnected me to Dembo and Malamini, who asked if I would visit them. Around the same time, a friend named Bouna encouraged me to visit him in Dakar, Senegal. It seemed like now was my time. One day I put together an itinerary, made travel arrangements, and soon after, I left to spend about two weeks in the area. Arriving in Dakar, I settled into a hotel in a lovely neighborhood, and I spent several days with my friend, getting reacquainted with another musician I'd known, and staying out late to listen to live music. On the appointed day, I met with Papa at the Dakar airport, and together we flew to Banjul, the capital of Gambia. He insisted I stay at his compound for the first few days. His home was located in a small village with sandy streets and no streetlights. It was lovely to spend time with his large family of two wives and 11 children.

Papa made contact with Dembo and Malamini, and a few days later he escorted me by private car to their family compound in Brikama. He left after a short while, and I settled into my room at Konte Kunda, the ancestral home of Alhaji Bai Konte, where I would be in the company of master musicians and friends from many years ago. The compound was a large walled parcel of land that included several small homes and outdoor sitting areas, and my room was in the area where Dembo and his family lived. After meeting some family members, I was shown around the neighborhood, and we had a bite to eat. Malamini asked if I would come over to his side of the compound later in the evening, and we agreed on a time for my visit. I settled in with Dembo and his family, and we talked about the past and present, about his father's passing, our times together in New York City, and about mutual friends. Dinner was fish with peanut sauce and boiled rice.

Around 8 p.m. I walked over to Malamini's house, and I found him in the courtyard, sitting on a straw mat at a fire, preparing boiled millet with milk and sugar. He offered me some, we sat near each other on a small bench, and we began to reminisce about our times together during his performances in the USA. His kora was nearby, and at one point, he reached for it and began to softly play a mid-tempo traditional groove in 4/4 time as we continued to talk. He asked about my life, where I was living, and we spoke about mutual acquaintances. "Oh Babou, it is very good to see you again," he said. His playing grew stronger and louder now, and as a definite melody arose from his kora, he continued... "I remember we have good times together. Thank you very much." Then he seamlessly sang this line: "Oh Babou, Babou Haddad." This gesture filled my heart, and I smiled deeply and looked into his eyes. He continued playing the groove, occasionally adding flourishes and glissandos, and then I suddenly realized what was happening. For years I had known about the praise song tradition, whereby *griots* compose melodies and lyrics in gratitude for others' good deeds, which they then perform in order to preserve oral history. Here I was, in Brikama, Gambia, and one of the great masters of the tradition was playing a praise song for me, Babou Haddad. He continued… "I remember when we come to New York City with my father, and you pick us up and take us to the concert, and then you pay dinner for us." As the music groove grew stronger with his narration, my eyes grew wider with surprise, but I also found it hard to continue to stare into his eyes because deep emotion was arising within me. "And I remember you always help to make our concert, to make a good concert for us." And then again, the refrain: "Oh Babou, Babou Haddad." With that, something even more amazing happened. One by one, his family members began to slowly process out of the house and into the courtyard, playing traditional instruments and singing the refrain in harmony: "Oh Babou, Babou Haddad." Several koras were now playing all around me, there in the moonlight, and Malamini's daughter echoed her father's singing as he layered spoken words of praise and melodic improvisations over a soulful and hypnotic groove. He continued: "And I remember we stay at your house for one week. You give us food, and you not take any money from us." The entire group was now singing "Oh Babou, Babou Haddad."

The ceremonial song continued for several minutes, and during an instrumental break, some of the musicians took solos over the baseline melody. Suddenly, I began to realize that what had appeared to be spontaneous was actually planned in advance. After I'd agreed to visit his house in the evening, Malamini had returned home and had composed and practiced a song with his family members to play for me in gratitude for my friendship with him over the years. When that thought sank in, I experienced a feeling I'd never felt before in my life: a deep connection through music that went beyond melody, rhythm and performance. I was experiencing the West African *griot* tradition from a very different perspective. This wasn't music merely for entertainment – it was ceremonial in nature. Instead of listening to a praise song written about a folk hero or a patron of the arts, I was experiencing the song as the person for whom it was written. I was the subject of – and the reason for – the song.

Malamini playing his kora

Notation of the praise song refrain

"Brain no good."

I've always enjoyed visiting Egypt. There's a certain familiarity I feel, whether because of my half-Arab blood, or the ease that I experience with the people I meet there. I taught courses in Cairo on several occasions, and whenever I had extra time before or after my next assignment, I would visit archaeological and tourist sites. On one visit, I had a free day before leaving the country, so I decided to visit the Egyptian Museum, a large pink stone building in central Cairo's Tahrir Square. The museum houses a staggering 120,000 ancient Egyptian artifacts and a large collection of mummies and sarcophagi.

As I approached the building and began to climb the steps to the entrance, I was approached by a smiling man with very kind eyes who explained that he was an official tour guide. He pointed to his badge and license number, and asked if he could be my guide to the museum that day. I thanked him and replied that I preferred to tour the museum on my own. With great patience and an enduring and lovable smile, he explained that the museum was vast, that many artifacts weren't labeled correctly, and that a guide would be very helpful. I hesitated, and he continued: "This is my country and my culture. I would like to share it with you. Don't worry, it is not expensive for you. I can show to you things that maybe you cannot understand if you go by yourself." I was sure I didn't want a personal tour guide for the whole time at the museum, but this short, older man with a receding hairline and the sweetest sparkling eyes you could ever imagine was hard to resist.

"Well," I said... "I don't want a guide for a long time at the museum. Can we spend only a short time together?"

"Yes, of course," he quickly answered. "I show to you only the highlights, maybe 30 or 45 minutes, and you can pay me what you like, whatever you like, and then you can stay by yourself. It's OK?"

So off we went, climbing the stairs to the entrance. He waited as I bought my ticket, and we walked past the first small gallery and entered a large rectangular atrium. Over the next half hour or so, my guide showed me some of the highlights of the museum, including jewelry, statuary, funerary masks, and mummies. We saw Tutankhamun's mask, one of the most recognized works of art in the world, and the Narmer Palette, possibly the earliest artifact of recorded history in the world, dating back to 3,000 BC. I was glad to have hired my friendly guide because of the great amount of background information I learned in our short time together. But what I was about to see, and what he was about to say to me, is what I would remember for the rest of my life.

We entered a large hall filled with mummies and sarcophagi. After viewing some of the more highly decorated coffins, he led me to a large glass case where several people were gathered. It was the mummy of Rameses II, one of the most important pharaohs of ancient Egypt who reigned from 1279 to 1213 BC. His body had been so well preserved that his facial features were clearly visible after more than 3,000 years. He even had a clump of henna-stained hair on the left portion of his head. His forearms, hands and fingers were wrapped in gauze, and his upper torso was covered with two sheets of linen, giving the appearance of a vest. As I stared at Rameses' body, my guide told me all about the mummification process, beginning first with removing the organs, and then embalming the entire body with powder made of locally sourced mineral salt. Finally, the embalmers wrapped every part of the body with strips of gauze, which were coated in resin. I asked about the removal of organs prior to mummification, and he told me that the most important organs were removed and stored in four ceremonial canopic jars, or *aljaraar alkanubia* in Arabic. "First, they leave the heart in the body because it is the energy, the soul. Then they take out and put organs in different jars, and they keep the jars near the mummy." He pointed to a nearby case where I could see examples of decorated canopic jars. Then he continued: "So, they clean the whole body inside and they remove four organs. They take out stomach, intestine, liver, and lungs, and they put each one in a special jar. Like I say before, they keep heart in the body, but the brain, they don't keep it."

"They don't keep the brain?" I asked.

"No," he said. "Brain no good. They throw it away. Ancient Egyptians think brain sometime make problems, and they don't want to keep it for afterlife. They think brain no good."

Brain no good! That thought resonated with me immediately. I know for sure that my brain has gotten me into trouble on many occasions. Of course, the brain produces and interprets motivation, emotions, learning, speech, movement, and so many other important things. The brain can also be a troublemaker though, especially when it's under duress, or responds to preconditioning, or when it hasn't yet fully developed. Sometimes the brain thinks too much, worries too much, fears too much... and in younger people, it often gives way to action without good judgement. It controls and affirms our thoughts (however misguided they may be); it regulates emotions (including negative ones like anger, jealousy, hatred and prejudice); and besides, it's hard to turn the damn thing off!

Don't get me wrong, I'm glad I have a healthy brain, and I'm grateful for the ways it has guided me in positive ways. But increasingly, as I get older and view my life's trajectory, I must agree with the ancient Egyptians – and I bet you do too – that in many cases... "brain no good!"

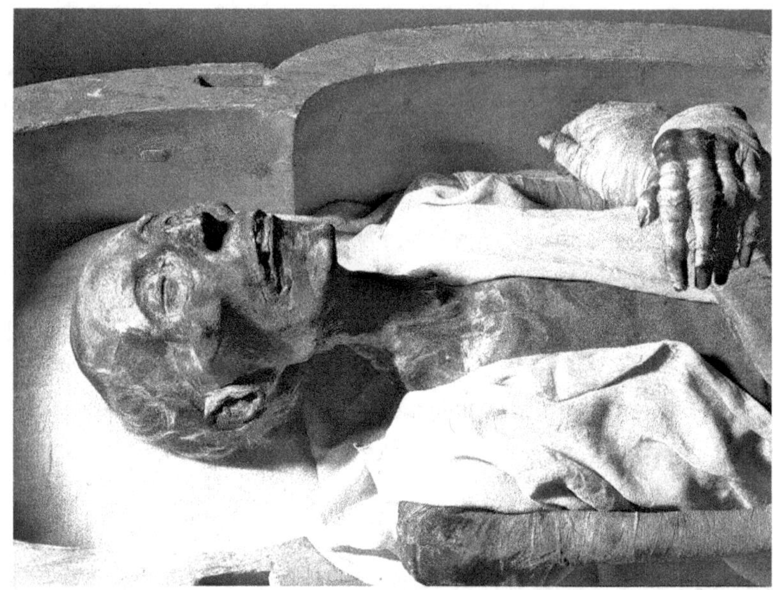

The mummy of Rameses II

Canopic jars at the Egyptian Museum

The green wave

At age 88, and while she was still in good health and spirits, I relocated my mother to my hometown, where she delighted in the company of new friends and experiences, and truly enjoyed the last three years of her life. Her decline began with a nasty fall, and spanned a period of about six months. She broke her leg, underwent surgery, and remained in the hospital for one week. Her dementia was also increasing, and she had some memorable one-liners during that first stay in the hospital: "Why am I here?" "Is this a hotel?" ... and my favorite one: "Am I starring in a movie?" Usually, I was able to distract her from excessive confusion with jokes, snacks, music, wheelchair excursions, and visits from local friends, but from that point on, she required my care on a daily basis.

She returned to the hospital a few months later because she was extremely weak and delirious. Her renal function had decreased; her lungs were retaining fluid; and she had developed atrial fibrillation. After a few days, the hospital discharged her, and I was lucky to get a room at the same rehab facility where she had previously stayed. Some of the nurses already knew her, and the director and staff members were extremely supportive to me. I spent every day at her side, and a few faithful friends also visited her during the last few weeks of her life.

My mother passed away in May at the age of 92. I was sitting in a chair at her bedside and reading a book when I heard a change in her breathing. I placed my hand on her head, leaned forward to speak softly into her right ear, and said: "Mom, you can go to heaven now. Do you see God? Do you see a light? If you see a light, Mom, go to it. Don't worry about me. I'll see you when I get there." A few seconds after I finished speaking, my mother raised her chest cavity, and then she exhaled deeply. At first, I wondered if it was another episode of the apnea she'd recently been experiencing, but this time I sensed that something was different. Then, as I stared at her face, I saw a green wave of light begin to quiver right above her head. It was an undulation of energy that slowly began to rise from her head and move upward from the bed. Despite my shock at this sight, I knew that many traditional cultures believe that the soul needs to pass through to the outside, into the ether, in order to be free. As soon as I remembered that, I glanced at the window in the room and noticed that it was closed, so I quickly went to it and flung it wide open. While standing there, I saw the green wave rise up from the bed and move very slowly in the direction of the open window. Then it suddenly dissipated.

I had at the ready a large frame drum, some rose water, lavender essential oil, and the book on death and dying rituals that I had been reading. I had wanted to do something spiritual and ceremonial when she passed, so as her body lay there, apparently already devoid of her spirit or soul, I began an odd-meter drumming pattern, and I succumbed to its trance-like effect. It was a musical prayer: an offering of love to accompany her transition to the next realm. I must have drummed for three or four minutes, making sure to circumambulate her body three times. I remember looking upward at one point, and silently asking my father to take her hand. After the drumming, I remained standing for a few moments, motionless and trembling. I put the drum on a table nearby, and then I examined her body to look for the signs of death that I'd learned about. I reached for her hands and saw that her fingertips had turned purple and her nails had turned completely white. I untucked the bed sheet and removed her right foot to see the same condition. Her eyes were closed, but her jaw remained slightly open. I touched her face, and I kissed her one last time.

I left the room to notify the staff that my mother had passed, and to request help. Moments later, a sweet nurse named Edna came into the room and expressed her condolences. She asked if I wanted her to wash my mother's body, and she seemed surprised yet pleased when I replied that I had planned to do the very same thing. She returned a few moments later with a tub of warm water, to which I added rose water and many drops of lavender oil. We soaked two washcloths in the ablution, assumed positions on both sides of the bed, removed her hospital gown, and began to ceremonially wash her body from top to bottom while I read aloud a body-washing prayer from my book. "I bless your hair that the wind has played with. I bless your eyes that have looked on us with love. I bless your ears that listened for our voices. I bless your throat that called out to me when I was in danger. I bless your arms that embraced me. I bless your hands that have shaped wonders. I bless your breasts that nurtured me."

From head to toe, we symbolically anointed the parts of her body that corresponded to each verse of the prayer. As my voice trembled and my eyes welled with tears, I could hardly read the print from the book that I held extended in my left hand. At one point, I looked at the nurse, and she too had tears flowing. When we finished the washing ritual, she thanked me for the deep experience we had just shared, and then she looked at my mother's body and said: "Oh, Gracie, you told me so many stories about your life, and you always made me eat those coconut candies that I like so much."

The protection spell

One year, I decided to take a short trip to Northeastern India to make a pilgrimage to the land where the ancestral teacher and spirit guide of traditional Thai medicine once lived. This man, Jivaka Kumarabhaccha, was a contemporary of the Gautama Buddha, and he lived in the same region where the Buddha spent a period of his life. I'd known about Jivaka for many years, and had become particularly interested in him while researching and writing my first book on traditional Thai massage. For that project, I'd transcribed and edited stories about him from Buddhist scriptures, and other sections of the book discussed the facts and myths surrounding this Indian Ayurvedic doctor. Doctor Jivaka personally knew and treated the Buddha as a physician, and he eventually became revered by Thai Buddhists as the spirit guide of traditional medicine.

I was in Thailand at the time, and as I began to plan for the two-week journey, I asked one of my teacher guides, Tevijjo Yogi, for his advice about an offering of some sort that I could bring to and leave at Jivaka's land. Yogi was steeped in knowledge of Thai Buddhist traditions, including incantations and traditional medicine, and I asked him to help me prepare for a ceremony (*puja*) at this sacred place where both Jivaka and the Buddha once lived. He agreed to make special offerings for me to take on my trip, which he placed inside a small brass container commonly used to hold altar relics. I flew from Chiang Mai to Bangkok a few days before my flight to Kolkata so I could spend time with him and retrieve the offering. On one of those days, he brought me to meet one of his own teachers, an elevated *reusi*, and an advanced practitioner of esoteric practices.

In Thai Buddhist society, *reusis* aspire to live in balance with natural law, and they often serve as spirit intermediaries. They wrap their long hair in coils on their heads, and dress in white, brown or tiger-print robes. *Reusis* practice esoteric sciences such as healing arts, alchemy, incantations and magic, palmistry, meditation, traditional medicine, and astrology. They often specialize in one of these areas, and are regarded as regional guardians of that particular body of knowledge. Traditionally, they lived ascetic lives as hermits in caves and forests, but in modern times they live wherever they can best serve others, including in villages, towns and cities.

After traveling in a hired car for some time, we arrived at a neighborhood of streets lined with trees, and we entered the home and place of practice of Reusi Bpoo Sompit. Yogi would be consulting with him about some matters; another spiritual seeker from Italy would be receiving a sacred tattoo (*sak yant*) in an adjoining room; and I was invited to sit in the main room and observe him as he went through a day of work and spiritual support to members of his community. Reusi Sompit was seated in a chair on a platform, and those who sought his help would make their requests from the floor in a kneeling position. I watched as he blessed objects, chanted, wrote in a book, and occasionally spoke to my teacher guide. At one point, a woman asked to be seen by him. She had come to ask for an incantation, presumably so she could make her way out of financial difficulty. She brought her pocketbook as a symbolic item and asked him to bless it so that her problems might be eased. After a few moments of quiet time, he took the pocketbook from her hands and began to chant and write inside it with a pen that had no ink. After that, he opened the latch and directed his incantations inside the bag, and then closed the latch again. The woman seemed content that her pocketbook had been charged with good energy.

She left some money in the offering tray, she bowed, and then left the building. Sometime later, there was a knock on the door, and we were all summoned outside to witness yet another blessing. This time it was a man who had just purchased a motorbike, and he also wanted it blessed. As Reusi Sompit exited the building, some people gathered outside. Children stopped playing their games and crouched in a semi-circle as the *reusi* began the blessing ceremony. First, he used a white paste to paint a sacred symbol with his finger on the windscreen of the motorbike while he recited a mantra. Then he spun his body around to hold the handlebars and chanted prayers aloud while he beeped the horn of the motorbike. He did it in a call-and-response fashion, first chanting some words, then beeping the horn with the same cadence as the previously spoken words. It was a bit comical, and some of the children started giggling. At the end, the man thanked the *reusi* with a bow of deference; he made a donation; and he rode away on his newly-blessed motorbike.

Back inside the building, I took my place on the floor toward the back of the altar room. Shortly afterward, Reusi Sompit asked a number of questions about me, and my teacher responded to each of them in Thai language. Upon learning that I would be departing shortly to deposit the blessed objects on Jivaka's sacred land, he offered to give me a protection blessing for my journey. At that moment, another person asked to borrow my camera so he could take photos of the blessing. I felt honored and excited to be able to receive a blessing from such an elevated master. He summoned me to the altar, and I learned that he would be giving me a protection amulet. As I assumed the correct posture for such occasions by putting my hands together in prayer position and bowing my head, I was told to recite the words *so maa re sa* repeatedly as an affirmation of my acceptance of the blessing. He began by reciting prayers in Pali language with a strong voice and in a fast cadence. In his left hand he held the metal protection amulet. It had engraved characters in Khmer language, and in-between his recited incantations, he occasionally blew on it. He continued the recitations as he sprinkled my head with holy water using a wooden whisk that he held in his right hand. From time to time, he reached back to dip the whisk into a wooden bowl containing the ablution water. My eyes were fully closed, and as the water hit my head and face, it ran down my neck and onto my shirt. I continued to repeat the acceptance mantra, and a few moments later I began to feel something in my abdomen and viscera. It was a movement sensation, an unusual feeling of tightening or constriction that I'd never felt before. I wasn't nervous or tensing my stomach muscles... I was open and loose and breathing deeply, and yet I felt something moving inside me as I knelt there and received the magic spell. It was very powerful, and I remained there with my eyes closed for the entire ritual. At one point I felt the bamboo whisk touch my head, and I heard Reusi Sompit blow air from his mouth onto the amulet and then onto my head. This action symbolizes the final transference of energy from the charged amulet to my body. After the blessing was over, he came closer to me, touched my head, closed my hand around the amulet while he recited a few words in Thai, and said, "Good luck, good luck."

I slowly opened my eyes and slightly raised my head to acknowledge him visually with a smile. As I did this, I realized that I was in an altered state. My stomach and chest seemed tight, and my mind was unfocused and foggy. Sensing that the blessing was over, I began to move away from the altar by sliding back on my knees without turning my back, but Reusi Sompit spoke, and Tevijjo translated that he now wanted to make sure that the protection spell had fully taken hold. I agreed, and as I slid back into position at the altar, I again assumed a deferential stance with my palms together, my head lowered, and my eyes fully closed. I felt his fingers touch various spots on my neck and on the back of my head as he softly spoke some words. I learned later that he was anointing me with medicinal oil that had been blessed during a fire meditation ceremony. After the anointing with oils, he held the top of my head tightly with his five fingers, and as he recited some prayers, I felt something along the left side of my neck. After that, he reached over my shoulders to raise my shirt and expose my bare back, and then I felt a series of soft slaps on my back. My eyes were closed, I had no idea what he was doing, and I felt a cold sensation with every blow. After a few moments, there was a pause, and then I felt a strong strike on my back, and then several others, five in total. I thought I heard people in the room gasp each time I was struck, but I didn't know why. After the last strike, there were a few seconds of silence as I felt my shirt being lowered, and then I heard a few final words of approval in Thai language.

I slowly raised my head and opened my eyes to thank the *reusi* for the blessing, and only then did I notice that he had a large machete with an ornate handle in his hand. I could hardly believe my eyes as I stared at that long blade. At the same time, a few people in the room moved forward to examine my back and my neck. Two neighborhood people who were watching the ceremony through the open front door also came in to examine my back and neck, and to see for themselves that I hadn't been cut and that I wasn't bleeding. I had been forcibly struck on my back five times with the blade of a sharp machete, and it had also been run against my neck in a slicing motion a few seconds earlier. There were some red marks where the impact of the sharpened steel had come in contact with my body, but my skin had not been pierced, and I was not bleeding.

My stomach and chest felt like they were enveloped in a suit of armor, and my head felt like it had taken a trip around the galaxy. I now had a powerful blessing, a protection amulet, a super-charged group of magic talismans in a brass container that I would soon be bringing to India, and a set of directions about how to perform the *puja* ceremony at Jivaka's home. I'll never forget the excitement of that day and the anticipation I felt about the experience that awaited me, which I'll tell in the next story.

Reusi Sompit, holding the amulet and sprinkling holy water

Sliding the machete against my neck

Pilgrimage to Rajgir

As described in the previous story, I'd decided to travel to a small town in northeastern India to pay homage to Jivaka Kumarabhaccha, a legendary physician and a supporter of the first order (*sangha*) of Buddhist monks. I'd thought about visiting the town of Rajgir after I read a research paper about the excavation of the ruins at a site called Jivaka Amravana, dating from the 5th century BC. He was a special person for me, and the more I practiced Thai massage, the deeper a connection I felt toward him. At times, strange things happened while I was working with clients and students, things that to me could only be explained by a connection to Jivaka as a spirit intermediary. My idea for the pilgrimage was to bring something representative of Thai medicine, and to place it inside a portion of the stone foundations of the buildings that once served as his home and herbal apothecary. Finally, I was going to visit his spirit energy where he once lived, and bring him a special blessed offering from Thailand.

I decided to first visit several musician friends in Kolkata, and then to travel onward into rural India to the holy site. After four wonderful days with my friends, I flew to Patna and spent the night at a hotel. Early the next morning I hired a car and driver for the three-hour bumpy ride to the village of Rajgir. Once there, I checked into a room at a Buddhist monastery, and I set out to learn how to reach the site. I brought a small backpack with a plastic bottle of water, my camera, and a brass container filled with magic talismans that was prepared for me for this very purpose. I also had 16 sticks of incense, special mantras and prayers written on a few index cards, and a set of instructions for carrying out the *puja* ceremony in the correct manner. As I ventured onto a dusty street that led to a narrow road, I learned that the ruins were several miles away and that the primary means of transport in the town was the *tanga*, or horse-drawn cart. I waited on a sleepy corner until a *tanga* approached, and the driver and I agreed on a price to take me to the holy site. Once we arrived, he offered to wait for me, but I told him I would be staying there for some time, and he left. Reusi Sompit, the shaman who had given me a strong protection spell just a few days before, told me that before I did anything at the site, I first had to ask for permission from the local spirit guides. My hope was to leave the magic brass offering hidden somewhere on the land, to pray, and then to remove some earth from that place to give to my teachers and other special people in Thailand and elsewhere. In this way, it would be a symbolic spiritual exchange from Thailand to India, and back to Thailand again.

Once at the site, I thought of looking for a place to leave the offering, but first, I took some time to take it all in. The place had an amazing stillness that I've experienced in only a few other places around the world. I was finally at Jivaka's mango grove and home, and I could hardly contain my joy. I spent a few minutes just standing there, and then I began to circumambulate clockwise, looking, walking, breathing, and sensing. I was all alone, except for a few monkeys who were calling from the trees. After one slow walk around the entire site, I began to wonder where I could leave the offering and perform my ceremony. I also wondered how I would collect the samples of earth since I didn't see anything nearby that I could use to scrape the hardened, parched dirt. As I thought about that, I was drawn to something on the ground ahead of me. It was a bone, perhaps a femur or a tibia. I didn't know if it came from a monkey, a dog, or another animal, but it seemed perfect for the job of digging, so I bent down to retrieve it, and I continued my circumambulations. Eventually, I stopped at a point at the northwest corner of the left elliptical garden, and I sensed that it would be a good place to leave the offering. I looked down and noticed that one of the stones on the face of the foundation seemed a bit uneven. I bent down and placed my hand on it, and the large block of stone, about a foot long, yielded toward me somewhat magically. I gave it a slight tug to partially reveal the ancient foundation behind it, and I pulled apart a few smaller rocks. Then, with the bone, I scraped away the hardened earth and mortar behind the stone, and I fashioned a small niche where I could place the offering. I had already dug a hole for my 16 sticks of incense, and my index cards with the mantras, prayers, and other instructions for the ceremony were laid out on the ground. I lit the incense and began to assume a kneeling position to begin the ceremony, but as soon as I knelt down, I felt something on my right knee. Thinking I had knelt on a pebble, I brushed my knee with my hand and resumed the kneeling position, but the painful sensation was still there. I came into a squatting position to take a look, and I noticed that my right knee was swollen. I hadn't hit it against anything or hurt it in any way, but it was throbbing, and when I touched it, I could feel there was liquid building up inside. In just a few seconds it had swelled to more than one inch high. I remember saying aloud: "Well, this isn't good," and I wondered if the spirit guides were trying to tell me something. After a few moments, however, I rationalized that I wouldn't be doing anything that would desecrate the site and that my intentions were pure, so I once again assumed a kneeling position, shifting my body-weight mostly to the other knee, and I began the ceremony. I asked the spirit guides for permission to leave my offering and to remove some earth to bring back to Thailand. In customary form, I prostrated to the Buddha, the *dharma*, the *sangha*, to my parents and to my teachers, and then I turned my spiritual focus to Jivaka. I thanked him for his guidance in my practice, and for the connection that I shared with my teachers and colleagues in Thailand and elsewhere. In a soft voice, I said aloud: "I didn't come here to ask for your help, but I guess now I'll also ask you to please watch over my knee." I took the brass offering, held it high to offer a final prayer, and placed it in the little nook I'd carved out with the animal bone. Following the directions that I was given, I said another prayer, blew on the object, meditated for a few minutes, and placed some earth into a plastic bag to bring home. Then I closed up the exposed area with the original stone, and I filled in the crevices and edges with compacted earth to keep it in place once again. It looked seamless.

I left that sacred place with the fragrant incense still burning and with the offering buried inside the northwest wall. Placing the bone in my backpack, I left the archaeological site, and I walked a few kilometers to the platform of a rickety cable car that took devotees on a scary ride a few hundred feet upward to a stupa atop the Rajgir Hills. After visiting the temple, I walked downhill to a precipice known as Gridhakuta Hill (Vulture Peak), which, according to tradition, is where the Buddha often went to meditate. Its location is mentioned in Theravada and Mahayana texts as the place where the Buddha also delivered several important sermons to the first order of monks. I arrived there just as a few tourists were leaving, and I sat there to meditate and to try to take my mind off my swollen and painful knee. I was all alone in that sacred spot, and it was so beautiful. I would have stayed longer, but I wanted to return to my room to decide what to do about my knee. I took a horse cart back to the monastery, and within a short period of time I decided to change my travel plans and return to Thailand immediately. I reasoned that my work was done in Rajgir, and that I wouldn't want to be stuck in a little town in the hills of rural India in case I needed serious medical attention. I went online with my laptop, paid all the rebooking penalties, and made changes to my air tickets. Very early the next morning, I set out to the railroad station on a *tanga*. It was the first and only time in my life that I'd taken a horse to a train. Upon arriving in Patna, I took a taxi from the railroad station to the small airport there, and within a few hours I was back in Kolkata. By then I had become sick with nausea and a migraine headache, and I was also very light-headed. I checked into the fanciest hotel I could find near the airport, and I fell asleep for a few hours. By late afternoon I was feeling better, but my knee was hurting quite a bit, and it was swollen and throbbing. The next morning, I flew to Bangkok and made a quick connection to another flight to Chiang Mai. By late afternoon, I was safe and sound, back "home" in my apartment off Huay Kaew Road, and away from the intensity of India.

The next morning I went to Ram Hospital, a short walk away from my apartment, where I often went for medical treatment. After a short wait, I was seen by an orthopedic surgeon, Dr. Paiboon, who diagnosed my condition as excess fluid in the bursa. We decided that he would aspirate the fluid, but when he did that, more than two vials of blood emerged from my knee.

Shocked, he asked: "What did you do?"

"Nothing," I said.

"What you mean? You not have trauma to the knee? You not remember anything? You not fall or hurt yourself?" I answered no to all of his questions. He replied that it was nearly impossible for something like this to happen without a direct blow of some sort to the knee. He even said to me wryly: "Maybe you have sex with a Thai girl, and you rub your knee on the rug?"

"Doctor," I exclaimed with a silly look on my face, "I told you I did not have any trauma there. It just happened spontaneously when I was making a *puja* in India."

He shook his head and repeated that it was very unusual for blood to appear in the knee bursa without any blunt force trauma, and that if my knee swelled up again, he would want to perform surgery. He told me there was a fifty percent chance that the knee would fill up again after the aspiration, and that I should stay in contact with his nurse about any further developments. He bandaged and wrapped some gauze around my knee, and I walked back home. When I awoke the next morning, it had become filled with more liquid and was swollen again. I waited a few days to see if it would subside, and then I returned to the hospital where a different doctor aspirated it a second time. While consulting my patient notes, he mentioned that Dr. Paiboon had recommended surgery and that I should definitely do that if my knee swelled up again. I thanked him and returned home. About three days later, it began to fill up again, but not as much as on previous occasions. I got up the courage to return to the hospital to see the second doctor, Dr. Preecha, and I asked him to aspirate the knee for a third time. At first he refused, saying that it was time to schedule the surgery with Dr. Paiboon. I asked him as sweetly as possible to aspirate the knee once more, and he eventually agreed, but only on one condition: that I would schedule the surgery. I reluctantly agreed, so he aspirated the knee, I received an appointment for surgery three days later, and I returned home.

By the next day, the knee had become swollen again. It didn't seem to be as inflamed as before, but I was concerned because I had made a commitment to undergo a surgery that I didn't feel was necessary. I suspected the disorder was related to the spiritual connection I had made at the holy site. After all, it suddenly happened just as I was about to make my offering. I spoke by phone to the teacher who had prepared the offering I'd taken to Jivaka's home, and he reasoned that what was happening to my knee was a type of karmic cleaning. I also believed that, and I sensed that I could begin to treat the condition myself in order to avoid surgery. I began to work the area with acupressure, and I applied ice and raw ginger to the knee at regular intervals. I meditated during the day and evening, and kept my leg elevated as much as possible. I made an anti-inflammatory poultice of fresh ginger, turmeric and Asiatic pennywort, and I applied the paste to my knee. I wrapped my knee in gauze, and I included the amulet that Reusi Sompit had given to me. After a while, I fell asleep.

By the next morning, the inflammation had subsided a bit. Encouraged, I spent the rest of that day working the energy lines of my upper and lower leg, and I continued with the herbal poultices, amulet placement, and recitation of the mantra for Thai healing arts. At one point I received a phone call from the hospital to confirm my appointment for surgery the following afternoon. I tried to remain as calm as possible, and I meditated and asked Jivaka for his intercession. On the advice of one of my Thai colleagues, I asked the spirits to forgive me for anything I had done in this life or in a previous life that had caused harm to any living thing. Eventually, with my knee wrapped in fresh herbal paste and my mind at peace, I feel asleep.

When I awoke the next morning, I took a moment to touch and hold my knee, and I hoped for the best. I sat on the edge of the bed and slowly unwrapped the gauze that held the poultice and the amulet in place. As I wiped away the herbal paste with a wet cloth, I could hardly believe my eyes: all traces of inflammation were gone! As I pressed around the patella, there weren't any signs of blood or synovial fluid in my bursa, and aside from the staining caused by the herbs, my skin was back to its natural tone. I stood up and walked around to be sure that the pain was also gone. My knee was back to normal, and I was delighted. After a few moments, I realized that I needed to call the hospital to cancel my appointment for surgery. I called and asked a nurse to have Dr. Paiboon return my call as soon as possible.

About twenty minutes later, he called. "Hello Robert, so I see you for surgery this afternoon at 3 p.m.?"

"Well, doctor," I said, "I don't need the surgery anymore."

"What do you mean?" he replied. "What happened, and why you cannot do the surgery?"

I explained that for the past few days I had been working on the energy lines of my leg and the acupressure points of my knee, and that I was using an herbal poultice and praying for it to subside.

"But blood cannot go back into the body from the bursa like that," he replied. "Are you sure the swelling is gone?"

Then I asked the doctor if he believed in *saiyasaht*, a Thai language term for shamanistic healing rituals using mantras, prayers, sacred objects and incantations. He chuckled when I said that word, and said that no, he didn't believe in it. I replied that I was a believer, and that by using an amulet and praying to *Chiwok* (Jivaka), my knee had healed, and that I needed to cancel the surgery. After a few seconds of awkward silence, he agreed to cancel the surgery, and he told me to contact him again if the swelling returned. I agreed to do so, and I thanked him very much for his care and his concern.

I sincerely believe that the problem with my knee was the physiological result of an underlying metaphysical condition. It happened to my right knee at the very moment I began to make the *puja*. The knee is a symbol of reverence, and the right side is the masculine side in Thai traditional medicine. I believe that some type of internal combustion resulted from the intensity of the protection spell, the amulet, the brass container holding magic objects, the mantras I recited, and the offering that I made at Jivaka's holy site in Rajgir, India. I am forever grateful to have had this amazing experience, and I'm especially happy that my karma got the good cleaning that it apparently needed.

The foundations at Jivaka Amravana

Tangas in Rajgir, Bihar

"This is going to be brilliant!"

I've been fortunate to know a few truly remarkable people in my life. One of these was a woman named Harriett Stevens. We first met at a party thrown by mutual friends, and we were both married at the time. After exchanging phone numbers, the four of us began to spend time together as couples, and we grew to be good friends. Harriett was a slim, short southern girl with an easygoing attitude, but she had health problems. When we met, she had already undergone a kidney transplant, since renal disease had destroyed both of her original organs several years before. She loved travel and hiking, and she was an accomplished tennis player. Unfortunately, the first transplant failed after a few years, and she returned to dialysis and was placed on a donor list for another compatible kidney. Luckily, she had another transplant a few years later, but that second kidney functioned only a short time until it also failed. She returned to dialysis, and as long as her blood was cleaned regularly, she led a reasonable life. Shortly after her second kidney failed, her husband left her, and they divorced. One year before that my wife had also left me, so Harriett and I shared a lot of talking, crying and confiding, and as we helped each other, our friendship grew to a new level of depth.

My mother Grace took a special liking to Harriett. They'd originally met when we were both married and when my parents would come to visit from New York. My mother had lost a kidney many years before, and that may have contributed to the special empathy and thoughtfulness that she seemed to have for Harriett. After my father's passing, my mother spent longer periods of time when she came to visit me. All my friends loved her, and eventually she relocated to my hometown. During that period, she and Harriett grew even closer. They would spend hours talking, sharing life stories, speaking on the phone, and laughing and giggling together. Harriett was deeply affected when my mother passed away. She kept a photo of Grace in her home and sometimes said that she felt closer to her than she did to her own mother.

As the years progressed, she became weaker, and her need for dialysis grew stronger. The hemodialysis machine she used in her bedroom wasn't doing the trick anymore, and her doctors prescribed a program of supervised peritoneal dialysis. This seemed to rejuvenate her spirits and her energy, but she had to go to a clinic three or four times a week for an hour of dialysis. Naturally, this new routine changed her life and added additional stress. All throughout the suffering and change, however, she never lost her spirit or her positive outlook on life. She was in serious pain on a regular basis, but she rarely complained. She developed an even more spiritual outlook on life than she had previously, and she never turned down an opportunity to be in the company of others, laughing, socializing, and even enjoying a nip of rum from time to time. I would often visit her at home or take her out to dinner. Whenever she was well enough, she attended parties and events that I held at my home. Everyone who met her was attracted to her outgoing and life-affirming personality. Even as she sat immobile in her wheelchair, a special type of social magnetism attracted others to her. One of my friends, Robert, had taken a special liking to Harriett. He began to visit her occasionally, brought her things to eat, made her laugh, and kept her company whenever he could. I appreciated that about him, since only a few other people were doing the same for her.

Eventually, she began a marked decline and needed to be hospitalized. She became listless, her heartbeat had weakened, and fluid retention had caused her legs and ankles to swell. I visited her as often as possible, stayed at her bedside, brought her special treats that I knew she enjoyed, and tried my best to ease her mind. Robert also visited her in the hospital several times. One night, just two days before she passed away, the remaining visitors returned home for dinner with their families, but I stayed a bit longer to keep her company. Around 8 p.m., Robert walked into the room, greeted her cheerily, and sat on the opposite side of the bed from where I was seated. The both of us kept her company, telling her jokes, making her laugh, and helping in any way we could until visiting hours were over.

At one point, we helped her as she struggled to become more comfortable in the hospital bed, and we adjusted the transparent tubes that carried the morphine drip to her veins. After a moment of silence, she craned her head toward me, opened her eyes slightly, and said softly: "Bob, I have a confession to make."

"A confession?" I asked. "What do you mean?"

She took a short breath, became visibly emotional, and explained that when she'd first met me all those years ago, she'd felt an amazing energy that she wanted to explore further, but because we were both married, she never said anything to me about it. She continued: "I've loved you for all these years."

"Aw, honey, I've loved you too," I replied.

"No," she answered resolutely, "I mean, I've been in love with you for all these years. Ever since we met, and through our marriages and divorces, I've been in love with you, but I never said anything."

I thought for a moment about what I could possibly say in response to that alarming statement, but before anything came out of my mouth, she continued: "But I've got to tell you, sweetie, I'm sorry, but I'm not in love with you anymore." She turned her head to the other side of the bed and said softly: "Now I'm in love with you, Robert. You've been so kind and sweet to me, and you always make me laugh and cheer me up. Now I'm in love with *you*."

At such a critical time near death, her "confession" was poignant, but it was also funny as hell. Her lips were trembling, and tiny tears were appearing on her lower eyelids, but Robert and I were grinning, and when she saw the expressions on our faces, she began to laugh, and that allowed us all to laugh and cry and then laugh again.

The next afternoon, I went to visit her, and I spent the greater portion of the day at her bedside. She was slipping fast, and the nurses and doctors didn't know if she would last through the night. She was largely silent, with her eyes closed, but every once in a while, she would speak to me or ask for a sip of water. I had my hand clasped in hers, and I remained silent as I tried to meditate and reflect on her impending death.

At one point, she squeezed my hand very slightly and said in a whisper: "Bob, are you there?"

"Yes, honey, I am right here with you," I answered softly.

With that, she turned her head very slowly toward me, strained to open her eyes a little bit, and said: "Wow, this is going to be brilliant!" Surprised, I asked what she meant. As she returned her head and closed her eyes again, she let go of my hand and made a slight gesture in the air. "I see all these wavy roads ahead of me... it's amazing," she mumbled. "There are wavy roads... and... there's a light at the end, a bright light." She fell quiet for a few seconds, and then she slowly continued: "Oh, it's getting brighter. Oh... that's beautiful, and... and there's a door up ahead, a gate, oh... Oh God, it's Grace. Your mother is there at the door... and... and oh, now she's opening the door for me." Then Harriett moved her hands and arms slightly, and began to call my mother's name: "Grace, Grace... She's at the door..."

I was spellbound and didn't know what to say or do. The only thing that occurred to me was to try to contact my mother metaphysically and ask her to take Harriett now. I thought to myself: "Mom, take her now. Take her hand and pull her in." I reached out to hold Harriett's hand, but she fell silent again and remained in repose. A few minutes later, I kissed her, and I took my leave. As I left the hospital and drove home, and all throughout the rest of the evening, I was unable to do anything except feel spiritually connected to her and to my mother. I also felt a clear and unafraid awareness and acceptance of death.

Harriett passed away in the middle of the night, an enlightened person, someone who was acutely aware of life, love, and death. She was so accepting of her destiny, and she even had the courage to look forward to her own death. After all, one of the last things she said before she died was "This is going to be brilliant!"

Harriett Stevens

The tej bet

I first became introduced to Ethiopian music in my late twenties. A wonderful musician and performer named Seleshe Damessae had emigrated from Addis Ababa to Vermont and was teaching there, and also traveling to perform at concerts throughout the USA and Europe. He would sometimes come to stay with me at my apartment, and I recorded and produced his first commercial album. Seleshe (also known as Gashe Aberramola) was an *azmari*, a professional poet-musician much like the troubadours of other African traditions, and his instrument was the *krar*, a five or six-string lyre believed to be the ancestor of the American banjo. After about ten years, he moved back to Ethiopia, and we kept in touch occasionally by email.

One day, many years later, I was speaking by telephone to another Ethiopian friend, a brilliant artist named Wosene Kosrof, who was living in California. Wosene, also from Addis, had lived in Vermont for a time, and knew Seleshe well. I was telling him how much I would like to visit Ethiopia one day and that I'd love to see Seleshe again. I asked him to let me know the next time he was going to Ethiopia, and that I would try to come and visit while he was there. He replied: "I'm going in two weeks. Why don't you come over?" I couldn't imagine doing a trip like that so quickly, so I told him I'd wait until the next time. But he insisted that now was the time. "Just change your plans and come in two weeks," he said. He gave me routing information and suggested airlines with the best connections to Addis Ababa, and I told him I'd look into it and get back to him.

About two weeks later, I found myself on an airplane flying to Rome, Italy, spending a few days with friends and family there, and then flying onward to Addis Ababa, Ethiopia. Wosene met me at the airport and transferred me to my hotel, which was centrally located and near a large park. He had invited Seleshe for dinner at a restaurant the following night, but he hadn't told him that I was coming to Addis. The plan was for me to arrive at the restaurant a few minutes early so our mutual friend would have a big surprise when he saw me. It all went as planned, and over the next few days, I spent time with both my friends, and also had plenty of time to tour the area on my own.

One morning, Seleshe called me at my hotel to say he would be picking me up about 5 p.m. that afternoon to take me out to drink some *tej*. A fermented drink made from local honey, water and a medicinal shrub called *gesho*, it is considered the national drink of Ethiopia. *Tej* is usually processed in small batches and served at local gathering places and bars known as *tej bet*. I'd had *tej* before, but I'd never been to a traditional Ethiopian watering hole, so I was excited about the experience. Seleshe had hired a car with a designated driver so we could drink as much as we wanted. We left the crowds and the commotion of the city, and began to climb winding roads up to the mountainous plains overlooking the valley. Addis lies at an altitude of 7,500 feet, and we must have climbed at least another thousand feet to get to the *tej bet*. Once outside the car, the air was still, and there were wide swaths of grassland as far as you could see. In the distance were rolling hills, and men with plumed headdresses were riding horses decorated with colorful woven bridles and saddles. It was unlike anything I could have imagined, and it was so beautiful... a perfect backdrop for a lovely time with an old friend.

Seleshe explained that there were a few types of *tej*: a sweet and relatively harmless version called *berz*; a medium strength brew; and then there was the strongest one, which had a high alcohol content. I asked which one he drank, and he replied that he would have the strongest one, but that it might be too strong for me. I looked at him with a funny expression, and I told him that I would also have the strongest one. After all, I was on vacation, we had a driver waiting for us, and there were no other plans for the rest of the evening. He asked if I was sure, and when I said yes, he called a waiter and placed our first order. A few minutes later, two small glass pitchers arrived, and my friend showed me the proper way to hold them. We touched our glasses in a toast, and we began to sip the honey mead, which was absolutely delicious. We talked about old times together and about things that had happened in our lives since we'd last seen each other. We also interacted with local people as we sipped our honey wine and gazed at a beautiful sunset from the high-altitude grassland above the city. Another round? Of course! The *tej* was smooth and sweet, but after about an hour, I began to feel its effect. It made me so happy and giddy. We told jokes to each other and laughed a lot. The sun had set now, so we ordered some food to fill our stomachs, and then we had one more round of *tej* before meeting with our driver for the ride down to the valley below.

By the time the taxi dropped me off at my hotel, I had no problem standing or walking, and my vision wasn't blurred at all. I didn't have a headache or nausea either, but something was different... I didn't feel drunk, but I did feel different! My brain was cloudy, it was a bit hard to concentrate, but I felt happy, so exceedingly happy. I went through the motions of washing up, brushing my teeth, and getting ready for bed, and before I knew it, I was sound asleep by around 10 p.m. The next thing I remember was a ringing sound that pulled me out of a deep sleep. It was the hotel phone on the nightstand next to my bed. "Who is calling me so early in the morning?" I thought. As I opened my eyes and reached for the phone, I noticed on my portable alarm clock that it was already 9 a.m.

"Hello?" I mumbled.

"Hi Bob, it's Seleshe. How do you feel, man?"

"Umm, hold on Seleshe, let me get out of bed." I pulled away the covers, and as I rose to stand up, I struggled to maintain balance, and I had to lean against the wall nearby. I was still inebriated. "Seleshe," I said, "I think I'm still drunk, man."

"I know, I know... me too," he said. "But do you have a headache or a hangover?"

"No, nothing," I replied. "I feel great, but I'm still high."

"Me too," he said, giggling. "It's because that *tej* we had... it's organic. No chemicals, only honey and herbs and the fermentation. That's why I wanted to take you there. And we had the strong one, too! OK, so I just wanted to check up on you, and I'll talk to you later. Have a good morning."

For the next six hours or so, I remained in a happy and inebriated state, smiling and chatting with others during breakfast, walking around the city, visiting tourist sites... still high from 9 p.m. the night before. I'd slept about 11 hours, awoke with no hangover whatsoever, and continued to be buzzed for half of the following day!

With Seleshe Damessae, drinking *tej*

One of the horsemen at the *tej bet*

The habibti

In my massage teaching career, prospective students would some-times contact me to ask if I'd be offering courses in their area. Often, the initial contact would be by email, and sometimes a video conversation would ensue. Such was the case with a woman named Laura, who once contacted me to ask some questions about advanced study. She was already practicing professionally as a massage therapist in southern Argentina, and said that she wasn't able to take a course I had given several years earlier in Buenos Aires. She had my first book on the topic, had followed my career, and wanted very much to study with me. She asked if I would be teaching another course in Buenos Aires any time in the near future. I wrote to her and told her that I had no plans to teach in Argentina soon, but that I would be teaching for several months in Europe during the summer. I sent her a link to my schedule, and she responded and said she would try to visit with her cousin in Madrid around that same time.

A few days later, she wrote again and said that she had made plans to participate in my courses in Spain and Croatia. In order to coordinate plans, I suggested that we speak by video so I could learn more about her study and practice experience. Later that week we had a video chat. She was a lovely person, a passionate therapist who had studied in Thailand and elsewhere. She said that she would arrive in Madrid before the course, and that the following week she would travel to Zagreb to take my one-week advanced course there. We discussed travel and lodging possibilities, and I told her that my host in Croatia sometimes offered his studio in downtown Zagreb so that visiting students from other countries could have free lodging. Laura didn't speak English, so I mentioned that one of my Croatian students also spoke Spanish, and that she might help in translating whenever necessary. A week later, during the next video chat, we confirmed her participation in the courses; we discussed massage-related issues; and we agreed to speak by video once again after she had finalized her travel plans to Europe. I was enjoying chatting with her, and I was also attracted to her.

Several weeks later, during another conversation, Laura told me that she would be arriving in Spain a few days before the first course began. She had never been to Madrid before, and I suggested a nice hotel near the train station where she could stay. Since I would already be there, we discussed the possibility of spending a few hours together one day so I could show her around the city. At one point, during an awkward moment of silence while looking at each other on the screen, I told her that I had to admit that I was attracted to her, and that I would need to keep this in check when we met since I would be her teacher. I assumed that she would laugh off the compliment and assure me that everything would be alright, but instead, she answered that she also felt the same way. I immediately responded that if she was planning to study with me, we couldn't be romantic together during the courses because I would never cross that line with a student. She nodded to indicate her understanding. There was a brief pause, and then I said that if we both wanted, we could meet and possibly be romantic before the first class was held. That way we would have interacted with each other before she became my student. My reasoning made no sense at all, but before I could finish my sentence, she said that my suggestion was exactly what she had been thinking. It was a bit awkward, but also comical, and exciting.

About one month later, I arrived in Madrid after teaching a course in London, and I settled in to visit friends and to catch up on some computer work. Laura arrived a few days later, and I met her at her hotel so we could greet each other in person. I knew she would be tired from such a long journey, so after dinner and a hug, I returned to my guest house about one mile away. The next day we traveled around the city, enjoyed each other's company, and spent two romantic evenings together. From that point onward, we stayed in separate hotels and had no sensual contact throughout the entire time in Spain or during the following week as I taught the next course in Croatia. After the second course was finished, we vacationed together in Spain and Portugal until we said goodbye and flew onward to different places.

We returned to our respective countries, and we stayed in touch every few weeks. During one of those conversations, we discussed the possibility of her coming to visit me in the USA. We decided on a time period that would work best for both of us, and shortly afterward we bought her tickets. About a week before her arrival, we had a video chat to discuss some of the things we could do while we were together. As the conversation wound down, she said to me: "Bob, *¿te puedo hacer unas preguntas?*" (Can I ask you a few questions?)

"*Claro que sí,*" I answered.

Then she asked in Spanish: "Didn't you once say that your mother was Italian?"

When I answered that yes, my mother was Sicilian, she responded that her mother's side of the family was also Italian, which I thought was interesting. Then she said that she knew that Haddad was an Arabic name, and she asked about my ancestry. Did I know where my ancestors were from? Egypt, Lebanon, Syria?

"Syria," I answered. "*Mi padre nació en Siria.*" (My father was born in Syria.)

"*Ah, Siria,*" she replied, intriguingly. She continued: "*Porque mi abuelo también nació en Siria.*" I could never have imagined that a woman with a Spanish surname would have a connection to the Middle East, let alone that her grandfather had been born in Syria.

Surprised at hearing this news, I joked with her, saying that now I understood why I liked her so much. "You're a *habibti*," I said. (*Habibti* is the female form of the Arabic word *habibi*, which is a term of endearment, something like sweetheart or dear.) We laughed, and I asked if she knew which city her grandfather was from.

"Aleppo," she answered. "*Nació en Aleppo.*"

I could hardly believe what she'd said, and through my surprise, I told her that my own father was born in Aleppo. We looked at each other on the screen, and a moment later I asked: "*¿Sabes si era musulmán o cristiano?*" (Do you know if he was Muslim or Christian?)

She replied that her grandfather was Christian, and I told her that my father was also Christian. The whole thing was getting strange, but I needed to continue the process of deductive reasoning, so I asked if, by any chance, she knew which Christian rite he belonged to. She answered that yes, he was a Melkite Christian. My father was also Melkite.

Now the stares and glances between questions and answers grew longer and deeper. What could possibly be my next question? I thought for a few seconds, and then I asked: "How old would he have been if he were alive today?"

She took a moment to remember how old he was when he died, and then added the number of years since he had passed away... "*Como 110 años, más o menos,*" she said. I quickly calculated the numbers based on my own father's death, and they were the same, about 110 years. I told that to her, and we remained immobile, looking at each other on the screen with eyes wide open. I scoured my mind for another question to ask, but there was absolutely nothing there.

Just then, she said in a soft voice: "*Pues, tengo que decirte otra cosa.*" (Well, I have to tell you something else.) "*El apellido de mi abuelo era Haddad, y lo cambió cuando llegó a la Argentina.*" (My grandfather's surname was Haddad, and he changed it when he arrived in Argentina.)

I was stunned when I heard this, and my visual and mental paralysis became even stronger now. It seemed like an eternity before either of us said another word. I was beginning to wonder if I'd had sexual relations with my cousin.

After that conversation, I decided to order two DNA kits, one in each of our names, so they would arrive in time for her visit. Early the next week, I left on a one-week journey to visit friends in Upstate New York and to attend the wedding of the son of my childhood friend, Pat. I flew into Albany, rented a car, and first visited my friend Dan and his family for a few days. After that, I'd planned to drive further north to visit my friends Robert and Helene before arriving at the wedding ceremony for the weekend. As I was driving to their house, Helene called me on the phone to say they were out shopping, and she asked if I could delay my arrival by about one hour. It was late afternoon, so I decided to go somewhere to have a beer and read a book that I'd brought with me. I drove into the downtown area of Kingston, NY, and stopped to ask two guys on the street if there was a brewery in town. They gave me directions, and within a few minutes, I was sitting at a nice bar, drinking a cold beer. At the bar, I made eye contact with the fellow sitting next to me, and we began to chat. He asked about me, and I told him I was passing time before going to visit some friends nearby. He introduced me to a young woman sitting to his left, his daughter Danielle, and said that they were celebrating her graduation. I congratulated her and asked what she had studied. She replied that she had just completed a degree in genealogy and was about to open a professional practice.

"Ooh, can I tell you a story and get your advice, please?" I asked.

I then recounted the whole story about the video chat with Laura, to their great delight. After their laughter subsided, Danielle asked if I would allow her to investigate the case further. She said that this was exactly why she had pursued a degree in genealogy, that she had software that could compare both of our family trees, and that she'd really like this to be her first investigation as a Certified Genealogist. "I'll even do it for free," she said. I told her that I'd want to pay her something for her services, but that yes, I'd be very excited to have her on board. We exchanged contact information, and we promised to be in touch. I went on to visit my friends, and I had a wonderful time at the wedding, where I was reunited with people I'd known since I was a young boy.

A few weeks later, Laura arrived for her visit, and I told her about the serendipitous meeting with Danielle and her father at the bar. One day, we deposited saliva into the DNA kits, each one marked with our names and personal information, and I sent them off to the lab. I showed her around the area, we traveled to the coast for a little holiday, and we had a lovely time together. On one of the last days before she returned to Argentina, I took her to a Middle Eastern restaurant in town, and by chance, the owner, Jamil, was there. We hugged and greeted each other, I introduced him to Laura, and of course, I couldn't resist telling him the whole story. Laura watched, without understanding any of the English, but being fully involved in the interchange nonetheless. Jamil laughed heartily at each part of the story, and when it was finished, I turned to him and said softly, "You know, I want to know if I'm having sex with my cousin." He replied, "No, don't worry. In the Middle East it's OK for cousins to get married. Maybe not first cousins, but second cousin and third cousin, no problem. Have fun and enjoy your time together!"

Laura returned to Argentina, and we stayed in touch occasionally. The DNA results slowly began to be revealed by email updates. First, the ethnicity estimates were revealed, which showed each person's percentage of DNA from certain regions and ethnic groups around the world. After that, we began following clues and hints in the massive online database to connect information and photos of potential family members to our family trees. Once both of us had assembled our family trees and accepted or rejected all the hints about other family members, Danielle took over. She asked for our profile and password information, and began to import all the data into a sophisticated software program designed for professional genealogists. In this way, she'd be able to make direct comparisons to our DNA profiles and family trees. After she began the process, more information became available, including photographs and documents of emigration. She sent me photos of the steamship my father had taken to Ellis Island, New York City, as a seven-year-old boy. Birth and marriage documents were discovered and saved online, and old photographs of grandparents and great-grandparents began to surface. Danielle corresponded with me every week as she continued to learn of new developments.

Finally, after weeks of following leads and comparing both our family trees, she wrote to me with her findings. Danielle said that after significant research, she wasn't able to make a direct blood connection between Laura's grandfather and my father, and that there didn't seem to be any connection between the two Haddad families living in Aleppo at that time. After that declaration, she wrote: "Congratulations!?" – with both an exclamation point and a question mark. But it was the next paragraph of her email that was a big surprise. She wrote that while researching Laura's ancestral background and family tree, she noticed something on her maternal (Italian) side that looked familiar. Danielle took note of it, checked her own half Italian genealogical background, and, believe it or not, she discovered that she and Laura were cousins! Naturally, upon learning this news, they sent each other photographs of themselves and their families, and excitedly called each other "cousin."

The whole reason for the investigation was to learn if Laura and I were related, but as it turned out, the genealogist and Laura were the ones who were related!

Amadu

I never had a dog, but I have had a few significant cats in my life. One day, shortly after moving to a new home in the pine forest, my wife and I saw a kitten peering through the glass pane of the front door. When we approached the door, it quickly turned away, huddled under a bench, and remained staring at us. We opened the door, and it ran away into the forest. The next afternoon it appeared again, and this time it seemed a little less afraid. We quietly opened the door just a few inches and threw a piece of food on the deck. At first it jumped away, but then it approached the snack, smelled it, and ate it before disappearing again into the woods. Over the next few days, this pattern repeated itself as we threw the food closer to the door each time. Eventually, we opened the door completely and placed the food just past the threshold. The stray kitty entered the house to eat, we closed the door behind her, and she never left again. That was Riley, the sweet and mellow female calico.

Later that year we thought it would be a good idea to have a companion for Riley, so we went to the local animal shelter and adopted a newborn male tabby with swirls of brown, white and orange against a backdrop of medium-gray fur. We called him Amadu, a West African name that seemed to fit him perfectly. Amadu (or "Ami") was a feisty and excitable little kitty, but he was also extremely affectionate. At first, there were some power struggles between the two cats, since Riley was older and defended her turf, but eventually they began to get along and became good friends. I installed cat doors so they could come and go as they pleased, without the need for a litter box in the house. They regularly spent a lot of time outdoors in the woods, playing with mice and lizards, chasing birds, walking all around the property, and returning to the house whenever they wished.

When my wife and I divorced, the cats remained with me. Shortly after the divorce, Riley didn't return home one night. She normally didn't stray far from the house, and this was concerning. I searched for her in the woods and along the gravel and dirt roads in the area while calling her name aloud. I posted flyers with her photo and my phone number on trees and in neighbors' mailboxes. It soon became apparent that she was almost certainly killed and eaten by a coyote. Amadu must have seen the attack, because in the following days and weeks, he was extremely paranoid every time he left the house. He would slowly and cautiously walk through the cat door, scanning from left to right with his head, something he had never done before. We both missed her very much. Riley had always favored my ex-wife, and it was symbolic that she had disappeared so soon after my wife left our marriage.

Ami and I spent the next 15 years together, and he was a faithful friend and a deeply spiritual being. Sometimes, if I were working at my desk, or lying down on the bed reading a book, he would approach me and just remain still, looking directly into my eyes for a long time. It was charming and endearing, but it was also a little spooky. In ancient Egypt, cats were revered as divine creatures with psychic or supernatural powers, and it sometimes seemed that he was communicating with me on a metaphysical plane. He and I remained deeply connected throughout his entire life. If we were both in the house and I had to do some work outside, I would call out to him and ask him to come along. Whether I was landscaping, cutting the lawn, chopping wood, or just lounging outside, Amadu would often be nearby, keeping himself busy in my company. Sometimes we would even go for long walks together. All I had to do was call his name and encourage him to follow. He was like a dog in this way, but much less needy.

Amadu lived an amazingly long and healthy life, but he began to decline late in his twentieth year. He moved slowly, meowed a lot, didn't eat or drink very much, and wasn't himself anymore. After a few months, he could hardly walk, so I brought him to the veterinarian, who discovered a large tumor in his belly. He told me that Amadu was probably in considerable pain, and that the most compassionate option was euthanasia. We made a plan to do it the following day, so I could prepare myself for the sad occasion and spend the rest of the day with my faithful companion. We returned home in the car together, and later that afternoon and evening, several friends came to visit Amadu for the last time, including my friend Della, who really loved him.

I had decided that I would bury him down by the creek. It was a special place on my property where I'd often go to reflect, read, or play music. Ami often walked to the creek with me, or casually visited me while I was already there. Sometimes we sat together and communed with nature, watched birds and squirrels, and enjoyed the rippling sounds of water. I gathered a few shovels, a wide piece of colorful felt cloth, and a few of his favorite things. My idea was to create a tomb, and to prepare it to receive his body the next day. I put everything into the wheelbarrow, including Amadu, and I slowly wheeled it down the path to the creek about 500 feet away. When we got there, the water was flowing over the boulder in the creek bed, the sun was shining, and it was very peaceful. I gently placed Amadu on the ground, determined the best spot for his grave, and began digging. He watched me for a while and then walked slowly to the water's edge, where he took a drink. It took about fifteen minutes to dig a square-shaped grave about three feet deep. I trimmed the sides with a long and narrow shovel so the walls would be as flat as possible. I had decided to create a stone marker for him, made of a large ceramic tile and inlaid glass squares, which I set in mortar. Once the grave was ready and the marker complete, I knelt down, unrolled the cloth to line the grave and walls, and placed a cat toy, some catnip, and a food offering at the bottom of the pit. As I did this, Amadu slowly walked over to where I was working. He meowed, and I called his name. I stood up, and I watched him approach the edge of the grave. He arrived at the edge, looked down into the pit, and then he raised his head and stared directly into my eyes. I was surprised by what had just happened, but then he did it once again, first peering down into the grave and then looking up at me. I became emotional, picked him up, and told him that I was, in fact, digging his grave. I cried and kissed him, and he purred as we rubbed faces and looked into each other's eyes.

The next morning, I returned from the vet's office with his body in a small box, and I carried out a final burial ceremony by the creek. After some moments of reflection and meditation, I positioned the box in the grave along with the offerings. Then I filled the hole, compacted it with earth and rocks, and I set the marker in place on a small bed of freshly-mixed cement. The following weeks were sad and lonely. Ami had a playful and magnetic personality, and everyone who met him enjoyed his energy. I missed his companionship and the spiritual connection that we shared. My friends called me from time to time, and helped to distract me from the grief that immediately followed his passing, but somehow, I felt his presence still in the house. His body was gone, but his energy seemed to be lingering. Then, a series of events proved that my suspicions were on target... his extra-physical energy was still in the house and on the property.

One night I was awakened around 2 a.m. by a noise in the house. At first I thought it was a soundtrack to a dream I was having, but the nature of the sound didn't match the dreamscape, and I awoke and lay in bed with my ears attuned. And then I heard it again... a scratching sound coming from the kitchen on the other side of the house. I listened again and then realized it was probably a mouse that had come through the dryer vent near the laundry area. Especially in colder weather, an occasional mouse would find its way into the house from outside, seeking warmth and perhaps a crumb of food on the floor. It was time to set my humane mousetrap again to catch the little creature and set him free. Scratch, scratch... I heard it again, but this time it was a louder sound, and I wondered how a little mouse could be making such a loud noise. I got out of bed in the dark, found my way to the hallway, walked past the guest bathroom and another bedroom, and stopped at the laundry closet. I stood there and waited in the dark until I heard the sound again, but it wasn't near the dryer vent... the noise was coming from the kitchen. I quietly slipped another ten feet into the kitchen, turned on the dimmer switch, and I could hardly believe my eyes. There, in clear view, was Amadu's ghost. As he sometimes did in real life, he was scratching at the door of a lower kitchen cabinet, the same one where I used to keep his cat treats. He turned his head to look up, as if asking me for a treat, and as I stared mesmerized at the apparition, it dissolved into thin air. Not surprisingly, I had a hard time going back to sleep that night.

A week or so later, again at night, I was reading in bed before going to sleep. I finished the chapter, placed the book on the nightstand, and turned off the reading light. Unwinding from a busy day, I lay there on my back for a few minutes, completely still, and tried to relax my mind. Suddenly, I felt a slight movement at the edge of the mattress near my left foot, followed by a few more almost imperceptible movements. Then I felt a slight pressure against my lateral leg, right above the knee. I knew immediately that it was Amadu. He generally wasn't allowed on the bed, but he would sometimes sneak a cuddle after I fell asleep, and when he did that, he would always rest his body against my leg. Emotion swelled inside me as I realized my little guy had come back once again for a visit. I reached down to "pet" the air while I called his name, and I fell asleep.

A few days after that, my good friend Ronee came for a visit in the late afternoon. We had made plans to meet at my house to play some music together and then go out for dinner. I was working in my office when I heard a knock at the door. I opened the door to greet Ronee, but instead of the usual hugs and smiles we always exchanged, he just stood there with a blank expression on his face. I asked what was wrong, and he answered that he had just seen Amadu on the walkway leading to my house. He saw him clearly as he approached the steps, but then the cat simply disappeared. "It was definitely Amadu," he said, to which I replied: "Oh yeah, he's been coming around lately."

Here's to Amadu the brown tabby: a lover boy with a unique and metaphysical personality, and a wonderful companion for so many years.

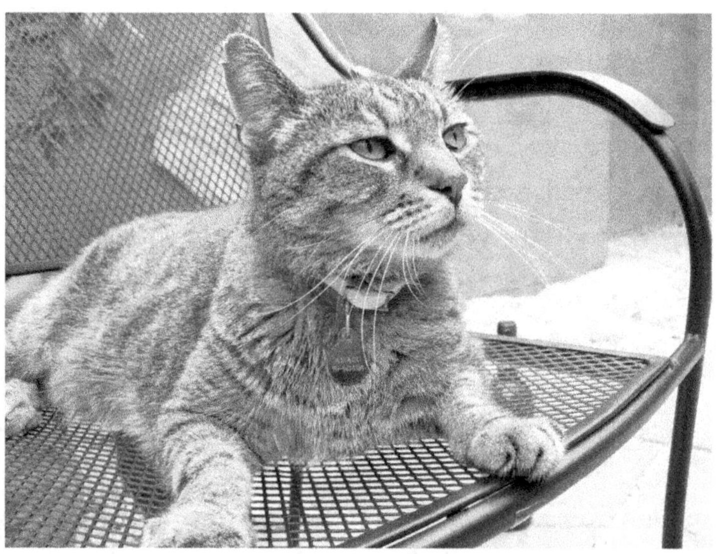

Amadu at age 18

The perfect toast

Once, when I was working in Europe, I had a three-day break in Croatia before flying to my next stop. One day, my student Lea (whom I'd known from previous visits) mentioned that if I had time, she would be happy to show me around Ljubljana, the capital of Slovenia. From Zagreb, it was only a two-hour train ride, so I jumped at the opportunity. I checked into a lovely hotel in the old city and began to explore the area. A few hours later, as planned, Lea arrived at my hotel with two of her girlfriends, intent to show me around town and give me a grand tour.

We walked on beautiful pedestrian bridges that cross over the Ljubljanica River alongside pristine white stone buildings. The Central Market, with its smells and samples of local food, was a gustatory delight. We traversed maze-like streets that gave way to plazas framed by old buildings and churches, and stopped for coffee and a chat at an outdoor cafe. Finally, we took a funicular to the top of a hill to visit the city's main attraction, Ljubljana Castle, which was built in medieval times. We explored the castle's tower and dungeon, and strolled on the ramparts that offer expansive views of the city. I was so grateful to have been invited by my delightful guests, and I was flattered to be accompanied by three beautiful Slovenian women for a few hours of sightseeing and fun.

After a wonderful afternoon of conversation, sights, smells and sounds, we decided to walk down the hill from the castle, have some wine together, and then go for dinner. The girls chose a bottle of local red wine, and they seemed excited to introduce me to a varietal grown only in Slovenia. The waiter brought our wine glasses and some cheese and bread. A few moments later he returned with the bottle, showed us the label, popped the cork, and poured wine into each of our four glasses. Lea picked up her glass and began to offer a toast. We all raised our glasses as she welcomed me to Ljubljana and said nice words about our times together as teacher and student. When it came time to clink our glasses, I extended my arm and touched my glass against Lea's, but within a few seconds she said with a slight grin: "Oh no, Bob. In Slovenia we cannot make a toast like this!" I didn't understand what she meant, but she continued: "After we touch the glasses, we must look into the eyes of the other person. That is the real connection."

Stunned, I realized that my eyes had remained fixed on the point of contact of the two glasses, even after the glasses had touched. She was waiting for me to visually acknowledge her to make a "real connection," but perhaps out of excessive caution, I hadn't done so. It was a startling realization. In my life, every time I clinked my glass against another glass, my eyes remained fixed on the glass after contact instead of looking at the persons I was toasting. I apologized and thanked her for bringing this to my attention, and we tried it all over again. One by one, we toasted each other by first touching our glasses and then immediately raising our eyes to make a direct connection with the other person. I was commended for my good work, and we all had a good laugh and a lovely time together.

Ever since that day, I do to others just as Lea did to me. When I notice that someone keeps their eyes downward after both glasses make contact, I stop the toast, and I tell the story about my first glass of wine in Slovenia, and then we do the toast all over again. Without fail, everyone enjoys this experience, and many people have later thanked me for bringing it to their attention. Some have even told me that they repeat my story to others when they engage in a toast with people who don't make direct eye contact after touching their glasses.

"If you're hungry, help yourself to the refrigerator."

The year following my mother's death was a difficult one. I was her sole caretaker for the last three years of her life, without any emotional or financial support from my two older siblings. I had relocated Mom to her own apartment not far from my home, where she met a completely new group of friends, got involved in social activities, and enjoyed a wonderful lifestyle close to me and my friends and community. When she finally passed, I lost all contact with my immediate family, but I held onto the memories of having loved her dearly, and having shared many deep and beautiful experiences together in the years prior to her death. Sometimes I could feel her presence – a feeling that she was near, and that we were aware of each other on a metaphysical plane.

For many years, I'd known and consulted with a well-known spirit medium named Sherrie Dillard, who lived in my area. An accomplished psychic, she'd worked with detectives investigating homicides, was an author of many books, and had dedicated years of her life to humanitarian service. I'd had numerous readings with her when my life was at a crossroads, or when I needed an outside perspective. This time, I'd contacted her to request a reading to communicate with my mother, because I wanted to know that she was truly at peace. In the years prior to her death, she had become angered and distressed by the selfish and controlling actions of my brothers. Even on her deathbed, she cried and asked why they had treated us the way they did. I was hoping that Sherrie (who had met my mother when she was alive) could make psychic contact with her so I could be sure she was truly resting in peace.

There was never anything strange or spooky about the psychic readings I'd had with Sherrie. She didn't directly quote anything that spirits "said" to her. Instead, she interpreted the energies she could feel and sense from a deceased person's spirit. When I called to make an appointment, she told me that she was fully booked and wouldn't be able to see me for about one month. She said that she'd put me on a waiting list, and that she'd call me when she got a cancellation, but I told her not to bother, and that I'd be back in touch with her again in the near future.

A few weeks later, while in a deep sleep at about 1 a.m., a dream I was having became sonically altered. The muffled laughter and vocal sounds that I heard seemed out of place. For a few moments, my sub-conscious mind struggled to make sense of the incongruity between the dream's content and its soundtrack. Somehow, I forced myself out of the dream. Lying in my bed for a few seconds with my eyes closed, I heard the sounds again — mumbled speech and laughter. To be sure I had fully exited my dream state, I opened my eyes and stared at the ceiling. As I listened attentively in an awakened state, lying on my back in bed, I heard them once again. They were coming from my living room, a female and a male voice making soft and unintelligible sounds, occasionally interrupted by giggling. At first, I wondered if two people had broken into my house, but I reasoned that if that were the case, they certainly wouldn't be talking or laughing. The female sounded just like my mother, but the male voice definitely wasn't my father's. I got up and slowly crept down the hallway. I entered the kitchen and turned on the light, and there was nothing. The front door was locked, and the outdoor sensor light was off. Having witnessed signs of spirits before in my life, I sensed that I had been visited by the spirit of my mother. After all, I'd been thinking of her very intensely over the previous few weeks, and it was conceivable that she'd come for a visit. Her giggling was probably a signal that she was alright – but who was the guy she was with?

I turned off the lights in the kitchen, stopped in the bathroom for a sip of water, and got back into bed. Before I could fall back asleep, I heard the laughing again. Convinced now that it was my mother, and determined to console myself with her presence so I could get back to sleep, I yelled out: "Mom, you're scaring the shit out of me! Could you keep it quiet out there? I'm trying to get back to sleep." The sounds immediately stopped, but then I laughed, thinking of what I had just done, and also knowing that my mother probably got a kick out of my humor. Then I added: "Oh, and if you're hungry, help yourself to the refrigerator. There's some good stuff in there." I continued to giggle for a few minutes in bed with my eyes closed until I eventually fell asleep.

The next morning, I was awakened by the ringing of my telephone. I jumped out of bed, quickly recalling what had happened the night before, hurried to the kitchen, and answered the phone. It was Sherrie, calling to say that she'd had a cancellation, and asking if I could come for a session that very afternoon at 2 p.m. I agreed immediately, and told her that my mother had appeared in my living room the night before, and that this was perfect timing. She replied that she wasn't surprised because she had also felt her presence. It wasn't until I hung up the phone that I realized I'd originally told her to not put me on a waiting list... but she had done so anyway, and now the timing for a session was extraordinary. Later that morning I called my friend Della to tell her about my mother's visit the previous evening, about the mysterious male voice, and that I had luckily gotten a last-minute appointment with Sherrie for that same afternoon. She was excited to hear the news.

I arrived for my appointment at Sherrie's office, and we started by discussing the goals for the session, and reviewing any questions I might want to ask of those we might contact. Once ready, we began as usual by closing our eyes, offering a brief nonsectarian prayer, invoking and thanking the spirit guides, and inviting them to make contact with us. After a few moments of silence, Sherrie said she was having trouble establishing contact with my mother. There was another spirit in the foreground, a man, and by trying to get our attention, he was preventing clear access to my mother. Sherrie had made contact with my deceased father in the past. "It's not your father," she said. "Should we speak with him?" I agreed, and then there was another period of silence as she began to communicate with the unknown male spirit. At one point, she opened her eyes halfway, glanced at me, and said: "Bob, do you have a deceased teacher?" I answered that yes, one of my main teachers of Thai massage had passed away about seven years ago, and that he and I were very close in the years before his death. She closed her eyes again, and then began to share thoughts and feelings about her interpretation of the spirit's energies. After a few moments, she said that he wanted to communicate to me that he was happy and proud of something I had done. She said that he was trying to convey that I was on the right path, and that he supported my efforts. There was nothing specific about what Sherrie was transmitting to me, no details about which things he was alluding to, and she didn't ask any leading questions either. Sherrie always offered a general interpretation of the matter at hand, allowed time for some discussion afterward, and then it would be up to the client to put the pieces together after the session. I liked that.

We said goodbye and thanked my teacher Asokananda, and Sherrie then attempted to make contact with my mother Grace. After a period of complete silence, I heard her say that it was sometimes frustrating when spirits wouldn't speak with her. She said that my mother was there, but that she wasn't responding to the request for contact. She opened her eyes and asked: "Why don't we ask your father? He always talks to me. What's his name again?" I reminded her that his name was John, and she closed her eyes once again to try to find him. After a few more moments, she said: "Oh yes, your father says that your mother is fine and that she's not holding any anger about anything." Then there was another pause, and she continued: "He says that they both know that you were the one... you were the one to help or to do something correctly. They both know that you did the right thing, or something like that, that they love you and that they're happy with you for something that you did. Does that make any sense?"

"Mm-hmm," I answered, still with my eyes closed.

"Is there anything else you'd like to ask?" she asked.

"No," I answered, "I think that's about it."

We bid farewell to the spirits with a closing prayer, and then we talked for a few minutes about the relevance and interpretation of what had just happened. I offered a few bits of information that she never knew, and the whole experience became even more meaningful. I thanked her for her great work, paid for her services, and exited the building.

I was in a buzzed post-session state on the drive home, yet elated and intrigued by the extra-physical connections I'd experienced. I parked the car, and just as I opened my front door, I heard the phone ring. It was Della, who was calling to find out about the reading that day. I told her what had happened – that my mother seemed to be fine, and that my father was the intermediary who transmitted the information. I also told her about the man who was vying for our attention before we made contact with my father. When I told her that Sherrie thought it was my deceased teacher, Della exclaimed: "Oh... so it was Asokananda who was with your mother in the living room last night!" I was shocked when she said that, but of course it all made perfect sense. I was so caught up in the emotions and afterthoughts resulting from the dramatic intuitive session that I hadn't made any connection at all between the previous evening's mysterious male voice and the appearance of my deceased teacher during the session.

In my life, I feel so fortunate to have had several meaningful experiences in the spirit realm, and I'm very grateful for each and every one of them. Call it what you may, but the soul, energy, or non-physical essence of people clearly endures when the physical body dies. I believe this with such conviction that no one could ever convince me otherwise.

Grace Haddad Ruggiero

Asokananda Harald Brust

Messages from Mexico

Later in life, I met a woman who took me on an intense and emotional ride that eventually ended in disaster. There were signs along the way – times when I wondered why she would say or do things that made no sense to me. But somehow, through her charm, beauty, sexiness, and sweet gestures, I was drawn into a deepening love affair over a relatively short period of time.

We began the relationship in a casual way. I was traveling regularly for work, and I wanted to know her on a much deeper level before making a serious commitment. At first, we'd see each other about once a week, but within a short period of time she wanted to get together twice a week, and then a few months later, even more often. Whenever I needed space or requested that we proceed more slowly and organically, she would accelerate the passion by being extra sweet and sensual; or she would do or say things to show her affection; or she'd buy me little gifts, even if they were insignificant and unnecessary. These actions fueled my interest in her and drew me closer, but they also distracted me from fully heeding the warning signs that were beginning to emerge.

After many years of being single, I was becoming intrigued by the idea that perhaps she could be my final partner in life, someone I could love and cherish and grow old with... all the traditional romantic notions about love and commitment that I hadn't considered for a long time.

Unfortunately, but ultimately very fortunately, that was not the way it would proceed. In the second year of the relationship, I began to see a side of her that was clearly unhealthy. She reacted to many things with excessive drama, would become defensive and argumentative for no apparent reason, and she crossed personal and ethical boundaries on a few occasions. My love for her had deepened based on the belief that she truly wanted to make a life with me, but the craziness had reached a saturation point. After almost two years in our relationship, she began to act in such insensitive and hurtful ways that I had no choice but to back away and take space for myself. I went away to the coast to be alone and to seek some clarity. While there, I confided in friends who affirmed her negative behaviors and encouraged me to leave her. I began online sessions with a therapist, I wrote in my journal, and I took long walks on the beach. When I returned home, we met at a neutral location, agreed to stop seeing each other, kissed, and went our separate ways. Within weeks she began dating someone else, but she continued to contact me, even though I'd asked her not to do so. I was hurting badly, wasn't sleeping or eating very much, and I needed time and space to begin a healing process. It reached such a point of discomfort that I decided to go to Mexico for a month to establish physical distance, to re-ground my heart, and to visit with friends.

On the day of my departure, I was sad and grief-stricken. I arrived at the Mexico City airport with a heavy heart, and I joined a line to clear customs and immigration. Passport in hand, all I could think about was how much I still loved and desired her, and how I wished things could be different. Those thoughts were on my mind even as I interacted with the customs agent, who smiled as he stamped my passport. Longing and pining for her, I picked up my bag and turned to enter the arrivals area, and there, right in front of me, something shocked me and stopped me in my tracks. It was a large strategically placed poster with an amazing message. In large bold upper-case letters, it read: "*Lo que deseas puede contener algo de lo que no quieres formar parte.*" (What you desire may contain something that you want no part of.) I stood there motionless for a few seconds, probably with my mouth agape. I then moved to a nearby wall, and remained there for a long time as I stared at the poster and pondered the synchronistic and spiritual significance of this message. I felt that it was clearly directed to me by the Universe, and it hit me very hard. It was true that I still desired her, but it was also true that both she and the relationship contained elements of which I wanted no part. I reached for a pen and a piece of paper to write down that sentence. At the bottom of the poster, in smaller type, were a few telephone numbers and other contact information to report occurrences of sex trafficking. After gazing at the poster and internalizing the message that was directed to my personal situation at that very moment in time, I picked up my bag to exit customs, turned to enter the arrivals lounge, and looked directly at a large welcoming sign that read: "*Bienvenido a México.*"

I believe in signs from the Universe and divine intervention. I don't necessarily believe in God in a traditional theological sense, but I am convinced that there is an extra-human power that guides, motivates, connects, supports, and heals, especially when a person is open and ready for positive change and transformation. The poster I saw upon my arrival at the airport, at the exact time that I was desirous of something that, in reality, was unhealthy for me, was a message from another realm that affected me deeply. It startled and surprised me, but I could never have imagined the other "signs" I would soon experience.

I visited Mexico City for a few days, and reminisced about the many times I'd been in that sprawling city, including when I studied there as a college student. I spent hours viewing amazing pre-Columbian artifacts at the Museum of Anthropology; I walked around the main plaza (*zócalo*); and I rode the metro to the neighborhood where I once lived. The sights, smells, sounds and memories were welcome distractions, but I was still conflicted and hurting about the failed romance. At the same time, though, I felt reassured and propelled forward by the wisdom written on that airport poster. Two days later I flew to Oaxaca, a beautiful mountain city I'd known from many years before, and where I would stay for the next few weeks. I checked into a hotel by late afternoon, and a short time later I decided to walk around town to become acquainted with the neighborhood, and then to take myself for a drink and dinner somewhere. In the few days since seeing the airport poster, I'd been processing the feelings it had aroused in me. I was certain that I'd loved this person with all my heart, and that I was capable of (and worthy of) unconditional and selfless love. After such a long time of being unpartnered, I was willing and able to compromise, to evolve together and work together. I was certain that I'd loved her in the deepest and most selfless way I had ever loved before. I recalled when I'd told her that my heart would remain open for a short while if she ever decided to change and compromise for the sake of our relationship. These were the thoughts that had been running through my mind that day. As I left the hotel, I walked down a small cobblestone alley, and there, on the right, was a large bench. It was made of cement, covered in smooth plaster, and painted dark red. And there, in bright white letters, were the following words: "*Te espero como se espera lo que jamás se ha tenido.*" (I hope (wait) for you as someone hopes (waits) for something that he has never had.) That sentence stopped me in my tracks because it precisely embodied what I was feeling at that exact moment in time. I stayed there for a minute, read and re-read the sentence, felt its message deeply, took a photo, and then slowly continued on my way.

My few weeks in Oaxaca went well, and I was able to focus on my work, socialize with friends, and ease my heart a bit. On one of the last days of my trip, I went to a restaurant in the neighborhood where I was staying, and I placed an order with the waiter. In recent days, I was feeling stronger in my conviction that although I did really love her, it was clear that she didn't love me unconditionally – her love was always conditional. I rationalized that she wasn't emotionally healthy enough for me, and that any attempt at a truly committed relationship would have ultimately failed. Sitting there at the restaurant, waiting for my food to arrive, I reminded myself that I had been blind to the warning signs and that from the very beginning, she and I were on a collision course. As I glanced around the room to observe the furnishings and art in the restaurant's beautiful courtyard, I suddenly noticed some decorative words painted high on the wall to my left: "*El amor es ciego. Por eso se estrella tantas veces.*" (Love is blind. That's why it crashes so often.)

This was now the third written message I'd seen in a very short period of time that directly correlated to my innermost feelings at each corresponding moment in time. During a time of deep inward reflection, emotion, and heartache, the Universe was somehow supporting me through these synchronistic occurrences. Synchronicity is something I've long believed in, and I've experienced it in other situations in my life. Far more than simply being in the right place at the right time, it is when elements within you and outside of you seem to combine, reflect each other, or confirm and validate thoughts, feelings and needs. Carl Jung described synchronicity as an acausal connecting principle in which events and energies in the external world align to one's perceptions or feelings, and may mirror, echo, or validate personal concerns. He also hypothesized that synchronistic events might be energetic manifestations that support the need to heal and grow. These synchronistic experiences were happening to me when my inner world of thoughts and feelings connected with the external world of people, places and things in Mexico. How could this be possible? I would think about something or feel a certain way, and then, as if by magic, I'd see a confirmation, validation, clarification, or assurance of some sort. The messages I was receiving seemed spiritual in nature, and they helped to momentarily soothe my sadness, worries and heartache. Were they external reflections of the spiritual part of my being? Was my soul exuding some sort of collaborative, reciprocal and numinous energy to reassure me and guide me forward? Were these really instances of "divine intervention?"

The first few months after my return home were very difficult. I had sessions with therapists who quickly identified her patterns as narcissistic in nature. I hadn't known much about narcissistic personality disorder (NPD), and my curiosity led me to a best-selling book on narcissism that was a revelation. It was the first book since my college years that I read with a highlighter. By the time I finished the book, the pages were awash in a sea of bright yellow, with handwritten notes in the margins. I contacted the author of the book, and I had an amazing and validating coaching session with her. I then had several sessions with a specialized therapist who helped "victims" of narcissistic abuse. I learned that unnecessary gifts, compliments and constant attention, and excessive communication were clinically labeled as "love bombing" tactics, used to lure and manipulate others in order to meet a narcissist's own goals or satisfy their own needs. I also learned that her constant demands for compliance and attention, her fits of anger, lack of empathy, hypersensitivity to criticism, unfounded jealousies, neediness, and her disrespect of my personal boundaries were all hallmark signs of narcissism.

After another period of heartache, and at the urging of therapists and friends, I finally decided to block her phone number and email address, and cease all communication with her. She had become toxic for me, and I had to abandon the idea of maintaining any sort of friendship going forward. My friends reminded me that I had "dodged a bullet" by ending it. It took me well over six months of no contact with her, plus occasional therapy, to recover from the heartache and abuse, but in the end, I emerged strong, content, and grateful. I knew in my heart that I was worthy of a healthy, compassionate, empathetic, supportive, truthful, loyal, and supportive partner, and I felt sure that I would never again ignore warning signs of unhealthy patterns in others. At the same time, I also knew that my capacity to love deeply and unconditionally still remained. In fact, it had grown even more resolute. I had left that relationship, but my capacity for love continued.

A few months later, I returned to beautiful Oaxaca for several weeks to complete a writing project and do some online work. I checked into a hotel on the very same block where I'd spent my first night almost one year before. I unpacked a few things, took a shower, and went out for a walk. An hour later, on my way back to the hotel, I remembered the red bench just a few hundred yards away, so I walked up the block to take another look at the message that had reflected my feelings so precisely the last time I was there. I approached the bench feeling strong and confident, and knowing that my capacity for unconditional love had been strengthened in the past year. I was excited to revisit that red bench and to re-read the message that had once spoken to me so deeply, but as I stopped in front of it, I was once again thrown into a visual and visceral shock. There was now a completely new message painted in the same bright white lettering, a message that once again spoke to me just as I was at that very moment in time. It said: *"Yo me fui, pero mi amor insiste."* (I left, but my love carries on.)

Nothing seems to happen by accident when the soul gets involved. It is the most intentional presence in life, whether we recognize its existence or not. It informs decision-making through thoughts and images; it fuels intuition; and combined with the element of synchronicity, it can speak through metaphors, symbolism, and other clues. In my case, my soul also seems to have one hell of a sense of humor!

The bench with the original message

The bench on my next visit

"Not cry."

One of my favorite small towns in the world, Mae Hong Son, is nestled in the rolling hills of northern Thailand. The central area of town contains two magnificent Buddhist temples (*wats*) whose gold and white reflections quiver on the surface of a large pond used at one time to bathe elephants. Over a period of about 15 years, I often went to Mae Hong Son to retreat from the busy pace of Chiang Mai, where I lived, studied, and worked each year for several months at a time. The town was also a point of departure to Wat Pa Tam Wua, a Buddhist monastery where I often spent weeks in silent meditation. Just a block away from the guest house where I always stayed was a small tour operator, Sawasdee Tours, run by Werun and Chan. Over the years, I'd gotten to know them, and I'd recommended visitors and tourists to use their services. Werun did driving tours in his small van, taking groups on excursions to hill tribe villages near the border with Myanmar, and to caves and other tourist spots in the general area. His wife Chan led day trips and overnight trekking adventures in the mountains to areas with waterfalls, elephants, and old-growth trees.

Whenever I was in Mae Hong Son, I always met them for coffee or a bite to eat, and sometimes we would have long and deep conversations. Werun was always especially friendly toward me, and he occasionally invited me for a drink or insisted on driving me wherever I needed to go, even though everything I needed was only a short walk away. One year, as we said goodbye to each other, he asked when I would be returning, and I told him that I'd probably come back in a month. He smiled and said that the next time I returned, he would invite me to their house for dinner so we could socialize on a deeper level. He made me promise to get in touch with him as soon as I came back.

About five weeks later I returned to Mae Hong Son for a week of peace and exploration. I checked into my guest house and walked up the hill to the main street to buy some fruit and snacks. On the way back, I saw Chan sitting near the tour shop, talking with another woman. She greeted me happily by calling my name out loud, and she invited me to sit with her and have a coffee together. While sipping our coffee, she asked one question after another about my life and my work in Chiang Mai. Then the conversation turned to meditation, and she asked if I was planning to spend time at the monastery on this trip. We continued the conversation as she asked more questions about my life, my health, and my home in the United States... all the while with her usual soft and friendly demeanor.

We chatted and drank coffee for what seemed like about ten minutes, and then finally, after a break in the conversation, I asked about her husband. "And where is Werun today?" I asked. "Is he working?"

"Oh, you not know," she replied, "he die."

"Who died?" I asked confusedly.

"Werun," she answered, "he die about one month ago." I could hardly believe what I understood her to say, so to be sure, I asked her once again who had died. She looked at me, smiled, and said that indeed her husband and my friend Werun had died.

"But I was just here last month," I said.

"Yes," she replied. "I think it happen maybe one week after you leave." She remained looking at me, motionless and with a soft expression on her face. I felt a bubble of emotion building inside me as she told me that he had suffered a heart attack and passed away quickly. The shock and sadness that I was feeling rose from my chest to my throat and head, and tears began streaming down my face.

Then an unimaginable thing happened. She looked at me with a serene expression and a faint smile, and she said: "Not cry, Robert. I always tell my son and family not cry when they think about papa, because then he can feel that they suffer because he die, and then maybe he feel bad and he also suffer."

I looked at her somewhat incredulously. I was still overwhelmed with shock and sadness about the sudden passing of my friend, someone who had hugged me only a month before and told me that when I returned, we would have drinks and dinner together at his house. I opened my eyes again to look at Chan, and she still had her gaze fixed on me with a soft smile on her face. It was such an unusual experience, something that in most circumstances would never occur in Western society. I would never expect someone to tell me not to cry when I learned that my friend had passed away, much less the wife of the deceased. I also struggled to understand how the spirit of a deceased person could also be affected by my own emotions. I'd heard that some Buddhists believe it can take days or weeks before one's spirit and energy are fully released from the body after death, but I had never been in a situation in my life when I was specifically requested to not cry. I looked at her, smiling at me with that sweet and peaceful face of hers. Then I dried my tears with my sleeve, swallowed hard, and took a deep breath.

She then told me a little more about how and when it happened, that he was a wonderful person, and that everything would be alright. We spent a few more minutes together, but I didn't know how to continue a conversation after that, so I stood up, held her hand, gave her my best wishes, and slowly walked back to my guest house. Over the next few days, I tried to visit her, but she wasn't at the office, so on the morning of my departure, I left a note for her with my condolences and some money, and I slid it under the door.

Ancient civilizations in Egypt, China, India, Africa, Australia, and throughout the Mid-East and Mediterranean regions used professional mourners to help comfort grieving families. Today, traditional societies all around the world still carry out funerary rituals that involve collective weeping and moaning over the loss of the deceased. Cleansing ceremonies, death wails, and grief rituals that involve crying take place over weeks or months in some cultures. Even in grief situations where communal crying is not the norm – such as at Western funerals, for example – bereaved families and friends are generally not expected to resist crying. Instead, they are usually held and comforted by others when they cry. But this was not the case with my friend Chan in Mae Hong Son, northern Thailand.

I'll never forget the one-of-a-kind experience when I had to modify my outward emotions to a way that was acceptable and appropriate to the grieving survivor of a recently deceased friend.

Chan on a hike

The goat herder

One year, during a break from working in Europe, a friend and I flew from Barcelona to southern Portugal for some travel and relaxation together. We arrived in Faro, rented a car, and set out to explore the beautiful countryside of the Algarve region, with its hills, beaches, and picturesque towns. The Algarve was populated in prehistoric times, and was settled by Phoenicians, Romans, and Arabs, among others. In addition to ancient Roman ruins, there are medieval castles and fortresses, as well as colonial-era churches, some of which were adapted from earlier Muslim mosques.

Fancy resorts are located alongside tourist beaches, but there are many small hotels and traditional guesthouses in beautiful inland and coastal villages. Over a period of ten days, we traveled to many of these towns, sometimes stopping for a day and night before moving onward. We drove past vineyards, and fig, carob and almond orchards, and we ate at fruit stands, local restaurants, and small cafes. I never missed an opportunity to speak Portuguese, and my desire to do so resulted in very sweet encounters with local people.

One day, as we drove through the countryside en route to our guest house, I noticed a man with about ten goats in a small area of a pasture adjoining the road. I asked my friend if we could stop and try to engage in casual conversation with him, and she agreed. I pulled the car over to the side of the road, and we both got out of the car and approached him. He was sitting on a small stool, milking one of the goats. I greeted him with, "*Olá senhor, bom dia.*" He smiled and asked how he could be of help. I was sure that our town lay just ahead to the left, but I started the conversation by saying that we were headed there, and I asked if, in fact, it was in that direction. He confirmed that it was just ahead, and then we introduced ourselves, mentioned that we were visiting the area, and began to make small talk. Occasionally, he would stop milking to gesture with his hands, or to get up from his stool for a quick stretch. Every few minutes, he would release a goat, grab another one by the leg, bring it closer to him as it bleated and objected, and then he'd begin milking once again. I asked if he used the milk for his own consumption, and he told us that he milked his goats twice a day, and that his wife made cheese, which was sold at local markets. I asked if there was a place nearby where we could buy the cheese, and he pointed toward an intersecting road and said there was a small store a few kilometers away. We asked about his family, and we told him how much we were enjoying our time in the Algarve and how different it was from where each of us lived.

Our friendly conversation continued for quite some time, and we kept him company as he went about his work. It was a beautiful day, and it was fun to be speaking with a local person in such a gorgeous pastoral setting. I imagined how uncomplicated and serene his life seemed to be – living in the southern Portuguese countryside with his wife, making goat cheese, and surrounded by natural elements. It seemed idyllic to me, and during a lull in the conversation, I looked at him and said: "*O senhor tem uma vida tão boa.*" (You have such a good life.) I went on to say that he lived in beautiful surroundings, where the local food and wine were so delicious, and the people were so friendly. I mentioned that it was wonderful that he and his wife worked together to make cheese, and that he was lucky to live in a quiet place without noise, traffic, or air pollution. He listened to me as I continued my praises, occasionally glancing at me from the stool while his hands directed squirts of milk from each udder into a metal pail below. I ended by reminding him that he was lucky to be living this type of life.

He looked at me, raised his eyebrows, and winced slightly as he replied: "*Pois amigo, nem sempre é tão fácil, sabe?*" (Well, friend, it's not always so easy, you know?) He then went on to explain how he had to walk long distances each day with a bad leg, how his wife was sick and required pain medication and regular medical attention, how his children lived and worked far away in the city and weren't nearby to help them, and how he had to make daily rounds with a cart to deliver his cheese. He continued by saying that the income they earned from the cheese wasn't enough to make ends meet, so to make extra money, he traveled one hour by bus several times a week to work odd jobs.

We looked into each other's eyes as he spoke, and by the time he finished explaining his true reality, I felt embarrassed and a bit foolish. I think I said something like: "*Sim, eu sei que a vida nem sempre é fácil, mas é tão lindo aqui.*" (Yes, I know that life isn't always easy, but it's so beautiful here.) "*É lindo, sim,*" (It is beautiful, yes) he replied, nodding his head slightly, his eyes pointing downward.

Here I was as an outsider, idealizing his "simple" existence, but in actuality, he was working very hard every day and struggling as an older man to make ends meet. I was perceiving his goats, his beautiful town, and his wife's cheese-making as charming and idyllic, but I hadn't "walked a mile in his shoes." During our short but deep conversation, I had failed to consider that "the grass is always greener on the other side," and that "you always want what you don't have." Instead, I was looking at his world through my very own pair of "rose-colored glasses."

To all those mentioned in this book, for having affected my life in memorable ways. --- To my parents Grace and John Haddad -- To family members and early friends: --- George Everett, Al Decresenzo, Brian Sabbagh, Pat Hamel, Nancy Vespoli, Marie Oliva, Anna Parla, Josephine Hamel, -- to my Haddad and Lociero cousins: -- Louis Peretti cousins: -- Paul deWolfe, Lue Simopoulos, Karen Oliva, Rocco Graziano, Arnaldo Cordero, Martin Kwapinski, jason Haddad, Dan Walker, Della French, Suzanne Diamante, Gosia Wojnicka, Robert Browning, Susan Preston, Paul Mazzio, Steve Haddad, Jim Oliva, Lynne Crawford, Ronnie Shadlack -- To some friends from adult life: --- David DiGiuseppe, Ann Green, Sue-Anne Solem, Ronee Fantozzi, Jay Yeo, Robert Agriopoulos, Bob Russell, Lilian Jacques, Elliott Shapiro, Timothy Kyle, Camine Pesapane, Holly Riddle, Mke Richmond, John Moore, Hélida Esther Cabrera de Bauer, Harriett Stevens, Peggy Wagner -- To inspirational musicians and friends through music: --- Ravi Shankar, Zakir Hussain, Alhaji Bai Konte, Dembo Konte, Malamini Jobate, Bickram Ghosh, Richie Havens, Ephat Mujuru, Dumisani Maraire, Leandro Apaza, Badal Roy, James Lascelles, Larry Karush, Martin Eagle, Tarun Bhattacharya, Harald Brust, Bill Burton, Randy Friel, Steve Gronback, Ed Habert, João parros, paul Fowler, paul Sonatupa, John Rassias, Cahyo Marzan, Maruja Apaza, Eli Alvarez, Cristina Muñoz, Cesar Muñoz, Steve Gorn, Johnny Hartman, Arooj Ahmad, purna Das Baul, Grupo Expresión, Selesñe Damessae, -- To inspirational teachers and helping guides: --- Raúl Rodriguez, Phra Ajahn Anake, Lek Chaiya Thiwong, Sharon Salzberg, Tanya Boigenzahn, Mark Wisdom, Mikiyas, Diane Ranes, Sherrie Dillard, Jo Jensen, Cristina García, Jack Schuller, Isabel Schuller, -- To a few colleagues: Kira Balaskas, Gary Keller, Harald Brust, Davor Haber, Pichest Boonthumme, Janice Gagnon, Carmen Germania López Zúñiga, Basilio Villacorta Sánchez, Ralf Marzen --- To my dear godchildren: --- Arjun Tamang, Maruja Apaza, Cahyo Marzan, -- To all my nieces and nephews --- Blessings and peace to these people for showing their true colors and for the hard but important life lessons: Ron, Charlie, George, Rich, Martha, Danielle, Kate, Tanya, Bouna, Laura, and others ---

Photo credits

A connection of ecstasy — photo of Purna Das by Bob Haddad; photo of Sherif Baba courtesy of Richard Shelquist, wahiduddin.net

A Gambian praise song — photo of Malamini courtesy soundcloud.com; music notation courtesy David DiGiuseppe

Amadu — Bob Haddad

Amazonas — photos by Bob Haddad

A most exquisite morsel — photo by Bob Haddad; image courtesy Alfaihaa

"Brain no good." — Rameses' mummy © history.com; canopic jars, Shutterstock.com

"¿Estás seguro?" — photo by Bob Haddad

"From your passport, of course." — photos by Bob Haddad

"Get me the hell out of here!" — Bob Haddad

"Help, Mighty Mouse, save me." — baby photo courtesy Bob Haddad; Mighty Mouse, Alamy K3743P, © Terrytoons, 20th Century Fox

Hitchhiking adventures — photos courtesy Bob Haddad

"I know you." — photos by Bob Haddad

Intuition, premonition, apparition — courtesy Bob Haddad

Ixcatlán and the mule kick — photos by Bob Haddad

Lulu and Richie — photo by Bob Haddad; album cover © Stormy Forest Productions, Inc.

Maha Shivaratri in Kathmandu — photo of sadhu by Prakash Mathema,
    © AFP, Getty Images; all other photos by and courtesy of Bob Haddad

Messages from Mexico — photos by Bob Haddad

Music of the World — stage photo by Ira Landgarten; image and logo
    courtesy Bob Haddad

"Not cry." — photo courtesy Nongnapat Chingta

"Oh madame, please don't say this word." — Bob Haddad

"Oh, nothing much." — photo © Ligmincha Institute

Paucartambo and the Panaderos — Panaderos 1989, by Shirley Mayhew;
    all other photos by Bob Haddad

"Photo for your mother." — photos by and courtesy of Bob Haddad

Pilgrimage to Rajgir — photos by Bob Haddad

Shona spirits — Ephat Mujuru by Greg Plachta; other photo by Bob Haddad

Sleeping on an Algarve Beach — photo by Bob Haddad

Spirit in the rice field — photos by Bob Haddad

Thai Healing Alliance International — logo by Bob Murray,
    courtesy Bob Haddad

The Bedouins near Aleppo — photo by J. Vondrakova, Shutterstock.com

The blind musicians of Cusco — photos by Bob Haddad

The protection spell — photos courtesy Bob Haddad

The tej bet — photos courtesy Bob Haddad

"This is going to be brilliant!" — Bob Haddad

"Two, please…" — photo © Etsy.com

"Well, good luck, and thanks for the drink." — photo of Johnny Hartman,
    Alamy.com P51A2; album cover, © Impulse Records

"You should start a publishing company." — photo of Chris Strachwitz by
    Alain McLaughlin, courtesy Arhoolie Records; photo of Bob Haddad by
    Anitta Frazier, The Durham Herald; logo courtesy Bob Haddad

About the Author

Born in New York to immigrant parents from Syria and Sicily, Bob Haddad became fascinated with travel, modern languages, traditional music, and world cultures at an early age. He has lived and studied in the USA, throughout Latin America and in Thailand, and his travels and explorations have taken him to over sixty countries, sometimes spending months or years at a time.

Bob has enjoyed varied careers as a language professor, music producer, and Thai massage therapist and teacher. His books on music education, Latin American folklore, and traditional Thai healing arts have been released by major, independent, and academic publishers. He speaks four languages and has basic knowledge of others.

The author offers these accounts of true stories from his life to share his magical and life-shaping adventures with others, and to spread awareness of the inherent wisdom gained by surrendering to the unknown.

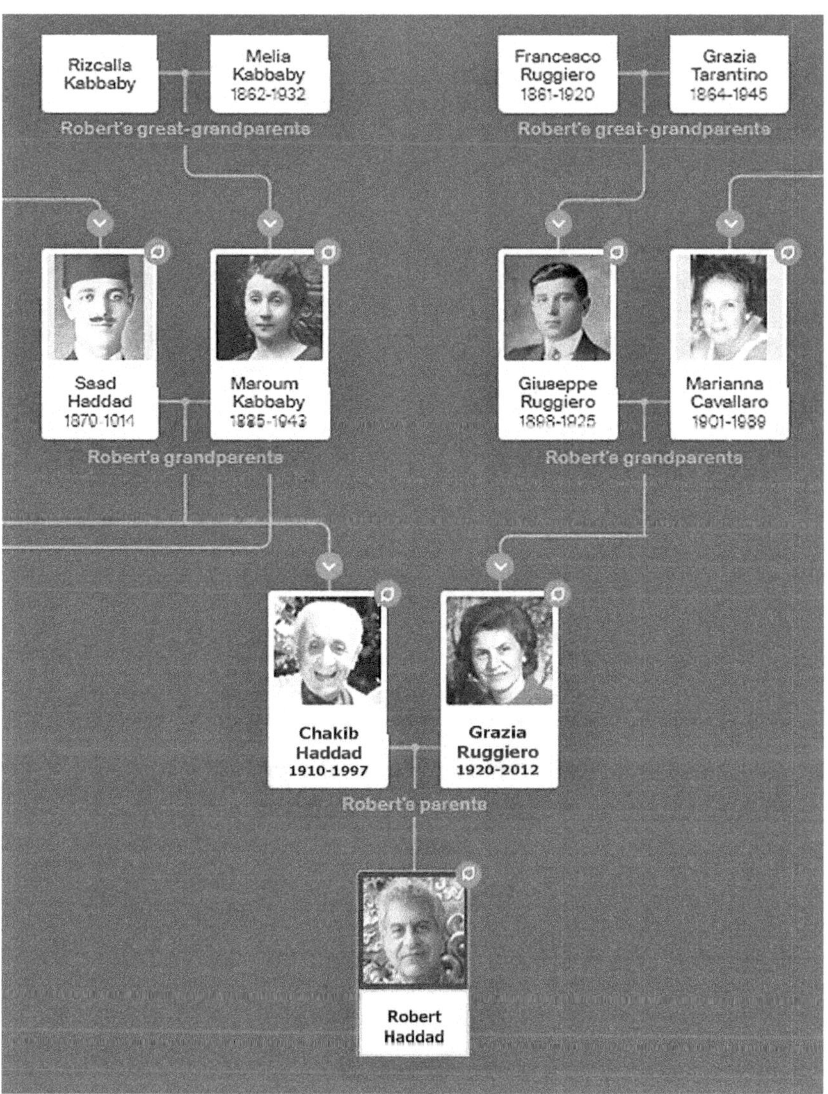

Family tree, four generations

Other books
by Bob Haddad

The Art of Thai Massage: *A Guide for Advanced Therapeutic Practice*
(Findhorn Press / Inner Traditions, Rochester, Vermont, USA,
ISBN: 978-1-64411-372-1)

Thai Massage & Thai Healing Arts: *Practice, Culture & Spirituality*
(Findhorn Press, Forres, Scotland, ISBN: 978-1-84409-616-9)

World Music: *A Cultural Legacy* (Glencoe McGraw Hill, Columbus, Ohio,
USA, ISBN: 0-07-824189-8)

American Music: *Hits through History*
(Glencoe McGraw Hill, Columbus, Ohio, USA, ISBN: 0-07-845743-2)

Mexican Tongue Twisters / Trabalenguas Mexicanos
(Bilingual Press, Tempe, Arizona, USA, ISBN: 0-927534-02-9)

Contributing Author: Glencoe World Geography
(Glencoe McGraw Hill / National Geographic, Columbus, Ohio, USA,
ISBN: 0-02-664173-9)